The New Humanitarians

Social and Psychological Issues: Challenges and Solutions
Albert R. Roberts, Series Editor

Finding Meaning in Life, at Midlife and Beyond: Wisdom and Spirit from Logotherapy
David Guttmann

The New Humanitarians

Inspiration, Innovations, and Blueprints for Visionaries

Volume 2
Changing Education and Relief

Edited by Chris E. Stout, PsyD

Foreword by Mehmet Oz, MD

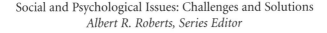

Social and Psychological Issues: Challenges and Solutions
Albert R. Roberts, Series Editor

Westport, Connecticut
London

Library of Congress Cataloging-in-Publication Data
The new humanitarians : inspiration, innovations, and blueprints for visionaries / edited
by Chris E. Stout ; foreword by Mehmet Oz.
    p. cm. — (Social and psychological issues: Challenges and solutions, ISSN
1941–7985)
  Includes bibliographical references and index.
  ISBN 978–0–275–99768–7 ((set) : alk. paper) — ISBN 978–0–275–99770–0 ((vol. 1) :
alk. paper) — ISBN 978–0–275–99772–4 ((vol. 2) : alk. paper) — ISBN
978–0–275–99774–8 ((vol. 3) : alk. paper)
  1. Philanthropists. 2. Humanitarianism. 3. Charities. 4. Social action. I. Stout, Chris E.
  HV27.N49 2009
  361.7'4—dc22   2008020797

British Library Cataloguing in Publication Data is available.

Library of Congress Catalog Card Number: 2008020797
ISBN: 978–0–275–99768–7 (set)
        978–0–275–99770–0 (vol. 1)
        978–0–275–99772–4 (vol. 2)
        978–0–275–99774–8 (vol. 3)
ISSN: 1941-7985

First published in 2009

Praeger Publishers, 88 Post Road West, Westport, CT 06881
An imprint of Greenwood Publishing Group, Inc.
www.praeger.com

Printed in the United States of America

The paper used in this book complies with the
Permanent Paper Standard issued by the National
Information Standards Organization (Z39.48–1984).

10 9 8 7 6 5 4 3 2 1

To all of those profiled herein and to all of those they help—you are all heroic.

Contents

Foreword: Honor Roll

From the time I first met Chris after our election as fellow Global Leaders of Tomorrow in Davos, Switzerland, for the World Economic Forum's Annual Meeting, I was impressed by his remarkable insight and diligence. Over the years, we have collaborated on various health-related projects, and we have shared profound sadness over many global tragedies.

Now Chris has embarked on a daunting challenge—that of compiling a Who's Who, or Honor Roll, of worldwide humanitarian organizations. Chris has taken his proverbial golden Rolodex of contacts and friends and compiled an impressive list that represents the "best of the best" in global human service organizations. Although Chris made his admittedly "biased" choices by going to the founders he already knew, he has nevertheless highlighted some of the best in the world–some well known, some almost unknown—but all that represent a sampling of the finest. Each is a testament to the power of the human spirit in the face of seemingly insurmountable challenges and deficits.

All the familiar bromides are absent from *The New Humanitarians*. Though it would be tempting to wring our collective hands at the enormity of the proverbial "world-going-to-hell-in-a-hand-basket," *The New Humanitarians* is a totem of real inspiration. Chris has highlighted organizations that favor results over standard protocol in accomplishing their work. Those herein are doing the difficult—not by following in other's footsteps, but by forging new paths and finding new solutions to mankind's humanitarian needs. The time has come for them to collectively tell their stories—a daunting task, but that is something Chris has experience with.

Someone once remarked that the core issue with Nazi Germany was *not* that there was a Hitler, but that there were *too few* Schindlers. *The New Humanitarians* gives us all hope that there is a new generation of Schindlers across the globe, and our imaginations can show us the differences they will make for the future.

Mehmet Oz, MD, MBA

Acknowledgments

First and foremost, I want to thank all of the people involved in the organizations profiled herein. Many people would not be alive or function at the levels they are without your vision and passion. Period. Full stop. It is your zeal that has so inspired me to publish these books. My thanks to each of you for taking the time to craft what has become this set. I am fortunate to call each of you my friend, and the world is blessed to have you. I also must apologize to those who lead organizations that are not included herein. It is a function of time and space—not having adequate amounts of either. Nevertheless, I hold a great and abiding respect for all of those working in the so-called humanitarian space. The world is in your debt.

Debbie Carvalko is my publisher extraordinaire at Praeger/Greenwood. Without her pitching my proposal, this project would not have been made into the reality that you are holding in your hand. She was a valued collaborator in the shepherding of the production of the manuscripts to final production. Debbie, you are amazing.

I was fortunate to gain valuable help in organizing, interviewing, and writing with a valued set of graduate student assistants: Annie Khan, Teresa Bartrum, Stephanie Benjamin, Mark Zissman, Valaria Levit, and Donald Bernovich. I would like especially to thank Patrick "Skully" Savaiano, who from the start displayed not only a keen sense of organization of the myriad of complexities that this project involved, but also demonstrated a wonderful balance of professionalism blended with a hip, e-mail-savvy communication style with some of the most prominent leaders in the humanitarian space. This is an incredible feat by an incredible person—tip-o-the-hat to you, Skully. And I would also like to particularly thank Myron Panchuk, who served as a fantastic resource and intellect to this project. I owe you my friend.

It was my mother who modeled rather than lectured about the importance of helping others. She provided me with an inspiring example that I can only hope to be able to mimic for my children. Thanks, Mom.

The support of my wife, Karen, is always invaluable, whether I am writing or not; and she was especially helpful in her ever-sharp review of many of the first drafts of what now appear herein, as well as tolerating my innumerable, long-winded, overly animated discourses about so many of the incredible stories and works of those profiled. Both of my children, Grayson and Annika, were valued partners in the early production steps of helping me stay organized with the chapters and whatnots of such a project. They were willing and able freelancers who could perforate pages as well as offer critique on some of my more complicated sentence-structuring problems. I thank and love you all.

Chris E. Stout
Kildeer, IL

Care to do more yourself? Please do! Here's how . . .

1. Visit CenterForGlobalInitiatives.org for more information on projects you can be a part of. If you don't see something you think you can help with, e-mail me at Chris@CenterForGlobalInitiatives.org and I may be able to connect you to another organization that can help, or we may be able to initiate work.
2. Consider suggesting *The New Humanitarians* to others and start a viral buzz! Think of all your contacts who may be interested in this book. If you go to www.Praeger.com and search for "The New Humanitarians" you can print a downloadable flyer for the book to give to interested others. You can also email the Praeger link to interested others as well as the CenterForGlobalInitiatives.org.
3. Inquire if your local or university library has *The New Humanitarians* in its collection, or on order. If you recommend it to them, they may add it and others can read it as well.
4. Request a presentation at your local college, university, public library, high school, church, mosque, synagogue, book seller, coffee shop, service organization (Rotary, Lyons, etc.), or book club by e-mailing a request to Chris@CenterForGlobalInitiatives.org or by calling 847.550.0092, ext. 2.
5. Request an interview by a broadcast, cable, or Internet television program, radio, newspaper, or magazine reporter. Media kits are also available by request to Chris@CenterForGlobalInitiatives.org or by calling 847.550.0092, ext. 2.

Introduction

Chris E. Stout

Welcome to a trip around the world. You will travel to six continents, led by men and women of various ages and backgrounds. Be warned: you may go to some fairly desperate places, but they all have a seed of hope. You will not be traveling as a tourist, but rather as an activist with more than three dozen organizations—each one incredible. Each chapter is a story, a story of need, of response, and of accomplishment. They are all at once different, but yet the same as being an inspirational account demonstrating the power of the individual triumphant over the challenges of poverty, illness, conflict, or a litany of injustices. My friend, Jonathan Granoff, President of the Global Security Institute, said of the project that it is a counter to the pervasive "pornography of the trivial" that infects much of what is in print these days. I suspect he is correct.

As a sad postscript but powerful testament to the seriousness of the work done by those profiled herein, a few days prior to this manuscript being sent in to the publisher, I was speaking with a representative with Médecins Sans Frontières who told me that three of their staff had been killed in a conflict zone in northwest Africa. My heart sunk on this news. Although I know such things happen—and with much more frequency than I usually let myself believe—I was more honored to get the stories of these heroic organizations out to a broader audience.

In these three volumes, readers will learn about individuals who have created organizations that:

- Break up human trafficking rings and teach citizens how to intervene in other injustices
- Go to conflict areas and put themselves at risk to end the conflict
- Help ensure elections are just
- Go to active war zones to administer emergency medical care
- Provide training and loans in order to empower people out of poverty

- Create a new language and then put it to use in developing education and job training programs
- Work to stop nuclear war and curb the development of weapons of mass destruction
- Create an ingenious for-profit organization that supports the not-for-profit work
- Solve a problem of medical supply shortages in the developing world while also alleviating medical waste problems in the developed world
- Export social services training into self-sustaining programs
- Create project-based trainings in order to increase capacity for global projects
- Treat immigrant and refugee survivors of torture in a culturally competent manner that is encompassing and holistic
- Help boys conscripted into being child soldiers adapt to a normal life
- Create the first not-for-profit pharmaceutical company to help in the battle of neglected diseases
- Advance education for girls where it is almost unheard of
- Integrate urban environmental design with democracy, civic participation, and social justice
- Bring the philosophy of "it takes a village to raise a child" to formative elementary school years, blend cultural heritage, and inspire students by mobilizing parents, teachers, and young adults
- Connect experts from a range of fields to work together on problems such as curing and preventing infectious and epidemic diseases, analyzing the risks of science and technology breakthroughs, and designing enforceable global health and environmental policies

CONTEXT FOR THE PROJECT

In developing my own nascent organization, the Center for Global Initiatives (profiled herein), I came to realize that there are many successful, groundbreaking models that already exist worldwide, but there really isn't a blueprint or a how-to on the subject. Although this is most likely due to the uniqueness of the organizations and their leadership examined herein, as well as their idiosyncratic approach to conducting their work, it is my hope that these volumes will provide readers a unique behind-the-scenes glimpse of the organizations and offer incredibly valuable insights, present insider experiences, and give advice that few would ever have access to from one organization, let alone from more than forty of the best-of-the-best.

I went about the selection process via the people I know. I met some in Davos at annual meetings of the World Economic Forum, or perhaps at a TED conference (back when Richard Saul Wurman still orchestrated them), or a Renaissance Weekend, or by being a co-nominee in the Fast Company Fast-50, or goodness knows where. I did not apply any scientific methods or algorithms to seek out the most cost-efficient organizations, those with the most stars on Charity Navigator, or those listed in a *Forbes* table. I was totally subjective and biased. I left my scientific method in the lab because I have been fortunate to have worked with some of the most innovative humanitarian organizations in the world, or to have collaborated with their incredibly talented founders/directors.

In fact, it is my experiences with these extraordinary people that led to my idea for this book project. There are many wonderful, long-standing organizations that do important work, but I found that many of the organizations I was working with were newer and, honestly, a bit more edgy. Many have more skin-in-the-game. These founders were on the ground and doing the work themselves, not remotely administrating from a comfortable office miles or a continent away. But don't let my capricious favoritism prevent you from researching the many, many other fantastic organizations that exist throughout the world. In fact, I hope this book may cause you to do exactly that. (I suppose I could have tried to get a book deal to compile the *Encyclopedia of New Humanitarians*, but I will leave that to someone with way more spunk than I.)

Though many of us are content in helping various causes by writing checks of support or perhaps even volunteering, the individuals profiled herein preferred to actually start their own organizations—to enact their passionate interests. So therein was the idea that crystallized the concept for this *New Humanitarians* project. I wanted to find out what makes these new humanitarians tick and how their brainchildren worked. Now, through this three-volume set, readers can, too.

From Braille Without Borders and Witness, to Geekcorps and ACCION, humanitarian groups are working worldwide largely in undeveloped countries to better people's lives. Whether they are empowering people with schools for the blind, intervening in human trafficking, giving the underserved access to technology, or helping individuals work out of poverty, the men and women of these innovative organizations offer their tremendous talent to their causes, along with great dedication and, sometimes, even personal risk to complete their missions. The work of these groups is remarkable. And so, too, are the stories of how they developed—including the defining moments when their founders felt they had to take action.

This project features a sampling of humanitarian groups across various areas: medicine, education, sustainable development, and social justice. These new humanitarians have been very successful with on-the-ground guerilla innovations without a lot of bureaucracy or baloney. They are rebels with a cause whose actions speak louder than words. They have all felt a moral duty to serve as vectors of change.

I did not want to be the author of *The Complete Idiot's Guide to Changing the World* or *Humanitarian Aid for Dummies,* but I did want to canvass the organizations whose founders I know personally and have had firsthand experiences with, as well as showcase others who are recognized pioneers, and have them describe in their own words where they gained their original idea, or what the tipping point was that so moved them to create their own organizations. I hope readers may gain not only inspiration, but also actionable approaches that are based on the real-world experiences of those profiled if they, too, care to take action.

Many of those appearing herein already hold world renown, so I hope this project will give readers the chance to learn the answers to questions rarely answered publicly, such as "How did you first get funding? Did you have false starts or failures? How creatively do you approach opportunities and obstacles—be they organizational or political? How do you create original solutions? What would you do differently today or what do you know now that you wish you knew then?"

COMMON DENOMINATORS

Even though the approaches of all these organizations are different, they do share a number of commonalities. At the time they formed their entities, each organization was novel in its approach to dealing with the problems it was addressing. The organizations were not restricted by past ways of thinking or acting. They created innovative approaches to produce something that was real and actionable from a concept and a vision. They developed practical approaches to solutions, some complex, some elegant, all robust and lasting. They were provocative. They were unhappy or unsatisfied with approaches others were using, and decided: if you can't join 'em, beat 'em. And they did just that—they cleared their own trails to sustainability for their organizations for the benefit of others.

They also either have a global reach or are at least not bound to the North or the West. These are "young" organizations with an average organizational age of fifteen years, with the majority being founded ten or fewer years ago. Thus, they are new enough to demonstrate generalizable methods to help readers in their own development of their work, while demonstrating sustainability and viability of their model and approach. Simply put, it is my goal to have this set of books demonstrate how these organizations make a difference. Each of them has taken an approach to their life and work by living like they mean it. While there is the essence of the power of one, it is one for all.

The organizations profiled in this three-volume book set differ in many other ways as well. Some have been recognized with many awards and accolades (MacArthur "Genius" Award recipients, fellows of institutes or think tanks, etc.), whereas others are newer or have such a low profile or are so remote as to not be picked up by any radar. I like that diversity. Some have incredible budgets and others almost none, but they all do amazing things with what they have. And with the increased exposure gained from being in this book set, they may be able to gain more people's awareness.

For example, Braille Without Borders is an organization created in 1998 by Sabriye Tenberken and Paul Kronenberg when they left Europe to establish the Rehabilitation and Training Centre for the Blind, a preparatory school for elementary-school children in the Tibet Autonomous Region (TAR). Before the center was opened, blind children there did not have access to education. These children were stigmatized outcasts who held little hope for integration or much of a future. Although there are many governmental and nongovernmental organizations that have set up eye clinics for surgery or eyeglasses, there is a large group of blind people that cannot be helped by these clinics. The center was created for them.

If this wasn't challenge enough, those in the TAR had no written form of communication. There was no Tibetan version of what many blind individuals use to read, known as Braille (invented in 1821 by Frenchman Louis Braille). So, of course, Sabriye *invented* a Tibetan script, or Braille if you will, for the blind. This script combines the principles of the Braille system with the special features of the Tibetan syllable-based script.

Impoverished countries worldwide account for nearly 6 million preschool and school-age children who are blind, and 90–95 percent of them have no access to education. Braille Without Borders wants to empower blind people in such countries so they can set up projects and schools for other blind people. In this way the concept can be spread across the globe so that more blind and visually impaired people have access to education and a better future.

It is people like Sabriye Tenberken and Paul Kronenberg and all of those herein who are taking the kind of action that William Easterly pines for in *The White Man's Burden*—they are interested in results and they deliver. They offer small-scale results that make a large-scale impact.

STRUCTURE

Readers will find that some of the chapters are authored by the founder or current leader of the organization profiled. Other chapters are the result of an interview. I wanted this book to be thematic and structured, but I also wanted to provide a wide berth for every organization to best tell its story. Thus, for some it is literally in their own voice, first-person. In other instances interviews were conducted and a story unfolds as told by the founder or current leader, the de facto coauthor.

I had established a set of standard questions that could be used as a guide, but not as a strict rule-set. I told every organization's leader that he or she could follow them or ignore them, or to choose whatever was appropriate. I was very pleased with the result. That is, most chapters cover similar thematic aspects— how they started, how they manage, and so forth. But I think I have been able to steer clear of the chapters looking like cookie-cutter templates with simply different content sprinkled in the right spots here and there. It was my hope to create a set of guidebooks, not cookbooks, and I hope you as a reader will enjoy a similarity between chapters in their construction, but great variability in their voice and creation.

I asked authors to sketch the background on their centers or organizations, when they started, canvass their history to current day, provide a description of their model, indicate how large they are, what type of corporate structure (non-for-profit, university based, etc.) they have, what metrics they use to track productivity or how they measure success, and biographical information about the founder.

I also had a set of curiosities myself: Where did the idea came from? What was the inspiration/motivation for the starting the organization? Was there "that one incident" (or the first, or the many events) that so moved the founder to no longer "do nothing" and take action. I felt that reading about specific cases or vignettes of groups or individuals who were helped would give a finer grain as to outcomes and impacts of such organizations. But I also wanted to learn how these organizations defined success. I think readers will be not only pleased, but inspired. I hope that readers will have their own passions sparked and have their desire to know (and perhaps, to do) more increased.

Organizing the chapters was a bit of a challenge. As you will see, there is much overlap between their activities, and many somewhat defy an easy categorization (which I like, actually), so I did the best I could to make what I hope readers will consider to be reasonable groupings. Or, perhaps this will at least cause readers to look at all three volumes!

And now, it is with great pleasure (and awe) that I introduce the *new humanitarians*.

VOLUME 1: CHANGING GLOBAL HEALTH INEQUITIES
Médecins Sans Frontières/Founded in 1971

I was in Geneva when I first met Doris Schopper, a physician who was involved in the founding of Médecins Sans Frontières (MSF), and she was an incredible person filled with energy and stories. As readers will find, this chapter provides a frank and transparent description of the chaos involved in the nascent years of MSF—quite the shift to the Nobel Prize–winning organization and operation of today. Médecins Sans Frontières is an independent humanitarian medical aid agency committed to two objectives: providing medical aid wherever needed, regardless of race, religion, politics, or sex, and raising awareness of the plight of people it helps.

Unite For Sight/Founded in 2000

If you ever want to feel inadequate, just look up Jennifer Staple. While most of us were struggling to get through undergraduate school, Jennifer, while at Yale, formed what has become an award-winning global enterprise doing incredible work. The organization's model serves as an inspiration regarding the power of making and acting upon connections. Unite For Sight implements vision screening and education programs in North America and in developing countries. In North America, patients are connected with free health coverage programs so that they can receive an eye exam by a doctor. In Africa and Asia, Unite For Sight volunteers work with partner eye clinics to implement screening and free surgery programs.

Scojo Foundation/Founded in 2001

In the small world of global efforts, I read a piece by Jordan Kassalow, OD, MPH, and I called him while he was at the Global Health Policy Program at the Council on Foreign Relations in New York, serving as an adjunct senior fellow. We had a wonderful conversation, and I have referenced his keen points on the deadly reciprocity of illness and warfare in subsequent talks I have given. He and Scott Berrie went on to found the Scojo Foundation. Their mission is to reduce poverty and generate opportunity through the sale of affordable eyeglasses and complementary products. Scojo Vision Entrepreneurs are low-income men and women living in rural villages who are trained to conduct vision screenings within their communities, sell affordable reading glasses, and refer those who require advanced eye care to reputable clinics.

Sustainable Sciences Institute/Founded in 1998

I tell people that Eva Harris, PhD, could make a lab out of a Jeep and that she is the spiritual cousin of MacGyver. I have read her seminal book, *A Low-Cost Approach to PCR*, and though not a biologist, I was astounded. We first spoke on the phone some years ago about the possibility of collaborating on a project together, and my astonishment continued. She developed the Sustainable Sciences Institute (SSI) and holds a mission to develop scientific research capacity in areas with pressing public health problems. To that end, SSI helps local biomedical scientists gain access to training, funding, information, equipment, and supplies, so that they can better meet the public health needs of their communities.

Institute for OneWorld Health/Founded in 2000

I first spoke to Victoria Hale, PhD, after she and her attorneys had been meeting with Internal Revenue Service attorneys to convince them that the Institute for OneWorld Health was indeed a NOT-for-profit pharmaceutical company. We were looking to collaborate on a pharmacogenomic project in which my Center would do the "R" of R&D and she would work on the "D," or development. We first met face-to-face in Geneva at the World Economic Forum headquarters. Today, the Institute for OneWorld Health develops safe, effective, and affordable new medicines for people with infectious diseases in the developing world.

Jamkhed (aka Comprehensive Rural Health Project — CRHP)/Founded in 1970

Shobha Arole, MD, came looking for me in Davos at a World Economic Forum Annual Meeting. I will never forget that, in our conversation, I presumed she needed help with getting some doctors to Jamkhed, but she quickly, and ever so kindly, told me that she was in the market for *students* so she could help train them before they developed their bad habits. And she and her father, Raj Arole, MD, are doing so, and quite successfully. Their Comprehensive Rural Health Project (CRHP) was started to provide healthcare to rural communities, keeping in mind the realities described above. It developed a comprehensive, community-based primary healthcare (CBPHC) approach. CRHP is located at Jamkhed, which is far away from a major city and is typically rural, drought-prone, and poverty stricken. One of the main aims of the project is to reach the poorest and most marginalized and to improve their health. In reality, perhaps not everyone in the world will be able to have equal healthcare. However, it *is* possible to make sure that all people have access to necessary and relevant healthcare. This concept is known as equity, and it is an important principle of CRHP. Health is not only absence of disease; it also includes social, economic, spiritual, physical, and mental well-being. With this comprehensive understanding of health, the project focuses on improving the socioeconomic well-being of the people as well as other aspects of health. Health does not exist in isolation: it is greatly related to education, environment, sanitation, socioeconomic status, and agriculture. Therefore, improvement in these areas by the communities in turn improves the health of the people. Healthcare includes promotive, preventive, curative, and rehabilitative aspects. These areas of integration bring about effective healthcare.

International Center for Equal Healthcare Access/Founded in 2001

I met Marie Charles, MD, MIA, in Quebec City at a Renaissance Weekend. I listened to her presentation on her Center's work, and I knew I had found a kindred spirit. In fact, at the time of this writing, it is looking promising that we will be working collaboratively together in Cambodia. Marie founded the International Center for Equal Healthcare Access (ICEHA), which is a truly remarkable nonprofit organization of 650+ volunteer physicians and nurses who transfer their medical expertise in HIV and infectious diseases (>7,000 aggregate man-years of human capital) to colleagues in more than twelve countries in the developing world. Rather than perpetuating a continued dependence on Western charity, this creates a sustainable system that allows these countries to provide healthcare to their own patients at the highest possible standards and yet within the existing resource limitations. As an interesting but crucially important side-note, the recipient developing countries themselves shoulder the major share of the program implementation costs, giving them a true sense of proprietary pride, value, and ownership as opposed to "receiving charity." ICEHA turns the paradigm of international development on its head.

Flying Doctors of America/Founded in 1990

Allan Gathercoal, DDiv, and I have been through a lot together—stuck in Nairobi, stuck in Burundi, bribing airport officials with lighters in Hanoi to bring medicines in, working in Bolivian prisons together; and, most recently, we met in

Cambodia. Allan is the founder of Flying Doctors of America, and his organization runs short-term medical/dental missions to the rural regions of Third World countries.

Marjorie Kovler Center of Heartland Alliance/Founded 1987

I'd speculate that Mary Fabri, PsyD, spends more time some years in Rwanda than in Chicago. She goes to where the needs are, and when in Chicago, the needs are at the Marjorie Kovler Center, where she is director and one of the clinical co-founders. The Kovler Center provides comprehensive, community-based services in which survivors work together with staff and volunteers to identify needs and overcome obstacles to healing. Services include Mental Health (individual or group psychotherapy, counseling, psychiatric services, and a range of culturally appropriate services on-site in the community), Health Care (primary healthcare and specialized medical treatment by medical professionals specifically trained to work with torture survivors), Case Management (access to community resources, including tutoring, ESL, food, transportation, special events), Interpretation and Translation (bridging cultural and linguistic barriers in medical, mental health, and community settings), and Legal Referral (referral and collaboration with immigration attorneys and organizations).

International Center on Responses to Catastrophes/Founded in 2002

Stevan Weine, MD, is a renaissance kind of guy. He can gain impressive NIH grants and awards while also writing about Alan Ginsberg and Bruce Springsteen (and take time to coauthor and present with me as well). I have had the pleasure of traveling to all sorts of places with Steve and meeting a fascinating group of activists, scientists, and intellectuals, all the while listening to some great music. He is a mentor, a role model, and a good friend. He also is the founder of the Center at the University of Illinois–Chicago, whose primary mission is to promote multidisciplinary research and scholarship that contributes to improved helping efforts for those affected by catastrophes.

International Trauma Studies Program/Founded in 1997

It was Stevan Weine who introduced me to Jack Saul, PhD, and took me to visit Jack's International Trauma Studies Program (ITSP), now at Columbia University. Jack's perspective is that recent natural and human-made catastrophes have highlighted the need for a multidisciplinary approach to the study, treatment, and prevention of trauma-related suffering. So, at New York University in 1997, he founded the original program. It is now a training and research program at Columbia University's Mailman School of Public Health. The program has been enriched by the participation of a diverse student body, ranging from mental health professionals, healthcare providers, attorneys, and human rights advocates, to journalists and media professionals, academicians, oral historians, and artists. Students and professionals are given the opportunity to develop and share innovative approaches to address the psychosocial needs of trauma survivors, their families, and communities. ITSP offers a dynamic combination of academic studies, research, and practical experience working with trauma survivors in New York City, the United States, and abroad.

Center for Health, Intervention, and Prevention @UConn/Founded in 2002

Jeff Fisher, PhD, invited me to his Center at UConn, and I had the flu. I would not have missed such an opportunity for the world. You see, the University of Connecticut Psychology Department's Center for Health, Intervention, and Prevention (CHIP) creates new scientific knowledge in the areas of health behavior, health behavior change, and health risk prevention and intervention. CHIP provides theory-based health behavior and health behavior change expertise and services at the international, national, state, university, and community levels.

REMEDY/Founded in 1991

REMEDY, Recovered Medical Equipment for the Developing World, is a nonprofit organization committed to teaching and promoting the recovery of surplus operating-room supplies. Proven recovery protocols were designed to be quickly adapted to the everyday operating room or critical care routine. As of June 2006, the REMEDY at Yale program alone had donated more than 50 tons of medical supplies! It is estimated that at least $200 million worth of supplies could be recovered from U.S. hospitals each year, resulting in an increase of 50 percent of the medical aid sent from the United States to the developing world.

Center for Global Initiatives/Founded in 2004

The Center for Global Initiatives (CGI) is my baby. It is the first Center devoted to training multidisciplinary healthcare professionals and students to bring services that are integrated, sustainable, resiliency based, and that have publicly accountable outcomes to areas of need, worldwide, via multiple, small, context-specific collaboratives that integrate primary care, behavioral healthcare, systems development, public health, and social justice. The word "global" is not used herein as a synonym for overseas or international, but rather local as well as transnational disparities and inequities of health risk and illness outcomes. The Center seeks to eschew the many disconnects between separation of body/mind, physical/mental, individual/community, and to offer a synthetic model of integration. CGI's philosophy and approach is always that of a collaborator and colleague. No West-Knows-Best hubris. Perhaps the most important aspects of the Center for Global Initiatives are the simplest: it serves as an incubator and hothouse for new projects; it helps to nurture, grow, and launch those projects as self-sustaining, ongoing interests; and after a project has taken hold, it serves as pro bono consultant to help those now managing the work with whatever they may need—materials, medicines, case consultation. About 90 percent of all CGI's projects have come about as a result of being invited to do the work. As best can be done, depending on the project, CGI seeks to blend primary care, behavioral health, and public health into an ultimately self-sustaining, outcomes-accountable, culturally consonant result.

VOLUME 2: CHANGING EDUCATION AND RELIEF
Braille Without Borders/Founded in 1997

Sabriye, Paul, and I used to joke about how we were likely the poorest attendees in Davos at the World Economic Forum. And in spite of our modest bank balances, I can tell you that they were two of the most powerful of the movers and shakers there. Braille Without Borders wants to empower blind people in these countries so they themselves can set up projects and schools for other blind people. In this way the concept can be spread across the globe so other blind and visually impaired people have access to education and a better future.

Room to Read/Founded in 2000

I heard John Wood talk about his post-Microsoft adventure of founding Room to Read. His brainchild partners with local communities throughout the developing world to establish schools, libraries, and other educational infrastructure. They seek to intervene early in the lives of children in the belief that education is a lifelong gift that empowers people to ultimately improve socioeconomic conditions for their families, communities, countries, and future generations. Through the opportunities that only an education can provide, they strive to break the cycle of poverty, one child at a time. Since its inception, Room to Read has impacted the lives of over 1.3 million children by constructing 287 schools, establishing over 3,870 libraries, publishing 146 new local language children's titles representing more than 1.3 million books, donating more than 1.4 million English language children's books, funding 3,448 long-term girls' scholarships, and establishing 136 computer and language labs.

Global Village Engineers/Founded in 1992

Chris Shimkus is a good guy and a good friend with whom I first connected in Geneva at the WEF Headquarters. He took one of those proverbial leaps of faith and left his "day job" to devote himself to the work of Global Village Engineers (GVE). GVE is a volunteer corps of professional engineers supporting the local capacity of rural communities in developing countries to influence public infrastructure and environmental protection. Its engineers choose to volunteer their skills to ensure the livelihood of these communities by building long-term local capacity, especially in situations of disaster prevention and rehabilitation and the need for environmental protection. They believe that infrastructure will best serve communities when they have the capacity to become involved from project inception through construction. Governments and project sponsors often do not invest in communicating basic facts to the community about design, construction, and maintenance. The mission of Global Village Engineers is to find these facts and develop the local capacity to understand such facts.

Common Bond Institute/Founded in 1995

I first met Steve Olweean, PhD, in an airport in Oslo—or was it Helsinki? We were on our way to St. Petersburg to the conference he founded. That conference was a lightning rod of connections with people I continue to work with around the world, from Sri Lanka to Tel Aviv, and that's just the tip of the iceberg of what Steve does. He founded the Common Bond Institute (CBI), which is a U.S.-based NGO that grew out of the Association for Humanistic Psychology's *International (Soviet-American) Professional Exchange.* The Professional Exchange was initiated in 1982 as one of the first Soviet-American nongovernmental human service exchanges. CBI organizes and sponsors conferences, professional training programs, relief efforts, and professional exchanges internationally, and it actively provides networking and coordination support to assist newly emerging human service and civil society organizations in developing countries. Its mission is cultivating the fundamental elements of a consciousness of peace and local capacity building, which are seen as natural, effective antidotes to small-group radical extremism and large-group despair, as well as to hardship and suffering in the human condition. To this end, enabling each society to effectively resolve and transform conflicts, satisfy core human needs within their communities, and construct effective, holistic mechanisms for self-determination, self-esteem, and fundamental human dignity and worth is the purpose of their work.

SWEEP/Founded in 2004

The Jane Addams College of Social Work, University of Illinois at Chicago (UIC), Addis Ababa University (AAU), The Council of International Programs USA (CIPUSA), and a network of nonprofit agencies are engaged in an exciting effort to develop the first-ever master's degree in social work in Ethiopia, through a project known as the Social Work Education in Ethiopia Partnership, or SWEEP. The undergraduate social work program at AAU was closed in 1976, when a military regime ruled the country. Now, with a democratic government in place since the early 1990s, the SWEEP project is working in collaboration with AAU's new School of Social Work and nongovernmental agencies in Ethiopia to develop social work education and practice.

CUP/Founded in 1997

The Center for Urban Pedagogy (CUP) makes educational projects about places and how they change. Its projects bring together art and design professionals— artists, graphic designers, architects, urban planners—with community-based advocates and researchers—organizers, government officials, academics, service providers and policymakers. These partners work with CUP staff to create projects ranging from high-school curricula to educational exhibitions. Their work grows from a belief that the power of imagination is central to the practice of democracy, and that the work of governing must engage the dreams and visions of citizens. CUP believes in the legibility of the world around us. It is the CUP philosophy that, by learning how to investigate, we train ourselves to change what we see.

Endeavor/Founded in 1997

Linda Rottenberg, who co-founded Endeavor, is a Roman candle of energy, enthusiasm, and brainpower. I met her through the World Economic Forum as a Global Leader of Tomorrow. She is amazing at delivering on what's needed in creatively intelligent ways. Endeavor targets emerging-market countries transitioning from international aid to international investment. Endeavor then seeks out local partners to build country boards and benefactors to launch local Endeavor affiliates.

ACCION/Founded in 1961

ACCION International is a private, nonprofit organization with the mission of giving people the financial tools they need—micro enterprise loans, business training, and other financial services—to work their way out of poverty. A world pioneer in microfinance, ACCION was founded in 1961 and issued its first microloan in 1973 in Brazil. ACCION International's partner microfinance institutions today are providing loans as low as $100 to poor men and women entrepreneurs in twenty-five countries in Latin America, the Caribbean, Asia, and sub-Saharan Africa, as well as in the United States.

Invisible Conflicts/Dwon Madiki Partnership/Founded in 2006

I just met Evan Ledyard at a talk I gave at Loyola University in Chicago, and he introduced me to the work he has done with an incredible group of students. Invisible Conflicts is a student organization that sponsors the education, mentorship, and empowerment of twenty Ugandan orphans and vulnerable children. A twenty-one-year civil war in northern Uganda, between the government and a rebel faction called the Lord's Resistance Army (LRA), has led to the forced displacement of over 1.7 million people into internal refugee camps. To support their rebellion, the LRA abducted more than 30,000 Ugandan children, forcing them to be sex slaves and to fight as child soldiers. Because of these atrocities, all of the DMP-sponsored children live in squalid conditions in and around the many displacement camps. Because life around these camps is marked by poverty, hunger, and little or no access to education, an entire generation of children find themselves denied a childhood and a chance to succeed in life.

BELL/Founded in 1992

Building Educated Leaders for Life, or BELL, recognizes that the pathway to opportunity for children lies in education. BELL transforms children into scholars and leaders through the delivery of nationally recognized, high-impact after-school and summer educational programs. By helping children achieve academic and social proficiency during their formative elementary-school years and embrace their rich cultural heritage, BELL is inspiring the next generation of great teachers, doctors, lawyers, artists, and community leaders. By mobilizing parents, teachers, and young adults, BELL is living the idea that "it takes a village to raise a child."

Hybrid Vigor Institute/Founded in 2000

I first met Denise Caruso at a TED Conference. She was just stepping down from her position as technology columnist at the *New York Times*, just before the tech bubble burst. Smart gal. I was immediately smitten by her intellect, and in subsequent emails and conversations, she agreed to help me in the pondering of my nascent ideas for my Center as she was building her Institute in the form of Hybrid Vigor. The Hybrid Vigor Institute is focused on three ambitious goals: (1) to make a significant contribution toward solving some of today's most intractable problems in the areas of health, the environment, and human potential, both by producing innovative knowledge and by developing processes for sharing expertise; (2) to develop new methods and tools for research and analysis that respect and use appropriately both the quantitative methods of the natural sciences and the subjective inquiries of the social and political sciences, arts, and humanities, and to establish metrics and best practices for these new methods of collaboration and knowledge sharing; (3) to deploy cutting-edge collaboration, information extraction, and knowledge management technologies, so that working researchers from any discipline may easily acquire and share relevant work and information about their areas of interest.

Our Voices Together/Founded in 2005

Marianne Scott and I had a wonderful conversation one Sunday night that I will never forget. Without repeating it, I do want to say I was touched by her humanity in a very powerful and lasting way, and I knew then that she needed to be represented in this project. Our Voices Together holds a vision of a world in which the appeal of lives lived in dignity, opportunity, and safety triumphs over the allure of extremism and its terrorist tactics. The people of this organization see a future where terrorist tactics are not condoned by any community worldwide. They understand that to achieve this, trust must be built on mutual trust and respect around the globe. They recognize the vast potential in engaging the United States in diplomacy by connecting communities. To this end, they promote the vital role of people-to-people efforts to help build better, safer lives and futures around the world.

Geekcorps/Founded in 1999

Ethan Zuckerman has a wicked sense of humor, and he is not afraid to use it. I last saw Ethan in Madrid at an anti-terrorism conference, and we spoke of wikis as a solution to a puzzle I was working on about Amazonian medical services. How obvious. Ethan is the founder of Geekcorps, which has evolved into the IESC Geekcorps, which is an international 501(c)(3) nonprofit organization that promotes stability and prosperity in the developing world through information and communication technology (ICT). Geekcorps' international technology experts teach communities how to be digitally independent: able to create and expand private enterprise with innovative, appropriate, and affordable information and communication technologies. To increase the capacity of small and medium-sized business, local government, and supporting organizations to be more profitable and efficient using technology, Geekcorps draws on a database of more than 3,500 technical experts willing to share their talents and experience in developing nations.

VOLUME 3: CHANGING SUSTAINABLE DEVELOPMENT AND SOCIAL JUSTICE
Witness/Founded in 1992

I first saw some of the work of Witness at the Contemporary Museum of Art in Chicago, and I was quite disturbed and moved by the images I saw—which was the point. I then contacted Gillian Caldwell of Witness about this book project, and I got the distinct impression that she wondered "who is this guy, and is he on the level?" So, with some emails back and forth, and the good timing of the WEF Annual Meeting, where she happened to be going, I gained some street cred with her as I'd been an invited faculty, gone to Davos a number of years, and knew Klaus Schwab, who had also written the foreword for one of my other books. Then she let me into the tent, and I am very glad she did. Witness does incredible work by using video and online technologies to open the eyes of the world to human rights violations. It empowers people to transform personal stories of abuse into powerful tools for justice, promoting public engagement and policy change. It envisions a just and equitable world where all individuals and communities are able to defend and uphold human rights.

The Community Relations Council/Founded in 1986

I worked on a three-volume book set (*The Psychology of Resolving Global Conflicts: From War to Peace*, Praeger, 2005) with Mari Fitzduff, PhD, and I had no idea of the violence she was exposed to in Belfast as a child growing up there. Now it makes perfect sense as to her development of the Community Relations Council. Its aim is to assist the people of Northern Ireland to recognize and counter the effects of communal division. The Community Relations Council originated as a proposal of a research report commissioned by the NI Standing Advisory Committee on Human Rights. The Community Relations Council was set up to promote better community relations between Protestants and Catholics in Northern Ireland and, equally, to promote recognition of cultural diversity. Its strategic aim is to promote a peaceful and fair society based on reconciliation and mutual trust. It does so by providing support (finance, training, advice, information) for local groups and organizations; developing opportunities for cross-community understanding; increasing public awareness of community relations work; and encouraging constructive debate throughout Northern Ireland.

Amnesty International/Founded in 1961

Amnesty International's (AI's) vision is of a world in which every person enjoys all of the human rights enshrined in the Universal Declaration of Human Rights and other international human rights standards. In pursuit of this vision, AI's mission is to undertake research and action focused on preventing and ending grave abuses of the rights to physical and mental integrity, freedom of conscience and expression, and freedom from discrimination, within the context of its work to promote all human rights. AI has a varied network of members and supporters around the world. At the latest count, there were more than 1.8 million members, supporters, and subscribers in over 150 countries and territories in every region of the world. Although they come from many different backgrounds and have widely different political and religious beliefs, they are united by a determination to work for a world where everyone enjoys human rights.

PeaceWorks Foundation and OneVoice/Founded in 2002

Daniel Lubetzky is one of those incredible people who turn on a room when they enter it. He does so not with bravado and brashness, but rather with a quiet power that captures those around him. He is a compelling person with a compelling mission. He founded OneVoice with the aim to amplify the voice of the overwhelming but heretofore silent majority of Israelis and Palestinians who wish to end the conflict. Since its inception, OneVoice has empowered ordinary citizens to demand accountability from elected representatives and ensure that the political agenda is not hijacked by extremists. OneVoice works to reframe the conflict by transcending the "left vs. right" and "Israeli vs. Palestinian" paradigms and by demonstrating that the moderate majority can prevail over the extremist minority. Although the needs and concerns of the Israeli and Palestinian peoples are different—Israelis wish to end terror and the existential threat to Israel; Palestinians wish to end the occupation and achieve an independent Palestinian state—the vast majority on each side agree that these goals are achievable only by reaching a two-state solution. OneVoice is unique in that it has independent Israeli and Palestinian offices appealing to the national interests of their own sides with credentials enabling them to unite people across the religious and political spectrum. It recognizes the essential work many other groups do in the field of dialogue and understanding, but OneVoice is action oriented and advocacy driven. It is about the process and demanding accountability from its members and from political leaders. A peace agreement, no matter how comprehensive, will be ineffective without populations ready to support it. The focus is on giving citizens a voice and a direct role in conflict resolution.

Nonviolent Peaceforce/Founded in 1998

Nonviolent Peaceforce is a federation of more than ninety member organizations from around the world. In partnership with local groups, unarmed Nonviolent Peaceforce Field Team members apply proven strategies to protect human rights, deter violence, and help create space for local peacemakers to carry out their work. The mission of the Nonviolent Peaceforce is to build a trained, international civilian peaceforce committed to third-party nonviolent intervention.

Peace Brigades/Founded in 1981

Peace Brigades International (PBI) is an NGO that protects human rights and promotes nonviolent transformation of conflicts. When invited, it sends teams of volunteers into areas of repression and conflict. The volunteers accompany human rights defenders, their organizations, and others threatened by political violence. Perpetrators of human rights abuses usually do not want the world to witness their actions. The presence of volunteers backed by a support network helps to deter violence. They create space for local activists to work for social justice and human rights.

Witness for Peace/Founded in 1983

Witness for Peace (WFP) is a politically independent, nationwide grassroots organization of people committed to nonviolence and led by faith and conscience. WFP's mission is to support peace, justice, and sustainable economies in the Americas by changing U.S. policies and corporate practices that contribute to poverty and oppression in Latin America and the Caribbean.

Southern Poverty Law Center/Founded in 1971

Throughout its history, the Center has worked to make the nation's Constitutional ideals a reality. The Center's legal department fights all forms of discrimination and works to protect society's most vulnerable members, handling innovative cases that few lawyers are willing to take. Over three decades, it has achieved significant legal victories, including landmark Supreme Court decisions and crushing jury verdicts against hate groups.

Human Rights Campaign/Founded in 1980

After having served as a federal advocacy coordinator on the Hill for the American Psychological Association for twelve years, and at the state level even longer, I have come to know and very much appreciate the twists and turns of law making and the body politic. I have also come to know and respect the impressive work of those in the Human Rights Campaign (HRC). They have evolved from battling stigma to being a political force to contend with—no easy task in the Beltway or on Main Street USA. The Human Rights Campaign is America's largest civil rights organization working to achieve gay, lesbian, bisexual, and transgender (GLBT) equality. By inspiring and engaging all Americans, HRC strives to end discrimination against GLBT citizens and realize a nation that achieves fundamental fairness and equality for all. HRC seeks to improve the lives of GLBT Americans by advocating for equal rights and benefits in the workplace, ensuring that families are treated equally under the law, and increasing public support among all Americans through innovative advocacy, education, and outreach programs. HRC works to secure equal rights for GLBT individuals and families at the federal and state levels by lobbying elected officials, mobilizing grassroots supporters, educating Americans, investing strategically to elect fair-minded officials, and partnering with other GLBT organizations.

Global Security Institute/Founded in 1999

Back in the late 1990s, as a member of Psychologists for Social Responsibility and living in Chicago, I was asked to represent that organization at a meeting called Abolition 2000. The goal of that group was to have abolished nuclear weapons by 2000. I had the chance to meet its founder, the late Senator Alan Cranston, and I was smitten. That movement evolved into the organization Jonathan Granoff now leads, known as the Global Security Institute (GSI). It is dedicated to strengthening international cooperation and security based on the rule of law with a particular focus on nuclear arms control, nonproliferation, and disarmament. GSI was founded by Senator Alan Cranston, whose insight that nuclear weapons are impractical, unacceptably risky, and unworthy of civilization continues to inspire GSI's efforts to contribute to a safer world. GSI has developed an exceptional team that includes former heads of state and government, distinguished diplomats, effective politicians, committed celebrities, religious leaders, Nobel Peace laureates, disarmament and legal experts, and concerned citizens.

Search for Common Ground/Founded in 1982

I first had the pleasure of meeting Susan Marks in Davos at a breakfast meeting in which we were to co-facilitate a discussion. I could not keep up with her! She had us all enthralled with her perspectives and experiences, and I was astonished. She and her husband John started the Search for Common Ground as a vehicle to transform the way the world deals with conflict: away from adversarial approaches, toward cooperative solutions. Although the world is overly polarized and violence is much too prevalent, they remain essentially optimistic. Their view is that, on the whole, history is moving in positive directions. Although some of the conflicts currently being dealt with may seem intractable, there are successful examples of cooperative conflict resolution that can be looked to for inspiration—such as in South Africa, where an unjust system was transformed through negotiations and an inclusive peace process.

Project on Justice in Times of Transition/Founded in 1992

Mari Fitzduff introduced me to Timothy Phillips in the context of working on this project, and needless to say, I was taken aback by their work. The Project on Justice in Times of Transition brings together individuals from a broad spectrum of countries to share experiences in ending conflict, building civil society, and fostering peaceful coexistence. It currently operates in affiliation with the Foundation for a Civil Society in New York and the Institute for Global Leadership at Tufts University. Since its creation in 1992 by co-chairs Wendy Luers and Timothy Phillips, the Project has conducted more than fifty programs for a variety of leaders throughout the world and has utilized its methodology to assist them in addressing such difficult issues as the demobilization of combatants, the status of security files, police reform, developing effective negotiating skills, political demonstrations, and preserving or constructing the tenets of democracy in a heterogeneous society. Through its innovative programming, the Project has exposed a broad cross-section of communities in transition to comparable situations elsewhere, and it has contributed to the broadening of international public discourse on transitional processes.

In recent years the Project has conducted programs that have helped practitioners and political leaders strategize solutions in a variety of countries and regions, including Afghanistan, Colombia, East Timor, Guatemala, Kosovo, Northern Ireland, Palestine, and Peru.

Exodus World Service/Founded in 1988

Heidi Moll was cheering my son and me on last fall in a five-kilometer run that was a fundraiser for Exodus World Service and other agencies. I first came to know of their refugee work via a church we used to attend, and it was remarkable. Exodus World Service transforms the lives of refugees and of volunteers. It educates local churches about refugee ministry, connects volunteers in relationship with refugee families through practical service projects, and equips leaders to speak up on behalf of refugees. The end result is that wounded hearts are healed, loneliness is replaced with companionship, and fear is transformed into hope. Exodus recruits local volunteers, equips them with information and training, and then links them directly with refugee families newly arrived in the Chicago metropolitan area. It also provides training and tools for front-line staff of other refugee service agencies. In addition, Exodus has developed several innovative programs for use by volunteers in their work with refugees.

International Institute for Sustainable Development/Founded in 1990

The International Institute for Sustainable Development (IISD) contributes to sustainable development by advancing policy recommendations on international trade and investment, economic policy, climate change, measurement and assessment, and natural resources management. By using Internet communications, it is able to report on international negotiations and broker knowledge gained through collaborative projects with global partners, resulting in more rigorous research, capacity building in developing countries, and better dialogue between North and South. IISD is in the business of promoting change toward sustainable development. Through research and through effective communication of their findings, it engages decision makers in government, business, NGOs, and other sectors to develop and implement policies that are simultaneously beneficial to the global economy, to the global environment, and to social well-being. IISD also believes fervently in the importance of building its own institutional capacity while helping its partner organizations in the developing world to excel.

LET'S GET GOING

I hope you enjoy learning more about these amazing individuals and their work. I certainly have enjoyed working with them and in completing this remarkable writing project. They all have the common denominator of changing people's lives, and isn't that truly the way to change the world?

Braille Without Borders: Do You Need Vision to Be a Visionary?

Paul Kronenberg and
Patrick Savaiano

"Dear parents, don't worry about your children. The farm is clean and the food is excellent." With these words, the deputy mayor of the city of Lhasa in Tibet saw a new group of blind students off to the Braille Without Borders training farm in Shigatse, accompanied by their parents and Wangchen Geleg, the vice president of the Tibet Disabled Persons Federation. The deputy mayor continued, "With the preparatory school in Lhasa and the vocational training center in Shigatse, Tibet's blind will be in a position to integrate themselves into regular schools or professions."

In September 2002, Sabriye Tenberken and Paul Kronenberg changed the name of their organization to Braille Without Borders. This name carries two significant meanings that serve as the foundation for their mission. First, the co-founders of Braille Without Borders (BWB) want to convey the organization's willingness to work anywhere in the world. Second, and more importantly, the organization wants to create an environment for the blind and visually impaired that is "without borders." In other words, BWB promotes the empowerment of the blind among all individuals and recognizes the right of all people to explore and set their own borders. BWB wants its students to gain the feeling that they belong in society, and that they have the right to exist and be treated as human beings. The blind and visually impaired often have borders and obstacles placed upon them, intentionally or not, by the sighted people of the world. This situation is accentuated in the developing areas of the world such as the Tibetan Autonomous Region (TAR) in which the blind have traditionally been excluded from most social activities and opportunities.

Based on World Health Organization (WHO) statistics, 161 million people live with a disabling visual impairment, of which 37 million are blind and 124 million have low vision. Every five seconds, someone becomes blind, and a child goes blind every minute. About 90 percent of these individuals live in developing countries of Africa, Asia, Latin America, and the Pacific regions. About 90 percent of the blind children in these developing countries have no access to education. Before Braille Without Borders began in the TAR, the region's blind children did not have access to education. They led lives on the margins of society, with extremely few chances of integration. According to official statistics, some 30,000 of the 2.5 million inhabitants of the TAR are blind or highly visually impaired. This figure is an average that is well above that of most areas of the world. The causes of visual impairment or blindness are both climatic and hygienic: dust, wind, high ultraviolet light radiation, soot in houses caused by heating with coal and/or yak dung, and lack of vitamin A at an early age. Inadequate health care also plays a major role, and cataracts are widespread. The Tibetan government and private organizations have set up eye camps to train local doctors to perform appropriate surgeries, but there remains a significant population of blind people in the TAR that cannot be helped in this way.

Braille Without Borders was founded with the intention of empowering blind people from areas like the TAR so that they can set up their own projects, schools, and businesses for other blind people. In this way, the concept of eliminating the borders that are placed upon the blind can spread worldwide so that more blind and visually impaired individuals will have access to education and opportunities to integrate into society as they wish. BWB also hopes to change the perception of others who view blind people as being less able to fit into society than sighted people. The hopeful and encouraging words spoken by the deputy mayor of the city of Lhasa exemplify an acceptance of the organization's mission and a shifting perception toward blind people in Tibetan society.

HISTORY OF BWB

In the summer of 1997, Sabriye Tenberken, a blind woman from Germany and co-founder of BWB, traveled within the TAR to investigate the possibility of providing training for the blind and visually impaired people of Tibet. She quickly realized that there were no programs in place for the education and rehabilitation for blind people in the TAR. She decided to take the initiative to found an organization that would alleviate this problem. A local school in the city of Lhasa provided space for the project, and a local counterpart took care of all of the official paperwork.

Tenberken had realized that she was blind at the age of twelve, after she met another girl who said she was blind even though she saw more than Sabriye did. While attending a school for sighted kids, Sabriye had been picked on by other kids, but she had never known why. She was also treated in a different way by teachers and parents of other (sighted) children. They spoke to her in baby voices, gave her the largest piece of cake, and sometimes spoke to her in loud voices as if she were deaf. Sabriye had never seen very well, and the realization that she was "just" blind was a great relief to her. Now she knew why she had been treated differently than other children her age. She chose to be transferred to a special school for blind children and quickly realized that she was not the only one who was unable to see. At this school, she gained a lot of self-confidence through activities such as mountain climbing, kayaking, downhill skiing, and horseback riding. Through this training, she developed a will to accomplish things that even many sighted children did not dream of doing.

Tenberken originally became interested in Tibetology after visiting a special exhibition on Tibet as a teenager. She and her fellow students were allowed to touch the different artifacts, and she became interested in what Tibet was about. She applied to study the subject at Bonn University. Since Sabriye was the first blind student ever to enroll in this course of study, no books in Braille were available. Even more significant, a Tibetan Braille script did not exist. As an extremely motivated individual, Tenberken decided to develop a Tibetan script for the blind instead of withdrawing from the program at Bonn University. This script combined the principles of the Braille system with the special features of the Tibetan syllable-based script. Her script was submitted for close examination to an eminent Tibetan scholar, who found it to be readily understandable and easy to learn. Until Tenberken developed this script for her studies in 1992, the TAR had no script for its blind people. To this day, the blind and visually impaired people in Tibet continue to use Tenberken's script.

In the summer of 1997, Sabriye went to Tibet to study the situation of blind people. On this trip she met Paul Kronenberg, a Dutch engineer, who was backpacking through Tibet. She told him about her idea for setting up a project for blind people, and he was the only foreigner on the trip who did not think Sabriye was totally insane. They exchanged addresses, and nine months later, when Sabriye had all the paperwork ready to return to Tibet to start the first school for the blind, she called Paul to say good-bye. Instead of responding with "I wish you good luck," Paul said, "I will come with you." The next day, he quit his job; only five days later, in May 1998, Sabriye and Paul left Europe to establish the first Rehabilitation and Training Centre for the Blind in Tibet.

They began their project with a preparatory school for blind elementary school children. They made the necessary arrangements for six children from different villages to board at the school. The children came from different parts of the TAR and had to get used to one another's dialects. A local teacher was found and, within a matter of days, she was fully instructed in the Tibetan Braille script. The children learned the Tibetan Braille alphabet on homemade wooden boards with Velcro dots and, within just six weeks, they knew each of the thirty Tibetan characters and could count in the Tibetan, Chinese, and English languages. This immediate success helped provide the foundation for a hopeful future for BWB.

VALUES AND BELIEFS

BWB holds several core values and beliefs that aid in driving its mission. The organization aspires to aid people with blindness and visual impairments worldwide, regardless of race, creed, national origin, sex, age, handicap, disease entity, social status, financial status, or religious affiliation. As mentioned above, the organization does not view blindness as a justifiable reason for placing borders around an individual's opportunities. Blindness is not a reason to be socially excluded; it is a personal characteristic or quality and not a stain or deviance. BWB believes that blindness is no longer a disability when (1) society accepts blindness as a part of life that is equal to sightedness, (2) people with blindness have access to opportunities that afford them the ability to learn empowering techniques and methods that compensate for their inability to see, and (3) people with blindness and visual impairments organize and empower themselves and self-assuredly fight for equal opportunities. BWB has organized its programs and mission to make headway in these areas, eliminate factors that contribute to the perception of visual impairment as a disability in society, and instill self-confidence in its blind students.

PREPARATORY SCHOOL FOR THE BLIND

The first step toward accomplishing these goals was the establishment of a preparatory school in 1998. Since the blind population of the TAR is so wide-spread, BWB decided that it would be best to have the blind children boarded in Lhasa at the Preparatory School for the Blind so they would both live and be trained at the center. From financial, organizational, and logistical perspectives, it would have been too complicated and difficult to set up individual training programs in the remote areas of the TAR. With the children boarding at the school, training and education could be provided much more effectively. Adjusting to a new environment and being separated from familiar surroundings made it necessary for the children to accept and learn new techniques for the blind as quickly and efficiently as possible. Additionally, the children would have the opportunity to communicate with other blind people and exchange experiences of common difficulties they had at home. So from the beginning, the Preparatory School for the Blind has provided classes and lodging for children and adolescents between five and fifteen years of age.

It is the organization's goal that during their one to two years' training, the children will gain enough self-confidence to cope independently with the difficulties of daily life. First, the students receive intensive training in orientation, mobility, and daily living skills. This training involves helping the students improve their orientation in a room and on the school compound, walk with a cane, eat with chopsticks, and develop daily hygienic skills. Orientation training is followed by training in the Tibetan, Chinese, English, and mathematical Braille scripts. In addition to the training in special techniques for the blind, the students are also instructed in basic colloquial Chinese and English language skills. The primary goal of the preparatory school is that after completion of the basic training, the young students will be able to integrate themselves into local "regular" elementary schools.

PRODUCTION OF EDUCATIONAL MATERIALS

Although Braille script is the basis of literacy for blind people worldwide, only a fraction of blind individuals are actually able to read it. As mentioned above, prior to Sabriye Tenberken's invention of a Tibetan Braille script, there was no means for the blind people of Tibet to become literate. Through literacy, the blind can gain access to knowledge and skills, so BWB makes it a priority to train its students in reading Braille. The organization believes that once literate, the children will have access to education, and therefore be more able to increase their self-confidence, learn a profession, and integrate into society. In order to provide reading and work materials for the students attending the school and the vocational training program, BWB established a workshop that produces Tibetan Braille materials. Eberhard Hahn, a blind German mathematician, developed a computer program to convert written Tibetan into Tibetan Braille script. Tibetan texts are typed into a computer through Wyle transliteration, and Hahn's program converts this transliteration into Tibetan Braille. The first Tibetan Braille books were produced through this process in August 2001.

VOCATIONAL AND SKILLS TRAINING

Although helping children gain education through literacy has been BWB's first priority, the organization has also focused on many different skills that can be developed by the blind children. Many of these skills can be directly applied to the future professions of the children. For instance, children at the school can be trained in Tibetan and Chinese medical massage, pulse diagnosis, and acupressure. In the autumn of 2000, two blind, educated medical massage trainers were located and brought to start this program at the school.

The students may also obtain musical training, and especially talented blind children are trained by a professional musician in singing, composing, and playing musical instruments. With the addition of the organization's organic training farm in Shigatse, BWB is making great progress toward gaining viable vocational opportunities for its students. Beginning in the summer of 2004, students have been able to take animal husbandry training, including the production of milk, yogurt, and cheese as well as agricultural training in the cultivation of vegetables and grain. During that same summer, the students began to receive training in making handicrafts, including knitting, weaving, and basket making. Finally, the students began to be trained in the use of computers. Through vocational and skills training, BWB hopes to provide its students with self-confidence as well as future career options.

Training Farm in Shigatse

As part of its mission to provide its students with vocational and skills training, BWB set up a forty-acre training "farm" in the Tibetan town of Shigatse, about 250 kilometers west of Lhasa, in the spring of 2004. Although the farm is essentially a vocational training center for blind young adults in the neighboring counties around Shigatse, it also provides residential facilities for blind students who have gained admission to the nearby government "regular" school. In 2007, seven more blind students from the project in Lhasa joined the three original students at the regular school next to the farm. The teachers at the regular school were so happy with these students that they have requested that the farm send as many as it can. Having these additional academic, blind students resident on the farm has created or renewed an academic interest in the blind vocational students who were already living there. These original vocational students have begun freely attending the tuition classes that the farm offers to the academic students from Lhasa.

The year 2007 marked the beginning of many new, exciting systems and programs on the farm. The training farm has goals to build up a quality dairy herd, improve the care and rearing of riding horses, and organize the piggery and poultry. The animal husbandry unit on the farm has been consolidated to one plot that used to be an army barracks. BWB has recently installed an environmentally sound toilet system that was pioneered by a German/Dutch association called Ecosan. This Ecosan system has been tested successfully in central Europe and Asia. Its central feature is the separation of urine from feces by means of a simple, yet clever, partition in the toilet bowl itself. Urine is directed into a holding tank so that it can be later used as urea on the fields. Feces are directed into a holding pit where they quickly compost. This system saves water by using materials such as leaves, ash, and earth instead, which are kept in containers nearby the toilets. By adding these materials to the feces receptacle after each use, the composting process begins more quickly. The students and staff were instructed in using and maintaining this new system, and learned about its advantages for the environment. It is a system that can be installed easily in the most remote, rural Tibetan homes. Furthermore, it provides input for organic agriculture and supports the importance of using organic methods in Tibetan soil, where the organic component can be less than 4 percent.

In the autumn of 2007, BWB began the final phase of its work on a composting factory at the training farm. The building was completed and features ten cubicles on one side for ten pairs of opposing composting boxes. This makes the compost much easier to turn, making it both blind friendly and sighted friendly. More cubicles line the other side for storing and mulching straw, grass, leaves, and paper. Mulching, cutting, and hacking machines in three different sizes are on-site as well. The new composting factory is situated adjacent to six organic greenhouses.

Michael Parent from Canada, the third BWB Westerner, introduced the "Mini Square Meter Greenhouses." These greenhouses work according to a method of kitchen gardening that has been practiced for many years on the terraced mountainsides of Darjeeling in India. This system is especially suitable for blind gardening. Each gardening bed is one square meter, and planting is accomplished by placing individual seeds through holes punched in a template. The beds are arranged adjacent to each other, and form a line as long or as short as required for the blind students who are gardening. The beds are separated from the path by a raised barrier to prevent the blind or sighted farmer from walking on the earth that contains the growing seeds. Since each bed is a meter wide, each plant in the bed can be attended to individually and conveniently. The beds are covered by shade cloth or plastic depending on weather conditions. This cloth or plastic is supported by arches, one meter high, that are made from any sturdy yet flexible material. These mini-greenhouses are exceptionally easy to maintain and inexpensive to construct. One bed costs approximately five euros and can be replicated easily by rural Tibetan households. Several local nongovernmental organizations (NGOs), as well as the Swiss Red Cross, have adopted this system and are implementing it in local villages.

In addition to the greenhouses, the farm has also benefited from the instruction of a German animal husbandry expert, Boris Schiele. In 2005 Schiele gave a course in the care of dairy cows to the staff and students. The emphasis was on diet as a main requirement in the production of quality organic milk. Students also learned how to use a computerized, individual feeding program made possible because BWB grows its own fodder in its own fields. The growing pattern of grains and fodder was reorganized with the dairy herd in mind. New stables were also constructed so that the blind could work there easily. The milk that is produced is used directly in BWB's cheese production unit. The popularity of the organization's organic cheese is growing. Two staff, one sighted and one blind, recently returned from a practical course in cheese production in Holland. Stores as far away as Shanghai have expressed interest in the unique blend of European and Tibetan cheeses being produced on the farm. BWB hopes that the sales of the cheese will help generate income to cover at least a portion of the organization's running costs.

Self-Integration Project

Shortly after BWB began its projects at the preparatory school and training farm, the positive impact that was being made on the students became apparent. Children who came from backgrounds in which they were completely excluded from society discovered that they were not the only ones living that way. The students were able to share their experiences, and they were exposed to blind teachers, who were able to perform the tasks necessary to that profession. All the students were treated the same. Within a matter of days, the students' will to learn grew stronger, and their self-confidence increased considerably. If a student complained that he or she could not perform a certain task, the teachers and staff replied that the blind teachers and Ms. Tenberken were able to perform the task— so the student should be able to as well. The students showed that their increasing self-confidence was an extremely important step toward possessing the courage to approach the daily tasks of life in society.

One day, a few of the students walked into the center of Lhasa, and some nomads very rudely shouted at them, "Hey, you blind fools!" Kienzen, the oldest of the small group, turned around and told the nomads that yes, he was blind, but he was not a fool. "I am going to school. I can read and write! Can you do that? I can even read and write in the dark! Can you do that?" The nomads were astonished: they could not read or write because they had never even visited a school. This experience sparked conversation and curiosity among the members of this nomadic group, and about six months later, they brought a blind boy from their region to the project. This example helps illustrate how important it is for all children to know and believe that they are valuable members of society. BWB wants its students to take pride in their blindness and to embrace it as a part of their quality as people. In other words, BWB hopes to have the children stand up in their societies and say, "I am blind. So what?"

In the Tibetan society, as in many societies, it is believed that blindness is a punishment for something done wrong in a previous life. Through its work in the TAR, BWB is helping to modify this perception of the blind. Because of plenty of media attention given to the organization, the project is visited by numerous Tibetan and Chinese people who are curious to see firsthand what is going on there. When they are confronted with happy blind children, they wonder how it can be that these children are being punished for past wrongdoing. Instead, the staff tells visitors that the children are not being punished, but that they have been presented with a challenge for their next life. This call for a new perception of the blind is acceptable because it fits within this cultural context. The visitors seem to be open to this idea and suddenly see the blind with new-found respect.

Initially, BWB planned to train special field workers to counsel the students through this significant transition on a regular basis. They received help from some staff members of the organization Save the Children, who visited the school weekly. However, after only a few months, the staff at BWB noticed that the students were doing extremely well on their own, and that they had integrated themselves into their classrooms and school. BWB's staff gave this some thought and realized that this process of integration the blind children were going through was an extremely important one. They wanted to name this process. They realized that they could not call it "re-integration" because the children had never before been successfully integrated. They also could not name the process "integration" because this did not fully capture the students' experience. As the blind students began integrating with sighted children, the staff noticed that the blind students were willing to show those around them exactly what they were capable of doing. They were willing to ask for help from sighted children when needed, and they were willing to help sighted children when they were able. They made friends as well as competitors in class, demonstrating that the integration was real, and that the blind do not need to receive special treatment. To describe this process, BWB came up with the term "self-integration." Ultimately, on their own, the blind children were able to gain a foundation of knowledge at the school and, more importantly, enough self-confidence to integrate themselves into the school, a profession, and daily society.

Massage Clinic

An amazing success story that has resulted from BWB's efforts in educational and vocational training was the opening of its Massage Clinic, which was founded in 2003 by the organization's first massage therapy graduates, Kyila and Digi. It is the worthwhile and promising result of more than three years' training in massage and physiotherapy. The clinic's founders have since been joined by three additional graduates, Tenzing, Tashi, and Drolma. The clinic has also expanded by renting and renovating five additional rooms. A variety of massages, including Chinese massage, Thai massage, physiotherapy, acupressure, and oil massage, are currently offered at the clinic. It is situated on the main road in the center of the city of Lhasa. The clinic has proven to be a star attraction for tourists, both Western and Asian, and has advertisements in the major hotels and restaurants of Lhasa. It has achieved a high degree of independence in that it no longer requires subsidies from BWB and handles its own accounting and management.

Not only has the clinic grown into a successful business, but the manner of appointing management has evolved since its inception as well. Originally, the traditional Tibetan attitude prevailed in that positions of responsibility would go to the eldest. No special talents or qualifications were required to gain positions of responsibility other than the accumulation of years. The eldest were also expected to earn the most money and work the fewest number of hours. Eventually, however, it was agreed that the manager should be the individual who could motivate, encourage, and communicate most effectively with colleagues, customers, and officials. Based on these criteria, seventeen-year-old Lobsang, the youngest among the staff at the clinic, was chosen to be manager, and the clinic has expanded under his leadership. It now boasts a neon sign overlooking the main road of Lhasa, and its staff members give numerous local TV and radio interviews.

TOTNES SCHOOL, ENGLAND

Another inspiring story began in 2007 when two of the organization's blind students took part in an English course at the Totnes School in England. Kyila, also co-founder of the Massage Clinic, graduated from the intermediate as well as the advanced intermediate courses offered by Totnes School. Nyima studied in the same school and graduated from the pre-intermediate section. They studied with sighted students from Europe and Asia, and the Braille script and learning materials that they used were partly printed in BWB's Braille printing house, partly provided by the Royal National Institute for the Blind (RNIB). Like their fellow sighted students, Kyila and Nyima were integrated with local host families and were soon able to find their way around Totnes. Neither of them had problems finding friends, and thanks to the enthusiastic help of their teachers and hosts, they were able to follow the classes successfully. They were soon able to make small trips on their own, and even traveled to London by themselves.

During their stay in Totnes, Kyila and Nyima wanted to go to visit a school for the blind in England to get some ideas for their own school in Lhasa. BWB staff were uneasy at first, fearing that those at the English school would get the impression that the school in Lhasa was rather backward in comparison. BWB did not want its students to be discouraged, but the staff was surprised to find that the students' reaction was quite different than expected. Understandably, the Lhasa blind students were amazed at the advanced computer equipment and the technical knowledge of the English blind students. However, the Lhasa students also seemed amused by the "interesting" but "unnecessary" gadgets the English were using, such as machines that tell the blind if a glass is full or not, whether or not it is raining outside, and whether or not the sun is shining. Kyila and Nyima mutually agreed on one point: their classmates at the school in Lhasa were more advanced in the use of Braille than the blind students they met during their stay in England. "They just work with talking books and speech synthesizers," said Nyima. "This has nothing to do with real reading." Kyila noted that although blind students in Tibet have no problem using a white cane as a walking aid, "blind people in England seem to be shyer. They don't want to be acknowledged as a blind person and so they cannot imagine traveling independently."

THE NEW INDEPENDENCE

The observations noted by Kyila and Nyima are evidence that the organization's goals are being achieved by its students. Not only are the students concerned with learning and integrating into society, but they see the real opportunity to lead independent lives. As part of this "help for self-help" mission and to augment the process of "self-integration," BWB entered into a do-it-yourself phase in 2006 that continues to this day. This phase has marked an ongoing effort to put more responsibility in the hands of the Tibetan staff of the organization. For instance, important tasks that were once performed by founders Tenberken and Kronenberg, such as bookkeeping, scheduling, planning of curricula, and meeting with officials, have been handed off for the most part to their Tibetan colleagues. This important step toward project independence has not come easily. In fact, some staff members could not cope with this new situation and the greater responsibilities that came with it, and unfortunately they chose to withdraw from the project. However, several former students of BWB have since stepped up and replaced those staff members. The new and very young colleagues of the BWB staff are highly motivated and engaged with the project. They have felt free and confident enough to work on developing new teaching methods and plans and in this way create new structures within BWB.

The high level of motivation of the new teachers is not always welcomed by some older staff. "They're still too young!" complained a longtime teacher about her new colleagues who were once her students. "I don't want to be given orders by my former students," grumbled another teacher. The cook moaned that it was never this strict before. "How old do you have to be to have your own ideas?" answered Kyila, who recently returned from her year's study in England with interesting new ideas and plans for the project. Kyila, together with Yudon, a former student who has studied in a "regular" school in Tibet, have reformed the English and Chinese curricula and have organized new teaching materials. They have also, on their own, redecorated, rearranged, and reorganized the organization's early childhood training, called the Mouse Class. Gyenzen, a former student, now heads the Braille Printing Division and takes care of the students' needs for Braille textbooks. These young teachers have been called the Gang of Three, and they are attempting to break old, negative work habits that have been established over time. "We can run the project independently only if we work together," agree Kyila, Yudon, and Gyenzen, who seem surprised and disappointed at the reaction of some of their older colleagues. Tenberken and Kronenberg have tried to stay out of these internal conflicts as much as possible, but they have reported feeling quite happy about the fresh air and the positive mood this new, young staff has brought to the project: "Their influence transfers to the kids. We hope and trust, too, that our rookie management will be open to advice from their elders while keeping their youthful enthusiasm." Over the last decade, the co-founders of BWB have watched their mission take shape.

NEXT STEPS: THE INTERNATIONAL INSTITUTE
FOR SOCIAL ENTREPRENEURS

Given all that has been accomplished by BWB with relatively limited funding, it is amazing to consider the organization's lofty future goals. The organization believes that the current situation—an extreme lack of education for blind people in the developing world—can be changed, particularly by visionaries who are blind or visually impaired. In order to make progress toward this ultimate goal, BWB has established the International Institute for Social Entrepreneurs (IISE) in Kerala, India, and hopes to officially open this international center for social enterprises in January 2009. The IISE will train blind individuals (age eighteen and over) who have the right initiative, motivation, and skills, and who want to develop social projects in their own countries based on the model that has been established in Tibet. BWB recognizes that visually impaired people who have overcome obstacles in their lives, such as co-founder Sabriye Tenberken, are problem solvers. These individuals have great empathy toward social problems because they have experienced many firsthand. This is why BWB has chosen to focus on attracting IISE participants who are blind or partially sighted.

The campus of the IISE is located in a pristine little village by the Vellayani Lake, approximately 15 kilometers from the center of Trivandrum, the capitol of Kerala state in India. It has been built in an environmentally friendly, ethnic style that is based on the ideology of the late, renowned architect Laurie Baker. The center has incorporated rain water harvesting, solar and wind energy, waste management systems, and the Ecosan waste treatment system used at the training farm in Shigatse. It is built on two plots of land, one used for the school campus and the other to house the staff headquarters. The overall concept is to design this project as a model for all future institutions of its kind.

BWB would like its applicants for training at the IISE to be creative, innovative, and motivated. The visually impaired and blind students must be able to read and write in either enlarged print or English Braille script. Thanks to the hard work of the local administrative director, Tigi Philip, and a highly motivated group of professors, the framework of the curriculum has been completed. Over a course of one year, the students selected to attend the IISE will be trained in fundraising, public relations, management, project planning, computer technology, English, and communication skills among others. The students will be given the tools necessary to set up their own schools for the blind or visually impaired, improve existing schools, or start other social projects in their own countries.

To support Braille Without Borders with a donation, or volunteer your services, please visit their website at http://www.braillewithoutborders.org for more information.

BIOGRAPHIES

Sabriye Tenberken studied Central Asian studies at Bonn University. In addition to Mongolian and modern Chinese, she studied modern and classical Tibetan in combination with sociology and philosophy. Since no blind student had ever ventured to enroll in these kinds of courses, she could not fall back on others' experiences. She had to develop her own methods to come to terms with her course of studies. As a result, she decided to develop a Tibetan script for the blind. Sabriye coordinates and counsels the BWB project. She is responsible for the training of teachers and trainers for the blind, and initially she taught the children herself. Further, she selects and supervises all staff members. Sabriye is also responsible for fundraising and communication with official and sponsoring organizations.

She has written three books in which she tells about the history of the project and the way she dealt with becoming blind: *Mein Weg fuehrt nach Tibet* (*My Path Leads to Tibet*; Arcade Publishing, New York); *Tashis' New World*; and *Das siebte Jahr* (*The Seventh Year*). The first book has been published in eleven languages, including English.

Paul Kronenberg has been working with Sabriye since May 1998 to establish the Rehabilitation and Training Centre for the Blind in Tibet. He also worked part-time as a designer and construction coordinator for the Swiss Red Cross in Shigatse. Paul has a technical background. He graduated in four different studies: mechanical engineering, computer science, commercial technology, and communication system science. For several summers during his studies, Paul worked for different organizations in development projects in Africa, Eastern Europe, and Tibet. Paul is responsible for all technical aspects and maintenance in the center's program. He trains people in bookkeeping, office work, and the use of computers. Along with being responsible for communications and fundraising, Paul started up the production of Tibetan Braille books and supervises all construction activities within the project.

ORGANIZATIONAL SNAPSHOT

Organization: Braille Without Borders

Founders: Paul Kronenberg and Sabriye Tenberken

Mission/Description: According to WHO statistics, 161 million people live with a disabling visual impairment, of whom 37 million are blind and 124 million have low vision. Every five seconds someone becomes blind, every minute somewhere a child goes blind. About 90 percent of these individuals live in developing countries of Africa, Asia, Latin America, and the Pacific regions. Moreover, nine out of ten blind children in developing countries have no access to education. Braille Without Borders wants to empower blind people from these countries so they themselves can set up projects and schools for other blind people. In this way, the concept can be spread across the globe so more blind and visually impaired people have access to education and a better future.

Website: braillewithoutborders.org

Address: Förderkreis Blinden–Zentrum Tibet—Braille Ohne Grenzen e.V.

c/o Paul Kronenberg

Im Auel 34, D-53913 Swisttal, Germany

Phone: 0049-2226-913403

Fax: 0049-2226-913404

E-mail: blztib@t-online.de

2

Room to Read: The Democratization of Literacy

John Wood and Patrick Savaiano

MISSION

Room to Read was founded on the belief that "World Change Starts with Educated Children," and that education is the key to breaking the cycle of poverty. The organization strives to provide children with access to education, one child at a time, one school at a time, and one village at a time. The overall goals of the organization are best summed up in its mission statement:

> We partner with local communities throughout the developing world to provide quality educational opportunities by establishing libraries, creating local language children's literature, constructing schools, providing education to girls, and establishing computer labs. We seek to intervene early in the lives of children in the belief that education empowers people to improve socioeconomic conditions for their families, communities, countries, and future generations. Through the opportunities that only education can provide, we strive to break the cycle of poverty, one child at a time.

Room to Read focuses on countries that lack the resources to educate their children. It currently operates in eight countries—six in Asia (Cambodia, India, Laos, Nepal, Sri Lanka, and Vietnam) and two in Africa (South Africa and Zambia)—with plans to expand throughout Asia, Africa, and Latin America in the years to come to better meet the needs of children throughout the developing world.

John Wood, Founder and CEO, launched Room to Read after a trek through Nepal. He visited several local schools and was touched by the warmth and enthusiasm of the students and teachers, but also saddened by the shocking lack of resources that were available to them. Driven to help, Wood quit his senior executive position with Microsoft and built a global team to work with rural villages to build sustainable solutions to their educational challenges. He continues to be inspired by meeting people around the world who have a thirst for education, such as witnessing children in Vietnam reading toothpaste tubes because they literally had no books. "What most inspires me is that this is one of the great challenges of today's world," says Wood. "Can we reach out to the 800 million people in the world who lack basic literacy and give them the tools they need and the opportunity to break the cycle of poverty through education? In itself it's inspiring because it's doable. We live in an age of unparalleled prosperity, yet something as basic as literacy is missing from this many people. So in a way it's a very daunting task but also doable, and that inspires me. We as an organization, collectively, can make a huge dent and do something about this problem." Individuals such as philanthropist Andrew Carnegie, Steve Ballmer (CEO of Microsoft), and President Jimmy Carter have helped inspire Wood to reinvent his career and create his vision to democratize access to books and education worldwide.

In founding Room to Read, Wood interwove proven corporate business practices with his bold vision to provide educational access to 10 million children in the developing world. His novel approach to nonprofit management called for several factors to ensure its success. First, it required scalable, measured, and sustainable results. Second, it required low overhead, allowing maximum investment in educational infrastructure. Third, it required that challenge grants be put in place to help foster community ownership and sustainability. Finally, the organization required strong local staff and partnerships in order to create culturally relevant programs. Over the last decade, Room to Read's staff and supporters have put his vision into practice.

HISTORY OF ROOM TO READ

The Room to Read story begins in 1998 with Founder and CEO, John Wood. In 1998, Wood was an overworked Microsoft executive looking for the quiet solitude of a trekking vacation. While backpacking in the Himalayas, Wood met a Nepalese man who invited him to visit a school in a neighboring village. Hoping for a chance to see the real Nepal, rather than his tourist's trek, Wood agreed. This short detour would change his life forever, for the man Wood met was a Nepalese education resource officer. Wood soon discovered that despite this man's huge heart and tremendous work ethic (traveling mountain passes on foot to visit his schools), he had very few resources to offer the schools in his charge. At the school, Wood came face to face with the harsh reality confronting millions of Nepalese children: there were almost no books. Wood was stunned to discover that the few books in the school library—a Danielle Steele romance, the *Lonely Planet Guide to Mongolia*, and a few other backpacker castoffs—were so precious that they were kept under lock and key to protect them from the children. As Wood left the village that day, the school headmaster made a simple request: "Perhaps, Sir, you will someday come back with books." This request would not go unheard. After returning from his trek, Wood e-mailed friends to ask for their help in collecting children's books and was overwhelmed with the response. Over

3,000 books arrived within the next two months. The following year, Wood and his father flew to Nepal, rented a yak, and returned to the village to deliver the books.

Soon after that trip, Wood made the decision to leave the corporate world in order to devote himself to starting a new nonprofit. In his memoir, *Leaving Microsoft to Change the World*, Wood explains, "Did it really matter how many copies of Windows we sold in Taiwan this month when there were millions of children without access to books?" In late 1999, Wood quit his executive position with Microsoft and started Room to Read. With Room to Read, Wood sought to combine the corporate business practices he had learned at Microsoft with an inspiring vision: to provide the lifelong gift of education to millions of children in the developing world. He contended that with nearly 800 million illiterate adults worldwide and more than 200 million children without access to school, a non-profit "with the scalability of Starbucks and the compassion of Mother Teresa" was required. Beginning in Nepal, Wood and Dinesh Shrestha, future Nepal Country Director, began working with rural communities to build schools and establish libraries. To date, Room to Read has created over 440 schools and more than 5,100 libraries.

In 2000 Room to Read began the Room to Grow Girls' Scholarship Program after recognizing that many girls are denied access to education because of cultural bias. This scholarship fund targets young girls and provides a long-term commitment to their education that lasts an average of ten years. There are now more than 4,000 girls on Room to Grow scholarships. In the summer of 2001, Erin Keown Ganju joined the organization as CEO and was instrumental in its expansion into Vietnam, where she had previously worked for two years. Erin quickly became Wood's partner as the two of them continued to push hard to expand Room to Read's geographic and programmatic presence. With growing demand for Room to Read's services, expansion continued into Cambodia in 2002, followed by India the next year. In 2003 Room to Read also began publishing local language children's books, in addition to providing donated English language books used to stock its libraries. Room to Read works with local authors and local illustrators to develop new children's books and publish them in-country. To date, 226 local language children's book titles have been published.

The year 2004 was also very significant for Room to Read: the organization celebrated one of its first major milestones on April 29 with the opening of its one thousandth library in Siem Reap, Cambodia. Later that year, just days after the December 26 Asian tsunami devastated thousands of villages, Room to Read launched operations in Sri Lanka in order to rebuild schools and help ease the suffering of children there. In addition to expanding into Sri Lanka in 2005, Room to Read also launched programs in Laos, its sixth Asian country. On September 2, just eighteen months after its one thousandth library ceremony, Room to Read opened its two thousandth library, once again in Cambodia. The year 2005 ended with another huge milestone, the donation of the millionth book. Room to Read's five-year strategic plan was completed in 2006, and in December 2007 the organization opened its five thousandth library in Nepal. Room to Read continues to expand its programs, locations, and capacity to carry out its mission into 2008 and beyond.

ROOM TO READ'S PROGRAMS

Providing quality educational opportunities in the developing world is not a simple task. Each new country offers a unique set of challenges and opportunities, every region has its strengths and weaknesses, and every community has its own needs. For these reasons, Room to Read employs local teams led by a local director in each country. It hires local staff who are personally vested in their nation's educational progress and empowers them to make key programmatic decisions. Team members speak the language, know the customs, and understand what it takes to implement each program successfully. They ensure that programs are of the highest quality and are designed to meet each community's specific needs. With input from these local teams, Room to Read has developed a long-term, holistic, and multipronged approach to address a range of educational needs and create lasting change for children in the developing world. The organization's five core programs include the School Room Program, the Reading Room Program, the Local Language Publishing Program, the Computer Room Program, and the Room to Grow Girls' Scholarship Program.

School Room Program

Adequate schools are often scarce in rural areas of the developing world, a factor that contributes to poverty and limits economic development. It is not uncommon for young children to walk several hours each way just to attend school. Many of the schools that do exist are often ramshackle collections of crumbling bricks, loose sheet metal, and dirt floors. Although these structures are no longer safe for children, they continue to be used because the community has no alternative. In other villages, the school structure might be sufficient, but classrooms are grossly overcrowded, with as many as eighty students jammed into a room designed for forty. Unfortunately, these schools cannot count on outside help because government funding for education is scarce. In many countries, the government does not sponsor certain components of education such as preschool, which is the building block for a successful primary and secondary education. Although many communities in the developing world are committed to universal education, they do not possess the resources to achieve that goal in the near future. To help address these issues, Room to Read's School Room Program partners with local communities to build several types of schools to meet the specific needs of each village and culture.

In Laos, Nepal, and Vietnam, Room to Read constructs four- to fourteen-room buildings for primary and secondary schools that currently have unsafe structures or overcrowded classrooms. The organization might assist in completing school construction projects that have been delayed or help to identify communities that are in need of schools. For example, Room to Read partnered with the local community to expand the Shree Janakalyan Lower Secondary School in the Dhadhing district of Nepal. In the past, young students who completed fifth grade had to walk a minimum of one hour each way on a busy highway to reach a secondary school. Tragically, every year some students were killed in road accidents. As a result, the community and school began expanding the number of grades they offered in order to make it a full secondary school (grades 1–10). Room to Read partnered with the community to add an additional six-room building to facilitate this expansion.

The vast majority of primary and secondary schools established by Room to Read include libraries, often the first library the students have been able to use. These libraries provide extracurricular reading materials as well as games and activities that nurture intellectual curiosity and improve reading and critical thinking skills. In addition, these schools include adequate toilet facilities, also rare in many developing world schools. These facilities improve hygiene and increase privacy, which leads to increased student retention rates, especially among girls. In Sri Lanka, Vietnam, and, to a lesser extent, Laos, Room to Read also provides access to preschool. Educational studies demonstrate that early childhood learning makes a significant and positive impact in the educational development of young students. Furthermore, preschools offer an organized learning environment in which small children can be nurtured. This arrangement frees up the time of parents, grandparents, and siblings (especially older sisters), who would otherwise be needed to provide care.

Room to Read understands that a child's education begins with an adequate learning environment. For example, in Vietnam, although the Education and Training Ministry understands the importance of preschool education, the funds to build preschools are simply not available. The government hopes that many of the poor local communities can contribute material and labor to construct community preschools on their own, but these communities are often too poor to do so. In the community of Tan Lap in Long An province, villagers realized that they urgently needed schools for their children. The villagers knew that if their young children could attend school, they could focus on farming and better support their families. In addition, a preschool would begin to teach the children the critical skills they need to improve their lives and lift themselves out of poverty. With the support of Room to Read, today thirty-one young students are learning, writing, singing, and dancing in their new preschool.

A Room to Read preschool usually consists of a one- to three-room building and includes appropriately child-sized furniture as well as lavatory facilities. These structures are well built, include plenty of ventilation, and have a strong roof to withstand the heavy rains of the monsoon season. Many have a school yard with a fence and gate to provide security, and some—depending on location—even have a playground for the children. By setting high standards and expectations,

Room to Read has partnered with local communities to build over 440 schools to date. Thousands of young students are now learning in safe, child-friendly environments that encourage their mental, physical, and spiritual development.

Reading Room Program

The concept of a school library is virtually nonexistent in many communities throughout the developing world. Because so many people in the developing world survive on less than one U.S. dollar per day, children's books are considered luxury items. In some cases, not a single book is available to children to encourage independent learning, intellectual curiosity, and passion for reading. Teachers lack the resources and expertise to establish libraries. Even when children have acquired the skills to read, many do not have access to books to practice these skills.

Without the existence of a children's book publishing industry, the variety of local language children's books available to young readers in many of these countries is severely limited. Books that reflect local culture in an artistic and engaging style are in short supply. In addition, although many rural schools teach English, most have no English language books. If there are no children's books to engage children and help them learn English, their curiosity, motivation, and ability to learn can be lost. Establishing libraries and filling them with children's books, both in English and in local languages, through the Local Language Publishing Program continues to be a cornerstone of Room to Read's mission.

The first step toward the lifelong gift of education is putting a book in the hands of a child. Room to Read's Reading Room Program seeks to facilitate this by establishing a library in every new primary and secondary school it builds, as well as in many existing schools. Room to Read creates a child-friendly learning environment, complete with as many as 300 to 3,000 age-appropriate, local language and English language children's books (the exact number depends on the country, the size of the space, and the type of library), furniture, games, puzzles, and posters. In these libraries, students find books that expand their world, teach them new ideas, and equip them with critical life skills. Furthermore, Room to Read provides training on proper library implementation with three years of support, which includes the provision of additional children's books and further training for staff.

Room to Read establishes Reading Rooms in several different types of settings that include schools it has helped to construct, schools that have applied specifically for a library, and other environments where children have a need to learn, such as orphanages, children's hospitals, schools run by other nonprofits, and community centers. The majority of libraries established by the organization are created within existing rooms and in partnership with a school or community. Because the school community provides a clean room, Room to Read is able to create a child-friendly learning environment quickly and relatively easily. One example of such a library is the Binh Xuan Primary School in Tien Giang, southern Vietnam. Here, the school board believed that having a library and books would boost the quality of education at the school and motivate the approximately 900 students and teachers. When they presented the idea to Room to Read's Vietnam team, they also offered to appoint a dedicated librarian to run the program.

Established in late 2005, the Binh Xuan Primary School Reading Room is divided into two parts: one area for bookkeeping and housing the books, and another area where students can sit and read. Located on the main floor of the school, the room was renovated and equipped with lights and electric fans to ensure a safe and comfortable environment for the students. All bookshelves, reading tables, and seats, sized for primary school students, are colorfully painted. A section of the floor is covered with bright foam where students can sit on soft pillows to play with educational games and read books. Over 600 English and Vietnamese books await the eager students. In addition, fun and educational posters are on the walls to attract students and inspire curiosity and an interest in reading.

Several of Room to Read's local teams have discovered that many highly populated schools want to become partners to establish larger libraries but simply do not have the capacity to dedicate rooms, because their schools are already too crowded. In 2005 Room to Read's team in Cambodia came up with a new approach called Constructed Reading Rooms (CRRs). CRRs are stand-alone library buildings, which are constructed and then furnished in the same fashion as the library rooms. Special care is taken to construct these buildings as model facilities to further promote the value of education in the community. Buildings are designed using local architectural styles in order to foster local pride and ensure that they fit in with their surroundings. Some of the CRRs are built in conjunction with Room to Read's Computer Room Program and include fully furnished libraries as well as computer labs.

One example of a CRR is the Teuk Thlar Primary and Junior High School located in the province of Banteay Meanchey in the northwest part of Cambodia. With nearly 2,000 students, the school's tiny library—two shelves, one table, and 200 books—was far from adequate. Despite the relative dearth of books in the library, it attracted many students daily. Unfortunately, the number of books was very limited, and neither the school nor the community could afford to construct a good library building or improve the single, existing room. By partnering with the community, Room to Read helped to change this situation. With the community contributing funds, labor, and security, the library opened in September 2005 and received over 5,000 unique visits in its first few months of operation.

Room to Read expanded the CRR model to Laos and Nepal in 2006 and is continuing to grow this important type of Reading Room so that all children, regardless of their school environment, can access children's books easily. Unfortunately, in many school communities there is simply not enough space to have a room that is fully dedicated as a library. To address these challenges, Room to Read's local teams find innovative solutions to best meet the needs of each school or community. The organization has established libraries in classrooms and community centers, and it has created mobile book carts that can move from room to room to ensure that children have access to books. Room to Read has donated over 2.2 million books and published an additional 2 million books representing 226 new local language children's titles to fill the shelves of its libraries. In Nepal and Cambodia, not only is Room to Read the largest nonprofit importer of English language books, it is also one of the top publishers of both Nepali and Khmer children's books.

The vast majority of Room to Read's children's books in English are donated by or purchased at a steep discount from large publishers such as Scholastic and Chronicle Books. Room to Read is then able to ship thousands of books at a time to its partner countries. These English language children's books are supplemented with self-published, local language books so that children have books in their own language as well as in English in order to foster a love for reading. Reading Rooms are typically established with an initial donation of several hundred books in order to evaluate how efficiently the books are used. Within six months to a year, if the libraries have a check-out system in place and children are spending time there to read, a second donation of books is provided. To date, Room to Read has established over 5,100 libraries in its partner countries. These libraries come in all shapes and sizes, but they have a common element: local teams work with the community to determine how best to provide access to children's books and create a child-friendly environment.

Local Language Publishing Program

Although Room to Read has successfully established thousands of bilingual libraries in developing countries, this is just one component of its work. In 2002 the Nepal team discovered that Room to Read's libraries were not being used to their fullest potential because students did not have access to quality children's books in their local language. Before learning English, these children first needed to learn to read Nepali in order to develop good literacy skills in the local language. Room to Read's Nepal team quickly determined that there were simply not many quality Nepali children's books available. Parents were too poor to afford reading material for their children, so publishers were not motivated to publish children's books in the local language. To fill this gap in high-quality children's books in the local language, Room to Read boldly decided to launch the Local Language Publishing Program. With seed funding provided by the Skoll Foundation in 2003, this program was launched to create and publish new, local language children's books, thereby giving children access to the type of books that will spark imagination, curiosity, and a desire to learn to read.

To support its commitment to providing a lifelong education for all children, Room to Read began to produce age-appropriate and culturally relevant children's literature in local languages, so that children in the developing world have the same opportunities as those who grow up surrounded by children's books at home, at school, or in the local public library. The Local Language Publishing Program provides children with materials that will inspire them to read, expand their minds, and develop a lifelong love for reading and learning. Room to Read is significantly increasing the quantity and diversity of children's books currently published in eighteen local languages, as well as in English, by sourcing and publishing new children's literature within seven of the eight countries in which it works (with plans to launch the Local Language Publishing Program in Zambia, the eighth operating country, in the near future). Many of the books that are published by the organization are bilingual English and local language children's books that are especially beneficial to children because they can be used throughout a child's development. Initially, they can be read to stimulate a child's imagination and, later on, to reinforce reading skills in the local language and to aid in the initial study of English.

Room to Read works with local writers and illustrators to develop new, culturally relevant children's books. Many of these stories are adapted from local folktales, while others are sourced from various writing competitions and writers' workshops that are sponsored and held by Room to Read. The competitions and workshops are designed to promote a culture of writing, as well as reading, and to source and develop new creative talent. As a result, the books are appropriate to the local context, which is not always the case for children's books written for a non-local audience. Of all the manuscripts submitted to Room to Read, only the very best are selected for publication. The books are often field tested by children to garner feedback on plot, character development, and general suitability for the target age group. Bilingual books are subsequently translated into English, with the goal of maintaining the local flavor and integrity of the story. All the local language books are printed within the respective countries in order to create local jobs and promote the local economy. Room to Read aims to provide a variety of content to children in the developing world by covering a wide range of themes, including beginning words and basic vocabulary, the environment, health, math skills and concepts, morals and values, animal life, family life, folktales, and rhymes and poems. Room to Read is currently one of the top publishers of local language children's books in Nepal and Cambodia. Its goal is to be the "Dr. Seuss of the developing world." To date, Room to Read has published over 226 titles and printed over 2 million books in eighteen local languages. Because the books are published within the countries in which Room to Read works, it is possible to keep costs extremely low, approximately US$1 per book. Most importantly, young children in the developing world now have new, high-quality books to read and enjoy.

Computer Room Program

Opportunity is inherent in technology, and although computer technology has brought huge numbers of people across the globe closer together, thus far it has failed to reach the millions who lack access to the necessary infrastructure.

Nowhere is the "digital divide" more evident than in the developing world, where computers are available to less than 2 percent of the population.[1] Consequently, computer literacy is one of the largest unmet needs of educational systems, and it often holds young students back from being part of the global community and from improving their economic situation.

Computer labs can have a life-changing impact on children. The access provided by the labs allows students to develop computer literacy skills that can lead to further learning and job opportunities. Research shows that when teachers integrate computers and other technology resources into daily instruction, these resources can improve test scores; build students' communication and critical thinking skills; promote creativity, innovation, and collaboration among students; and increase students' community and global awareness.[2] Computer labs can have the added effect of improving attendance and reducing attrition rates by providing an incentive for students to stay in school.[3] Overall, computer labs help improve the quality and relevance of education in developing world settings and equip children with skills they will need in the twenty-first century.

With this in mind, Room to Read has developed the Computer Room Program. It is one of the last programs launched in Room to Read's partner countries, because it is beneficial to establish a working relationship with communities through the School Room or Reading Room Programs prior to investing in this more costly and complex program. Room to Read works with government schools and local nongovernmental organizations (NGOs) to make computer access a reality. Computer labs are established in schools and NGO-run community centers. The labs consist of six to twenty-one new computers (depending on the country and the size of room) with warranties, universal power supply (UPS) units, networking equipment and wiring, learning software, and voltage stabilizers. Other basic needs, such as furniture and a whiteboard, are often included as well.

An integral aspect to this program is the training provided to the computer lab teachers to help them develop a curriculum, improve their computer teaching skills, and ensure that hardware is maintained properly. The computer classes, and the teachers themselves, are periodically evaluated to quickly remedy any knowledge gaps and to reward successful programs with more computer resources. Over a three-year period, Room to Read provides follow-up training, as well as additional software and occasionally additional computers. Computer classes normally complement standard class time. In addition to teaching computer literacy and typing skills, the computers are used in conjunction with traditional classes to provide pragmatic application to relevant studies. Computer training and access are also often extended to members of the community after school hours.

One story of a successful Computer Room initiative comes from Battambang, Cambodia, where Room to Read established a computer lab for the more than 4,000 students at Net Yang Secondary School, a government school that caters to students from the surrounding rural areas. With many of his students too poor to afford access to private computer labs, the school director approached Room to Read to establish a computer lab within the school. His desire was supported by the rest of the school administration, all of whom were highly committed to meeting and fulfilling the Challenge Grant requirements. After its completion in June 2005, the lab began serving many of the 429 students in grade 9, which has had the highest drop-out rate. Students use the lab twice for two hours each week to learn computer fundamentals and English and Khmer typing. One teacher, Mr. Neng Iv said, "[The] computer room will help students to stay at school. Children will gain a good benefit by studying the life skill from this project. The gift from Room to Read Cambodia would improve the human resource in my school." Through its Computer Room Program, Room to Read is providing thousands of students in the developing world their first access to technology.

Room to Grow Girls' Scholarship Program

For many reasons, including economics and cultural bias, families in developing countries often fail to educate girls. In Cambodia, for example, girls' enrollment in school drops precipitously as they get older. At the primary level, 91 percent of girls are enrolled in school; at the secondary level, only 19 percent are enrolled; and at the upper secondary level (grades 9–10), the number drops to 7 percent. In Nepal, only 35 percent of women are literate. In India, the female literacy rate is 52 percent, and it is estimated that 35 million children are not attending school. If a family is able to send only one child to school, which is often the case in poor communities, it is almost without exception the oldest boy who is selected. In rural areas, girls are kept behind to work in the fields or in the home. They are often expected to marry and begin having their own children by adolescence. In urban settings, some girls leave schools to sell tourist items or work in factories; others fall into prostitution. Room to Read aims to keep girls in school, thereby empowering them to end the cycle of poverty.

The Room to Grow Girls' Scholarship Program has an immediate and direct impact on the lives of thousands of girls in the developing world. An education provides security and support to girls and empowers them to make informed life decisions. A solid education early in life is known to be a key ingredient for the improved status of women, which provides a ripple of positive effects throughout society. For every year a girl remains in secondary school, her wages increase 10–20 percent. An educated woman has fewer children, so population growth is slowed in resource-scarce countries. Infant mortality decreases by 8 percent for each year a woman stays in school. Family health and nutrition improve in the home of an educated woman. An educated woman is more likely to educate the next generation. These are all examples of how educating women can have a positive effect on families, communities, and countries.

Room to Read makes a long-term commitment to each girl on scholarship: as long as she attends classes and receives passing grades, her education will be funded through the completion of secondary school. This promise provides an incentive for her to do well in school and for the family to support her through the process. Currently, the majority of Room to Read's scholarship students range in age from five to ten years. Depending on the country and region, the scholarship covers all the needs of a young girl, including monthly school fees, school uniforms, books, stationery, backpacks, a female Room to Read staff member to oversee the program and mentor the girls, additional tutoring as needed, transportation (such as a bicycle or bus fare) for girls living far from school, lunch money for girls who live too far from school to eat at home, medical checkups and expenses, and field trips and workshops. The program officers work closely with the Room to Grow scholarship recipients and give them the support they need to be successful. They actively help to remove roadblocks the girls may encounter by meeting regularly with the girls, their families, and the school administrators.

Along the Vietnamese and Cambodian border, sex trafficking of young girls is all too common. Some families struggling to make ends meet or feed themselves are often forced to make unthinkable choices, including selling a child into trafficking. The ADAPT Program (An Giang Dong Thap Alliance for the Prevention of Trafficking) is a joint venture among several NGOs that seeks to prevent the trafficking of young women by enhancing their educational opportunities and improving their vocational options through a supportive web of services. Room to Read provides the scholarship component of this program. The ADAPT scholarship program is designed to be a collaborative commitment among the child, the adults in her life, the school, and Room to Read. The girl scholar commits to doing her best in her studies. In return, the parents commit to supporting her to continue her education. The school encourages her academic performance, and Room to Read covers the financial cost of her education. In 2007, over 4,000 girls from underprivileged families in Cambodia, India, Nepal, Sri Lanka, Vietnam, and South Africa attended school as Room to Grow Girls' Scholarship recipients. This program will continue to grow rapidly in the future so that more girls will have an opportunity to receive an education and improve their lives. "When you educate a girl, you educate the next generation."

CHALLENGE GRANT MODEL

A key aspect of John Wood's vision for Room to Read has been the Challenge Grant Model through which communities co-invest with Room to Read, facilitating the long-term sustainability of its projects after the local teams have moved on to assist other villages. New villages often raise a significant portion of the overall expenditure in the form of dedicated space, labor, materials, and/or small amounts of cash. These challenge grants act as catalysts for community building while also maximizing the local participation and expertise brought to the programs. In order to receive Room to Read's services, a community must sign the Challenge Grant contract. For the School Room Program, for example, this contract stipulates that the village must assemble a construction committee that meets regularly to ensure progress. An agreed-upon blueprint must also be used, ensuring that schools are built safely and cost effectively. Finally, the village must donate funds, materials, land, and/or labor to the effort. This model of community ownership produces a deep sense of commitment and a lasting impact on education in rural areas. Because of this approach, Room to Read's construction projects are sustainable institutions that are able to provide for the education of children in the long term.

Local Room to Read teams generally do not seek out future locations. Instead, communities must apply to Room to Read for assistance with a construction project. Once a community has been chosen as a future site for a Room to Read program, it must make considerable contributions to the process. The village must also pass Room to Read's thorough needs assessment. If a school would like to partner with Room to Read to establish a library, it is required to support the project by providing dedicated space, a dedicated librarian who commits to receiving Room to Read training in library skills, and, in the case of the library construction projects, materials and labor to aid in construction. If a school community has been chosen as a future site for a Room to Read computer lab, it must provide the teachers to run the lab (at least one teacher must go through Room to Read training), committed oversight of the ongoing project, and lab security. Furthermore, the school community is responsible for funding ongoing maintenance and electricity associated with the lab as well as Internet access, if available. Through the implementation of the Challenge Grant Model, and the intimate involvement of local communities, the organization helps to ensure that Room to Read's programs are successful and sustainable.

MONITORING, EVALUATION, AND CREATIVE PROBLEM SOLVING

Room to Read is committed to ensuring the highest quality programs so that it can have the greatest impact on the lives of children throughout the developing world. To this end, each project is subject to monitoring and evaluation (M&E), both internally and externally. The in-country staff visit the programs regularly and use a variety of methods, such as interviews and surveys, with key stakeholders, students, and teachers to gather information about program effectiveness. Through this internal monitoring, the staff are able to provide useful feedback and to highlight areas for future program improvements. In turn, Room to Read as an organization is able to make modifications when necessary based on the feedback of local teams, teachers, and students. In addition to its in-country M&E staff, Room to Read has hired a global program officer devoted to overseeing M&E in all the countries and programs. This position exemplifies Room to Read's focus on M&E and its commitment to systematically monitor and evaluate its work. As of 2007, a formalized, global monitoring system had been implemented that uses a mixed-methods approach to collect data across all countries related to access, use, and sustainability of Room to Read's programs.

Room to Read also conducted an independent, external evaluation in 2005 of all its programs in four countries (Sri Lanka and Laos were excluded because they were new to the partnership at the time). To investigate the effectiveness of the programs, this evaluation employed a sixty-six-item survey that focused on teachers' and students' perceptions, attitudes, and self-reported behaviors with regard to each Room to Read program in each country. The questions focused on teachers' and students' involvement in the programs, their perceptions of the quality of operations, and the value and impact of the programs. In each country across each program, students and teachers rated the programs highly: 91 percent and 87 percent of respondents rated the Room to Grow Girls' Scholarship Program and the School Room Program, respectively, a four on a four-point scale; additionally, 82 percent, 80 percent, and 70 percent of respondents rated the Computer Room, Reading Room, and Language Room programs, respectively, a four out of four. In the Reading Room Program, students and teachers agreed that students were becoming better readers and were reading more often as a result of the program. The majority of respondents agreed or strongly agreed that each program was running well.

John Wood admits that there are many things he would have done differently had he founded Room to Read with the knowledge he has now. First of all, he would have hired more people more quickly. Because Room to Read was a start-up organization, Wood was naturally worried about money, payroll, and similar issues, but this worry led to his personally printing receipts, licking stamps, and running to the post office even two years into the project. He also wishes that Room to Read had begun investing in publishing local language children's books earlier. The sooner a new organization starts making a difference, the sooner the organization can scale. In hindsight, Wood also recognizes the importance of setting up strong systems—every kind of system: customer databases, project databases, financial systems, and more. Getting the programs started quickly became problematic once Room to Read realized that it had not put certain systems in place first. Wood and Room to Read are constantly learning, and through ongoing evaluation are committed to continue making improvements within the organization.

AWARDS, HONORS, AND PRESS

Over the past few years, Room to Read has received several distinguished awards, including the *Fast Company*/Monitor Group "Social Capitalist Award," the Skoll Award for Social Entrepreneurship, and the Sand Hill Group Foundation's "Social Entrepreneurship" Award. In addition to these organizational awards, Founder and CEO John Wood has been selected for several honors, including the Draper Richards Foundation Fellowship, the "Young Global Leader" Award from the World Economic Forum, and *Time* magazine's "Asia's Heroes Award." Room to Read has been featured in many prestigious newspapers, magazines, websites, and television shows, including the *Wall Street Journal, Fortune, Forbes, Business Week, Time, Town and Country, International Herald Tribune,* Bloomberg Television, CNN, and PBS programs.

NEXT STEPS FOR ROOM TO READ

Room to Read's job is not done. There are currently more than 770 million illiterate adults in the world, two-thirds of whom are women and girls. In addition, there are over 70 million children not currently enrolled in primary school and more than

150 million not enrolled in secondary school. The need for Room to Read's educational programs spans the globe. To respond to this worldwide demand for its programs, Room to Read is committed to expanding geographically. In 2006 it expanded to a new continent by launching operations in South Africa. In 2008 it began programs in Zambia, and it hopes to expand into two additional African countries by 2010. The organization also plans to expand into two additional countries in Asia by 2010, beginning with a launch in Bangladesh later in 2008. In addition, it plans to conduct initial research on expansion to Latin America beginning in 2009. As Room to Read expands further into Asia and Africa, as well as to Latin America, it will simultaneously maintain its commitment to increasing its activities and support within the countries where it is currently operating. Within the next three years, the organization's ambitious goal is to establish a total a 13,000 libraries and impact more than 5 million children. Ultimately, Room to Read's mission is to bring the lifelong gift of education to 10 million children in the developing world.

TESTIMONIALS

Your glorious help has changed our school, and inspired our students to improve their academic performance. The students at our school received some of the highest exam scores out of the Kaski district, the first time our school received such distinction. We are very grateful to you all.

—Udaya Karki, Principal, Harihar English School, Nepal

Before I saw the colorful Room to Read books, I thought reading was only for homework. Now, I can read books that are fun and learn about other places and animals.

—Puja, Class 6, Masbar, Nepal

On behalf of the teaching staff and students at the Le Ngoc Han Secondary School, I want to thank all of you in Room to Read for your generous gift of a computer lab. Your support will help our young generation face the challenges of the future.

—Dong Thi Bach Tuyet, Training and Educational Services, Tien Giang Province, Vietnam

My name is Kun Nara. I am a student in grade 9 of Net Yang High school. I am very excited about the gift from Room to Read Cambodia because I've never seen and had the opportunity to use this kind of computer technology before. My family is very poor. I don't have money to pay for the private computer school like some students in rich families. So this is a great opportunity for me to engage in this skill. Room to Read is amazing. I would like to say thank you to the donor who has offered great opportunities to the poor like us.

—Kun Nara, Net Yank High School, Battambang, Cambodia

My mother used to tell me that "girls who know how to read and write will only write love letters to boys . . . so it is better that girls do not go to school." Times have

changed since I was young and I know that going to school is the only way that [my granddaughter] will ever get out of this poverty we live in.

—seventy-nine-year-old grandmother of a Room to Grow scholar, Cambodia

ORGANIZATIONAL SNAPSHOT

Organization: Room to Read

Founder and/or Executive Director: John Wood

Mission/Description: Room to Read partners with local communities throughout the developing world to provide quality educational opportunities by establishing libraries, creating local language children's literature, constructing schools, providing education to girls, and establishing computer labs. We seek to intervene early in the lives of children in the belief that education empowers people to improve socioeconomic conditions for their families, communities, countries, and future generations. Through the opportunities that only education can provide, we strive to break the cycle of poverty, one child at a time.

Website: roomtoread.org

Address: Room to Read

The Presidio

P.O. Box 29127

San Francisco, CA 94129 USA

Phone: +1.415.561.3331

Fax: +1.415.561.4428

NOTES

1. Chinn, M. & Fairlie, R. (2006). "ICT use in the developing world: An analysis of differences in computer and Internet penetration." NET Institute Working Paper No. 06-03 (http://ssrn.com/abstract=936474).
2. Apple Classrooms of Tomorrow (ACOT). (1996). *Changing the conversation about teaching & learning technology: A report on 10 years of ACOT research*. Retrieved December 6, 2007, from http://www.apple.com/education/k12/leadership/acot/library.html.
3. Rusten, E. (2003). "Using computers in schools." In Academy for Educational Development (AED)/LearnLink, *Digital opportunities for development: A sourcebook on access and applications*. Retrieved December 8, 2007, from http://learnlink.aed.org/Publications/Sourcebook/home.htm.

3

Global Village Engineers

M. Christopher Shimkin and Annie Khan

Global Village Engineers (GVE) is a nonprofit engineering initiative whose purpose is to create a global program through which highly skilled and experienced engineers can be of service to the world community and address vital worldwide social, economic, and civic needs.

GVE is composed of a volunteer corps of professional engineers supporting the local capacity of rural communities in developing countries by demystifying aspects of public infrastructure construction and environmental protection projects. GVE's engineers choose to volunteer their skills to assure the livelihood of these communities by building long-term local capacity, especially in situations requiring disaster prevention, rehabilitation, and/or environmental protection.

We believe that infrastructure will best serve communities when they have the capacity to become involved from project inception through construction and finally with long-term maintenance. Governments and project sponsors often do not invest in communicating basic facts to a community about design, construction, and maintenance issues. Our mission is to find these facts and develop the local capacity to understand such facts. We join efforts with knowledgeable nongovernmental organization (NGO) personnel, who use their new technical understanding to organize more effective public advocacy efforts.

After GVE volunteers work in the field to assess the engineering needs of a given project, they work with their NGO counterparts to formulate a strategy to impart the technical information in a simple and accessible manner based on cultural understanding and sensitivity. They also act as project catalysts and liaisons among the engineering designers, advocacy and environmental organizations, policy makers, and the impacted community organizations.

GVE VOLUNTEERS

GVE volunteers also have the opportunity to practice specific skills and enjoy the satisfaction of teaching new skills to people who deeply appreciate their value in maintaining their very survival, not to mention setting the foundation for their economic development. GVE volunteers follow up their assessments and initial trainings with ongoing dialogue and additional trainings with the communities until community members feel comfortable acting alone.

The volunteer corps of professional engineers is a vital component of our organization. GVE has developed an active network of technical professionals whose expertise extends across many engineering disciplines, including wastewater treatment, information technology, environmental impact, roadway design and construction, water and air quality impact, hydrogeology, storm water management, water supply, natural disaster preparedness, hazardous materials/waste, hydrology, hydropower, solid waste management, bridges/structures, and flood control.

WHY IS GVE UNIQUE?

Global Village Engineers is an organization that recruits and manages a volunteer corps of civil engineers, environmental scientists, and other technical experts who work with rural communities and NGOs in the developing world. Its unique mission is to empower these bodies through education and training on infrastructure issues that impact them so that they become effective advocates on their own behalf. This mission is based on the fundamental principle that people are powerless when self-doubt prevents them from participating in the political and social systems that bring infrastructure to their local environments.

Today, there are organizations that mobilize engineers and engineering students to construct housing, small water-supply systems, and schools. These volunteers actually perform the work, and in doing so, supply a valuable development function. However, these groups tend to work on small, relatively uncomplicated projects; more importantly, they do not focus on educating and training their communities and NGOs about the scientific and engineering principles required to understand the technical details that describe a project's impact on a particular community. In the GVE model, however, stakeholders learn from GVE volunteers how to integrate technical facts into their strategies for participating in the planning, design, and implementation of a project. It is this education that allows community members to deal effectively with the private and public agencies that all too often control or impact their local environments—often to their detriment.

Another important and somewhat unique component of GVE's strategy is to capitalize on seasonal downturns in the civil engineering industry by providing working engineers with meaningful volunteer work that enriches their professional careers. The small- to midsized firms that provide many of GVE's volunteers rarely offer the international, cross-cultural experiences such as GVE's that many excellent employees want.

HISTORY

M. Christopher Shimkin is the founder of GVE. The idea for GVE occurred to Christopher after his experiences in El Salvador in the aftermath of Hurricane Mitch in 1992. Mitch caused unspeakable destruction to the homes and lives of people, especially in an area called Bajo Lempa near the Lempa River. To help prevent future devastation, funding was allocated to design and build a levee that would prevent the banks of the Lempa River from flooding, thereby protecting the people in this area. The individuals involved with overseeing the levee project did not fully comprehend the intricate design structure and nuances of such a project; as a result, they were unable to effectively evaluate the situation. Christopher was asked to meet with these individuals to help bridge the gap between design and implementation.

While assisting with this project, Christopher interacted with the local community, conveying some basic engineering concepts to them. The information he shared seemed to make a great deal of difference in the attitudes of these individuals. For example, he explained a basic protocol involved with building linear structures such as roads, levees, or bridges. Christopher explained that "stations" are used as guiding points. Stations are numbered stakes planted in the ground. Christopher explained to several community members what the numbers on the stakes meant. At the end of the trip, there was a summary meeting, and people were asked for feedback regarding what they learned. One farmer, who had limited formal education, stated that for the first time in his life, he understood what the numbers on the stakes meant, and how they translated to the design map. Such knowledge made a lasting impression on this individual because now it was easier for him to make sense of at least one aspect of the project.

For Christopher, this was the birth of the idea for GVE. Christopher was taken aback by the impact of basic engineering concepts and the power of such critical knowledge on these community members. Christopher experienced firsthand the implications of how empowerment of the local population, and how things that are taken for granted by some, can have a profound impact on the lives of others. Specifically, basic engineering knowledge can equip people with the ability to learn and understand how things are affecting their environment and, consequently, their lives. Furthermore, this knowledge can impact their rights and privileges, since their lives are directly affected. Christopher recognized the importance of information sharing: "If one person can be deeply affected by basic engineering information, then so can others."

Upon returning from his trip to El Salvador, Christopher proceeded to discuss his ideas with other engineering colleagues, who were also passionate about this plan. Christopher felt so strongly about the role he could play in helping others that he quit his job and founded Global Village Engineers. Everything came together, and it proved easy to inspire other engineers to join GVE. To date, there have been between 100 and 150 GVE volunteers. According to Christopher, "You're an engineer for a reason, and the reason is that there is a human being impacted by the work you do, and you need to understand that. You're not just building a bridge—the bridge has a purpose and it has an impact, not just an environmental impact . . . it puts it in human terms."

THE GVE MODEL

As stated on the GVE website (www.gvengineers.org), "GVE's mission is to support the local capacity of rural communities in developing countries to influence public infrastructure and environmental protection." GVE acts as a consulting agency by taking on the role of empowerment, so that individuals feel like a part of the process. GVE helps the local population understand the reasoning and importance of building a structure a certain way in their town or village. Communicating with the local population about the changes that may occur in their community helps alleviate tension over facts that may be misunderstood or not understood at all. This is an important step in rapport building, which encourages community members to feel comfortable talking about and sharing their concerns, including having someone understand their point of view. According to Christopher, "We consult, we listen, we explain, we educate, and we 'demystify' the process." GVE plays an integral role in breaking down communication barriers, thus empowering and helping communities collaborate for their own betterment.

Christopher strongly believes in GVE's role as a mediator and consultant, and he discourages the practice of having outsiders go into a country and build structures, since this would harm the country by taking away from their economy. GVE believes that these countries have qualified people available to work, and it is more important to work with the local populations.

GVE PROJECTS
Levee Inspection and Maintenance Guide Training

The damage inflicted on the people of the Lower Lempa by annual flooding highlights the need to invest in long-term technical solutions and appropriate land-use decisions in the Lower Lempa region of El Salvador.

As part of a comprehensive flood prevention plan, an earthen levee is being constructed on both sides of the Lempa River. Accompanied by United Communities, a grassroots organization of community leaders, GVE continues to observe the levee's construction.

GVE emphasized the importance of ongoing inspection and maintenance to keep levees in good repair. Ultimately, levee maintenance is the responsibility of the Lower Lempa communities. At their request, our engineers demonstrated various levee maintenance techniques in the field, and prepared a guide describing how to complete minor repairs and how to identify, record, and plan for major maintenance needs.

Las Colinas Landslide Mitigation

For the Santa Tecla, El Salvador, project, GVE is assisting communities that have been affected by the Las Colinas landslide as well as other communities that continue to be threatened by future landslides or mudslides. Over 500 residents died in the Las Colinas landslide. In addition to community participation in the project, the city of Santa Tecla has been an instrumental partner in working to find practical solutions to mitigating the risks of the communities. Local interest in the development of this project is very high. Therefore, the local media are always on hand to get the most recent developments from Global Village Engineers.

GVE Mentoring Assistance

Several projects illustrate the effects of GVE assistance and mentoring. One example involves a community in El Salvador that was built on the river banks. A hydropower facility was located close to this area, and community members thought the power facility was responsible for the frequent floods. People came to this conclusion because flooding occurred on sunny as well as rainy days. However, the river on which this community was built is approximately 350–400 kilometers long and stretches through three countries. Therefore, if it rained in Honduras three days before, by the time the water traveled to this community, it could be a sunny day there. Individuals were unaware of this principle of watershed hydrology. GVE explained the hydrology mechanics to the community members, helping them understand the factors that impacted their environment and indirectly preventing conflict between the community and the hydro facility.

In another example, GVE acted as a mediator. In engineering design, one of the main documents is called the design plan. One aspect of the overall design plan is the highly detailed technical specifications document, which lists all the technical requirements down to the sizes of different screws and the strength of metal required to sustain a structure. Someone had acquired the design plan for the levee in El Salvador, read that the levee was to be built for a "ten-year design storm," and misinterpreted the information. The person thought that a ten-year design storm meant the levee would only last ten years. This information was published in the local newspapers, which resulted in a local upheaval. The community felt betrayed and undermined: they did not understand that a ten-year design storm is an engineering term meaning the levee was designed to sustain storms of a certain size and statistical frequency. Deciding on a ten-year storm designation affects the height of the levee, allowing it to handle a certain amount of water from a storm of a certain size that has a 10 percent chance of occurring in a given year. GVE was integral in helping to defuse a highly volatile situation by explaining the meaning of this term to the local communities.

Another example of GVE at work involved a project in Nicaragua. GVE worked with a mayor who had many simultaneous projects and was having problems prioritizing the most important tasks, especially from a technical engineering standpoint. GVE guided her and informed her about the appropriate processes for hiring an engineer, the expectations she should have of an engineer, and the appropriate engineering costs involved. She was new to the position and the nuances of the role; GVE was there initially to help her organize and prioritize, and was also available for ongoing support when needed.

Project Update: Lower Lempa, El Salvador

In February 2005, GVE volunteers and the country director for Voices on the Border visited the United Communities of the Lower Lempa in El Salvador. The trip was focused on continued work with communities in Lower Lempa affected by annual flooding and was a tremendous success. The main objectives of the visit were to consolidate ongoing community maintenance of the levee, promote more systematic inspections of the levee, and continue communication exchanges with the communities.

Over thirty-five members from eighteen communities participated with GVE. Together, they reviewed the status of nearly half of the approximate 14.85 kilometers of levee already constructed. In the follow-up meeting, GVE volunteers reviewed basic levee construction and provided suggestions on maintenance concerns. GVE volunteers applauded community maintenance done so far, including the stone paving of ramps by communities on their own initiative.

The second half of the meeting was an open discussion around the improved structuring of maintenance and inspection teams, and the collective development of a reporting form for levee conditions that will be centralized, compiled, and distributed to the Ministry of Agriculture (government agency responsible for levee construction), GVE, local police, city government, and others.

Individuals Touched by GVE

Concepcion (Conce) is a farmer, with a wife and two kids. He has a first-grade education and lives in the Lower Lempa area of El Salvador. GVE has been working with Conce on the levee project for approximately two or three years. GVE taught Conce simple field techniques to check if work should or should not be conducted on a levee at any given time. For example, an important aspect of a levee, which is made of soil, is that it should not have too much water or it should not be too dry. The method used to determine this involves rubbing some of the dirt together in one's hand. If there is some dirt left on the hand, it means one thing, and if there is no dirt in the hand, it means something else. Conce was taught this method.

One day, Conce was in the field with an engineering inspector while work was being conducted on the levee. Conce decided to check the conditions of the levee by the method he had been taught. After conducting this basic inspection, he realized that the conditions were not appropriate to conduct work on the levee. At this point, Conce informed the bulldozer operator about his concerns and requested that he stop work. The bulldozer operator was demeaning toward Conce since he did not believe that Conce had the appropriate knowledge regarding levee construction. However, the engineering inspector vouched for Conce's knowledge and demanded that the bulldozer operator stop working. Conce has repeated this story on many occasions because he felt empowered, important, and appreciated. The basic information he was taught gave him self-confidence and respect.

Another individual named Fernando was also personally touched by GVE. Christopher was at a meeting with representatives from the Japanese, American, and Salvadorian governments as well as various other community members. Someone asked Fernando what GVE had done for him and how the organization had helped him. Fernando said that two years previously, before the help of GVE, whenever he tried to contact various government representatives to request a meeting, he was ignored. After working with GVE for two years, Fernando gained the respect of the governmental representatives. As a result, he can now contact the government to request a meeting, and representatives would attend the meeting. Through the help of GVE, Fernando gained the respect needed so that he could participate in shaping the outcome of projects by gathering stakeholders on his own terms.

A consistent theme with these stories involves respect, empowerment, and the "voice" individuals attain through their interactions with GVE. Christopher believes it is important not just to convey information but to take in information, "to sit down and just listen . . . through listening one can learn many unexpected details; it is fascinating to hear someone, and it's exhilarating to be a part of the solution." Christopher understands the importance of gaining trust and building a relationship in order to help others. This is an integral part of the GVE model: the people-oriented aspect is what separates GVE from private companies. GVE is invested in understanding the communities where it is working and in helping community members feel secure with GVE and its intentions.

SECRETS TO SUCCESS

In order to obtain projects, GVE develops partnerships with big organizations such as Oxfam. Larger organizations have connections to smaller agencies in various countries where GVE works. Often, these larger agencies can connect GVE to other organizations and potential projects. In addition, Christopher has a network of people he contacts to determine if there are any projects where GVE can make a difference. Information about GVE is also spread by word of mouth, which is a testament to the work that GVE does.

GVE charges for projects depending on the size and funding of the organization. For example, larger organizations typically have funding available for their projects; smaller agencies, such as the Share Foundation or Voices on the Border, have limited funds. GVE will often fund projects involving smaller agencies. Generally, the operation of GVE involves minimal overhead, and it is based completely on the generous work of its volunteers.

Individual donations are the primary source of funding. Money is also provided through foundations and partnerships with various engineering companies.

Engineering companies will donate cash or give special compensation to their employees to work with GVE. For example, an employee can be granted three extra days of vacation, as long as he or she donates time to working on a project with GVE. In addition, volunteers donate their expenses, such as airfare and food. GVE actively hosts annual fundraising campaigns to obtain general funding.

THE GVE SUCCESS METER

When a community asks GVE to return, that represents a powerful marker for success. Since it is difficult to measure empowerment or the respect that community members gain, another measure is the number of individuals who actively maintain contact with GVE. However, this is also difficult to measure, since individuals from the regions in which GVE works do not have telephones or electronic forms of communication.

People benefit from the GVE-related projects because they are big projects, in the sense that these projects geographically impact many communities and thousands of people. Communities may be oblivious to the help they have received, yet they may notice that a river has not flooded in over three years. GVE worked on a project in Cambodia where the Sesan River runs out of Vietnam into the Mekong River, and every community on that river was impacted by the project. Although GVE did not meet with all those people, the project impacted them positively.

Success also comes through inspiring engineers. A lot of present-day engineering designs are done in the office, using computers. As a result, when engineers are granted the opportunity to travel and interact with various communities, it fuels their passion and helps them feel motivated about the work they are doing. According to Christopher, "It gives them a moral boost and makes them feel good about what they are doing by being able to go and share it with others."

CHALLENGES FACED BY GVE

Obtaining funding is difficult, especially for Christopher because he exhibits a level of passion that others may not share. Christopher has worked tirelessly to obtain funding. For example, he was in competition for one particular fellowship for two and a half years and, unfortunately, was not awarded the fellowship. To Christopher this is the most challenging and frustrating aspect of his job: the disappointment of not feeling heard, the inability to comprehend why others cannot see the valuable work that GVE has done/is doing, and the disbelief that others do not feel the same about helping improvised communities.

Such obstacles have not stopped Christopher from persisting. He continues to explain the benefit of the services provided by GVE, in the hopes that others will understand. If someone is not interested, then he will move on to someone else or use another strategy. It is this level of persistence, motivation, and drive that makes GVE the organization that it is.

To assist with GVE's growth, Christopher has implemented a board of directors and a board of advisors. They represent a core group of people who understand the mission of GVE. They play a critical role in sharing information and formulating creative solutions because they provide different perspectives and resources to explore avenues to help the growth of GVE.

INFLUENCES AND INSPIRATIONS

Christopher cites his parents not as mentors but as inspirational coaches. He describes his father as a self-inspired philanthropist and his mother as someone who understands the workings of philanthropy; passion from both parents to do right in the world has been instilled in Christopher. His parents helped to advise and guide Christopher when he first created the idea for GVE.

Christopher admires his parents' ability to adapt and understand situations where one has no experience. Neither parent had the remotest technical background, yet both quickly embraced the GVE concept from a humanitarian point of view. His parents can take a concept that one may have difficulty understanding and help someone feel intelligent.

Christopher is also highly self-driven. He explained that his inspiration comes from within. Since he is his primary source of inspiration, it is hard for him to grapple with the thought that others do not comprehend the mission of GVE. He believes that the best way to help others understand the importance of GVE's work is to help them feel the frustration an individual from the community may feel. This is accomplished through role plays that Christopher has his audience participate in whenever he is guest lecturing. Christopher truly believes GVE's mission; it represents a method of solving many problems while having a big impact on people's lives.

WHAT WOULD HAVE BEEN DONE DIFFERENTLY?

In reflecting on what he might have done differently, Christopher believes he should have fully engaged the engineering societies. Many people are attempting to do the same thing but in different ways; communicating with the engineering community might have produced a collaborative effort that would have generated better results. Part of Christopher's mission involved changing the culture of engineering. For example, in the legal profession, pro bono work is part of the culture; in the engineering field, this is not the case, nor are most projects implemented with the full engagement of all stakeholders. Christopher's idea was to recruit people and encourage longevity at work by asking employers to allot volunteers an extra week of vacation; in addition, he wanted to influence how engineers and engineering firms approach projects that have considerable community impact.

Christopher's ingenuity may be ahead of its time. GVE is focused not just on helping build physical structures but on building relationships with people and empowering them through communication and knowledge. Engineering firms are traditionally focused on concrete results.

THE FUTURE OF GVE

From an organizational point of view, there will be further development of the board of directors to support the growth of GVE. The GVE model has been proven, many people are embracing the concept, and the next important step is bringing engineering leadership at the board of directors' level.

Christopher has chosen a difficult path. "It's very hard, when talking about the funding stuff, when someone doesn't believe it and you start to question yourself. . . . I gave up a whole profession and career of thirteen to fourteen years and jumped into this without experience, thinking this is a great idea [so] why isn't everyone else jumping on the bandwagon?" Despite these challenges, Christopher has worked against the odds to empower others in developing countries, and his accomplishments speak for themselves. He is truly an inspiration to engineers and to anyone wanting to be a humanitarian.

RECOMMENDED BOOKS

The Civilized Engineer by Samuel Foreman
The Introspective Engineer by Samuel Foreman
The Existential Pleasures of Engineering by Samuel Foreman

Christopher believes that these three books put engineering in perspective, especially the first book, in terms of passion for human lives and human rights.

M. CHRISTOPHER SHIMKIN

M. Christopher Shimkin is a *summa cum laude* master's graduate in business administration from Northeastern University. Mr. Shimkin was selected as one of the World Economic Forum's 100 Global Leaders for Tomorrow for 2002.

Since 1982 he has been directly involved in community service work. Beginning as a class agent for the Eaglebrook School and responsible for postgraduation class fundraising, he then moved into local community as well as broader international involvement concerning education and the environment.

In 1992 Mr. Shimkin became a volunteer board member of the Millis (MA) Educational Resource Initiative Team and eventually was elected president. His success in attracting funds to support the initiatives of this nonprofit organization provided support for curriculum-enhancing programs within the local school system.

In 1993 Mr. Shimkin became a mentoring tutor for the national MATHCOUNTS program as well as a volunteer member of the Charles River Rail Association, working toward improved rail service in the suburban Boston area. In 1996 and 1997, he was appointed by the town of Millis to serve on the Open Space Plan Committee and Drinking Water Committee.

Mr. Shimkin has been an invited speaker at Oxfam America, the World Bank, Boston University's Center for Energy and Environment, Tufts University, Roger Williams College, University of Massachusetts, Brandeis University, and Northeastern University's Graduate School of Business Administration to speak about environmental professions and environmental impact evaluations. With regard to the engineer's role in international sustainable development, Mr. Shimkin was a panelist at the Engineers Without Borders' annual meeting, guest speaker at the Engineers for a Sustainable World (ESW) annual meeting, and at the Cornell University ESW chapter.

A graduate of civil/ocean engineering from the University of Rhode Island in 1989, he pursued a consulting career in environmental engineering, developing expertise in water quality evaluations, civil works infrastructure planning and design, and environmental regulatory compliance. His affiliations include

- University of Massachusetts–Lowell: University of Massachusetts Sustainable Development Advisory Committee.
- Boston Network on International Development: Board of Advisors

---

ORGANIZATIONAL SNAPSHOT

Organization: Global Village Engineers

Founder and/or Executive Director: M. Christopher Shimkin

Mission/Description: Global Village Engineers (GVE) is a volunteer corps of professional engineers supporting the local capacity of rural communities in developing countries to influence public infrastructure and environmental protection. GVE's engineers choose to volunteer their skills to assure the livelihood of these communities by building long-term capacity, especially in situations requiring disaster prevention, rehabilitation, and/or environmental protection. They believe that infrastructure will best serve communities when community members have the capacity to become involved from project inception through construction. Governments and project sponsors often do not invest in communicating basic facts to the community about design, construction, and maintenance. The mission of Global Village Engineers is to find out these facts and develop the local capacity to understand such facts.

Website: www.gvengineers.org

Address: Global Village Engineers, Inc.

6 Seward Ave.

Beverly, MA 01915 USA

Phone: +1.978-927-0219

Fax: +1.978-927-0219

E-mail: info@gvengineers.org

4

Common Bond Institute:
Vision and Journey

Steve Olweean

When vision is imbued with belief and presence in our day-to-day life, our actions serve to confirm and root it in reality.

—Steve Olweean, Founding Director, Common Bond Institute

Common Bond Institute (CBI) began essentially in the same form it has sustained throughout its existence. It began literally as a vision and intuitive journey. Over time, the journey increasingly required the creation of an organizational structure to allow the vision to be better planted in the corporal world for practical application.

Quite appropriately, CBI has maintained itself as a living "idea" rather than a brick and mortar "place" by establishing itself as a web-based, virtual organization, using the vehicle of increasingly accessible grassroots global communications, particularly the Internet. Through its extensive international network, CBI is able to link the commitment, energies, and resources of many collaborating organizations, groups, and individuals around the globe, forming intentional community and strategic alliances to address humanitarian needs in troubled and underserved regions of the world.

Collaboration is seen as the new standard for being an effective organization, and there is certainly a wealth of likely partners throughout the world these days. The daunting task of learning just how many like-missioned organizations exist at any one time increasingly underscores the fact that the world is experiencing an extraordinary surge in creative change agents coming forth and taking action to contribute to a palpable shift in consciousness toward a universal culture of peace. A benefit of actually being in this stream is feeling the sheer presence and force of this escalation, and how it is changing the course of reality.

CBI's particular story goes back to the 1980s and to an inspiring era of fledgling citizen diplomacy efforts in a polarized world split between the United States and the Soviet Union. This was a time of unprecedented and often uncharted opportunities for individuals to take dramatic steps in bridging the chronic gap of a seemingly intractable Cold War. These were heady days of collapsing stereotypes and grassroots bridges that circumvented institutional chasms created by hostile governments heavily invested in maintaining an "enemy" mentality. CBI was just one of the products that emerged from stepping into this unfamiliar space and engaging personally with those who, for all purposes and intents, represented the well-publicized, entrenched image of "The Other."

The name Common Bond emerged intuitively from the personal experience of reaching past artificial barriers to find and acknowledge our human commonality, and to experience a deep connection and belonging that neutralizes the energy of fear often felt when confronted with difference and the unknown. It also embodied the mission of traveling this same road through fear-based belief systems regarding the unknown within each of us that reflect outward into our relationships with others and the world.

HISTORY

In August 1990, Steve Olweean was a practicing psychotherapist in Michigan when two important events occurred that led him to organizing CBI. One was the escalating tensions of war in the Middle East as Iraq invaded Kuwait, and the second was his becoming involved in coordinating an international professional exchange visit to the then Soviet Union.

Steve's own long history as an activist in civil rights, social justice, and anti-war efforts in the 1960s and 1970s naturally drew him to what intuitively felt like a next step in this same journey: contributing to bridges being built through citizen diplomacy between the two most polarized parts of the human community—the United States/the West and the then Soviet Union—and an equally polarized region that impacted daily on the rest of the world—the Middle East. In particular, his many years of working as a psychologist and outreach crisis intervention worker in community mental health services for high-risk, marginalized, and underserved populations prompted him to use that professional and personal experience in finding ways he might contribute to improving the level of human services in these troubled societies. The goal, then as now, was to seek ways to increase the capacity of local communities to empower and heal themselves.

Kuwait

The 1990 Iraqi invasion of Kuwait brought with it a tragic impact on civilians caught up in the violence. By February 1991, when Iraqi troops left Kuwait, news of large numbers of civilians suffering from emotional, psychological, and physical trauma spread throughout the world. This suffering was compounded further by massive numbers of Iraqi civilian victims as a result of the Gulf War.

While listening to a National Public Radio (NPR) interview, Steve heard a Kuwaiti doctor being asked if his hospital needed more medical supplies, equipment, and physicians. The doctor was blunt: his words were, "We don't need equipment or supplies—we need therapists. There is an epidemic of psychologically traumatized victims that is growing every day, and we don't know how to treat them."

Assuming there must be a relief effort in the works to address this great need, Steve called the Free Kuwait office in Washington, D.C. As a father of two young children at the time, he was unable to volunteer to go to Kuwait for an extended period himself. However, based on his experience as a trauma therapist and his personal background as an Arab American Muslim, he was interested in orienting Western therapists to the Middle Eastern and Islamic culture they would need to be sensitized to in attempting to operate effective treatment services. In speaking to the director, Steve was surprised to find that not only was there no such mental health relief effort under way, but that the office was desperately trying to find a way for one to be organized.

After conversations with both the Free Kuwait office and the Kuwaiti embassy, where he gathered details on what services currently existed in Kuwait and what relief organizations they were aware of, it became apparent that although there were numerous efforts to provide relief services and supplies for the physical needs of food, clothing, shelter, and medical supplies, there was little if any organized service at the time to address the intense psychological needs of the population. The Red Cross and other organizations, including the UN, had conducted surveys and determined trauma was pervasive, that there was indeed a great and growing need for help, and that the indigenous services were far lacking or nearly nonexistent to address the massive need. At the time, though, no organized program was in place to actually provide services. Over the weeks and months that followed, there were a number of small groups and individuals that traveled from the United States to Kuwait on their own to offer treatment services. Steve provided consultation to several of these groups and individuals. He linked the Free Kuwait office, the Kuwaiti embassy, and the main hospital in Kuwait City with various trauma treatment groups and institutes to assist in generating more direct services. It was clear from these conversations that there was a profound lack of trained therapists in Kuwait, and that the true solution would be in providing vital practical training to local therapists rather than relying on bringing in outside services.

It was during this time that Steve also realized the serious limitations of existing treatment models for situations like Kuwait, and he began exploring new models for providing emergency psychological trauma treatment to large populations of victims in regions where services are either underdeveloped or compromised by social upheaval. This would eventually lead to conceiving of the Catastrophic Trauma Recovery model used by CBI in its trauma treatment training project serving local counselors in underdeveloped regions of conflict, including communities in the Middle East such as Palestine and Iraq.

Soviet Union

At the same time that the crisis in Kuwait was unfolding, Steve became involved with a Soviet-American professional exchange. In those early days, the level of practical training and skills in all areas of human services, and particularly in mental health, social work, and medicine, was seriously lacking in the USSR, and Soviet colleagues were desperate to obtain any skills possible to help them assist with the overwhelming and rapidly growing need for treatment services in a society literally teetering on the edge of collapse.

Beginning in 1983, the Association for Humanistic Psychology (AHP) had forged an immensely challenging, annual international professional exchange to the Soviet Union, initially shepherded by a core group of pioneers, including Fran Macy, Tom Greening, Anya Kucharev, and Paul Von Ward, and continued tenuously from year to year. The purpose of the exchange was to initiate contact with Soviet colleagues and nurture relationships that might be built on for future cooperation if the opportunity arose.

These were difficult years of intensified animosity and polarity between the two societies, with the saber rattling of a Star Wars weapons race and Ronald Reagan's depiction of the USSR as the "Evil Empire." As tensions rose, AHP became even more committed and determined to continue its exchange, even as the extraordinarily difficult process of obtaining visas and travel permissions had to be reinvented each year in the face of many obstacles placed in the way by both U.S. and Soviet bureaucracies. Members of the delegations would push to make travel arrangements and then simply begin their journey, sometimes while still awaiting final confirmation that their visas would be accepted at the border. Citizen diplomacy was not only unvalued during this period; it also was suspect and considered an obstacle to other agendas. Ironically, there was agreement on this point by many citizen diplomats: that established political agenda of maintaining the logjam of mutual animosity *was* circumvented and jeopardized by grassroots citizens reaching out across both sides of a line drawn in the sand. This conclusion only motivated many citizen diplomats in general to redouble their efforts.

In 1986 Carl Rogers, one of the founders of AHP, traveled to the USSR and drew national acclaim from Soviet government officials. Even they were aware of this internationally renowned psychologist and peace-building activist. In 1987 Virginia Satir made the trip as travel logistics very slowly began to improve. On the heels of these visits, in 1990 Steve took on coordination of AHP's exchange as the Soviet Union entered the years of Perestroika and Glazunov, and immediately began building on the vital groundwork previously laid by his colleagues. This was a period when it was increasingly possible to stay with Soviet colleagues in their homes—an act hereto illegal—and to begin cooperating on joint efforts together, rather than simply meeting briefly from time to time once a year in a hotel or public place. It was also a time of rapidly increasing ability to communicate directly around the globe—initially by rare and expensive fax and phone, and eventually by the truly paradigm-shifting vehicle of the Internet. The realm of the possible rapidly and dramatically changed, and continued to change as new and expanded levels of cooperation opened literally from month to month.

Steve led regular professional delegations to the Soviet Union one or two times a year on whirlwind, two- to three-week trips to St. Petersburg, Moscow, Vilnius, Riga, Kiev, Tblisi, Odessa, and other cities in the communist world, visiting colleagues hungry for professional contact with the West. Once there, meetings with Soviet colleagues were arranged based on who and what location was available at the time, often improvised from day to day. The mutual desire to be together and know each other was powerful and urgent, and it galvanized people into creating all sorts of arrangements to overcome the barrage of barriers and "official denials" to meeting. In retrospect, there was also an amazing degree of naïveté and daring, particularly on the part of the much more vulnerable friends and colleagues in these communist countries. Yet it is believed it was this kind of willingness to create such opportunities and to act on them, together with many such efforts occurring during this same pivotal period, that helped contribute to the rapid and unprecedented opening between the two polarized societies. In terms of his personal experience in this stream of activity and consciousness, it was the energy, promise, and practical hope of these early meetings that fed the dream from which CBI emerged.

Between trips, Steve maintained ongoing communication with colleagues to continue planning and preparing for ever-expanding collaborative efforts and projects. Each visit was packed with a schedule of training workshops and seminars, and intense brainstorming meetings that always went very late into the night, with much planning for how to exploit the remarkably mounting opportunities for collaboration. There was truly a mutual milking of the preciously private, concentrated time allowed to the American and Soviet colleagues, where both creative and ambitious projects were spawned and deep personal relationships formed. It was, in fact, the personal relationships, trust, and commitments that were to be the seedbed for all future efforts.

Following each exchange trip, Steve returned to the United States with an intense urgency to "do" something, to make use of these rare, new, and tenuous bridges while they were still at hand. Particularly since this was a time of great upheaval and crisis throughout the entire Soviet Union, and there was potential for both incredible new possibilities and devastating occurrences—including relapse into a closed dictatorial society—he was filled with a profound sense of urgency to act immediately before this tenuous opening might close. As the Soviet Union and its new incarnation, the Commonwealth of Independent States, convulsed, it was clear to anyone involved that the door could easily swing shut again at any moment on this entire region of the world.

Steve thought that acting immediately, even hastily, was the only logical and practical option. There was no time to weigh factors, measure feasibility, or carefully consider the depth of the commitment being initiated. Without purposely crafting a detailed path in advance, he and his colleagues found themselves in a position of trusted responsibility to act. This was less a cognitive experience as one of heart and the soul. On some level, the decision seemed to have already been made, and the focus was more on figuring out how to fashion the next step in implementing whatever was possible at the moment. It was not until he met with the AHP board again to present plans for moving forward with a list of collaborations that he realized a new chasm had opened, this time between the board and him.

Steve came to the AHP board with a great deal of enthusiasm and a barrel full of proposals and calls for action, fully expecting the ideas to be grasped and moved on immediately. However, most of the board—which had not been directly engaged in the exchange or vision—was unable to fully relate to the situation and was overwhelmed by the breadth of proposals. The fear of liability and of diverting time and resources from the organization's other activities caused great concern for many board members. As a result, the proposals were not accepted, and he left the meeting disappointed and frustrated. This was to become a discouragingly repeated experience in future board meetings.

Since at the time he was coordinating the International Professional Exchange and was also in the role of International Liaison for AHP, however, Steve was given latitude for whatever energies he wished to personally put into international relations and activities, as long as these efforts did not obligate the organization, put it at legal risk, or require its time and resources.

After the third AHP board meeting addressing the action proposals, it became evident that the vision Steve was following had outgrown the parameters of what the larger organization saw as its immediate priorities and capabilities, creating an impasse within the organization he had called his professional home in doing this work in the world. At the same time, those on the board who were sympathetic and supportive of his work counseled him to consider formally moving forward on his own, because, in reality, he had already been doing so for some time.

It was at this point that Steve transformed the vision he had been carrying and following all along into a separate organization and mission. Common Bond Institute was created as a leaner, faster, and bolder vehicle for continuing to follow and realize the vision in ways that put it into concrete practice in the world.

Relieved of the liability concerns and conflict with other organizational priorities, AHP was happy to move into the role of being a primary endorsing and supporting organization that did not need to engage its own resources.

The fall of the Soviet Union created more opportunities for open collaboration, and in summer 1992, Steve organized a three-month professional exchange visit to the United States for four key psychologists—three from HARMONY Institute for Psychotherapy and Counseling in St. Petersburg, Russia, and one from the Lithuanian School Psychology Service in Vilnius. Over the course of these three months, with an intense schedule of meetings, conferences, presentations, and networking conducted in a number of cities across the United States, a new and even deeper level of professional collaboration and friendship was forged. One of the key products of this time together was the creation of the first Annual International Conference on Conflict Resolution (ICR), and the launching of a larger vision of what they were co-creating together.

The ICR Conference was first conceived as a half-day seminar for perhaps fifty people to be held during Steve's next exchange visit to Russia. After a long discussion of possible topics for this new seminar, lasting into the early morning hours at Steve's kitchen table, the planning group decided that the focus would be the very process they had all experienced together: overcoming and bridging the initial artificial barriers between them to reach a common place of understanding, deep connection, and trust. The main topic was to be conflict resolution, and the subtitle was "Sharing Tools for Personal and Global Harmony."

The summer exchange ended in mid-August when the four colleagues returned home to Russia and Lithuania. During the interim months leading up to Steve's next trip to St. Petersburg in May, the only means of communication were rare faxes, brief phone calls, and hand-delivered letters. As news of the conference was publicized—primarily by distributed notices and word of mouth—the idea quickly took on a life of its own. The event site was changed twice from HARMONY's modest offices to a hotel, and then a larger hotel as the number of participants rose, and the dates were expanded to accommodate what was becoming a program of several days. Between August 1992 and early May 1993, the conference concept grew remarkably, from a modest half-day seminar for Russian and American participants to a six-day international conference with nearly 450 participants attending from a number of countries around the world.

When Steve and his colleagues again met each other as the conference opened in St. Petersburg, they shared their astonishment at what had been created. They realized then that their effort had hit upon a vital topic, time, and place to which many were drawn. As participants enthusiastically volunteered their perceptions of what the purpose of the conference was, it became obvious that each person brought with him or her a piece of the experience to invest in the community of the conference, and that the event itself was more of a vehicle for synthesizing the many diverse experiences into a common, co-created one for all. This was an invaluable lesson and set the frame for all future conferences, including the fifteen Annual ICR Conferences that have occurred to date, a number of related conferences on separate topics, and CBI's most recent initiative in launching another major annual international conference in 2006 and occurring each year since— the Annual International Conference on "Engaging The Other": The Power of Compassion. The image of a mandala has been used ever since as a working model: creating the center structure of programs, with opportunities built in for the participants to add to and complete the process.

In much the same way as these conferences, over the course of its history CBI's nature has been shaped by the metaphor of a mandala in pursuing its work in the world, through crafting possibilities for creative expansion and development of its programs, and inviting others to co-create new, innovative reflections of a core design.

COLLABORATORS

An account of CBI's history could not be complete without including the indispensable contributions of three key, long-time collaborators who have been involved in this journey from its beginning.

From very early on, literally in the formative days when CBI was just coalescing as an idea, Steve's daughters, Jehan and Jessie, contributed a phenomenal amount of their time, energy, skills, and heart to ensuring the often tedious nuts and bolts of organizing CBI's many efforts were accomplished. As they literally grew up in the midst of a flurry of activity surrounding these nonstop proceedings, each began to also grow into her own individual purpose for remaining a part of this work in the world, by taking on her own piece of the mission for herself. Today, while each pursues her own professional career, both continue to assist CBI as seasoned conference organizers and contributors to the programs and mission.

Sandra Friedman, past president of the Association for Humanistic Psychology and an early participant in AHP's Soviet-American Professional Exchange, as well as the co-founder with Steve of the International Humanistic Psychology Association, has been a strong supporter and consultant throughout CBI's existence. Along with Mark Pevzner and Alexander Badkhen of HARMONY Institute, Friedman has been a key contributor to the formulation of the conferences and training projects of CBI.

ORGANIZATION STRUCTURE, MISSION, AND STYLE
Structure

CBI is an international, nongovernmental, nonpolitical organization. It creates educational, training, conflict transformation, and humanitarian relief programs in various regions of the world, in collaboration with local partner organizations and groups. Its orientation is multidisciplinary and multicultural, and throughout its history it has been operated primarily by volunteers, in cooperation with other like-missioned organizations, large and small. Funding for its programs is obtained through conference registrations, donations, and occasional grants.

Philosophy and Mission

Cultivating the fundamental elements of a consciousness of peace along with local capacity building are seen as natural, effective antidotes to small-group, radical extremism and large-group despair, as well as the hardships and suffering of the human condition. To this end, enabling each society to effectively resolve and transform conflicts; satisfy core human needs within communities; and construct effective, holistic mechanisms for self determination, self esteem, and fundamental human dignity and worth is the purpose of CBI's work.

CBI is grounded in the application of humanistic psychology's principles in its commitment to capacity building at both the grassroots and social institutional level. It actively works to form strategic alliances and partnerships with organizations, groups, and individuals dedicated to nurturing global relationships while creating and promoting an authentic world culture of peace.

Style

By design, CBI's efforts are fundamentally collaborative for a larger impact. It maintains an extensive and expanding global network of partner organizations and groups that cooperate in pulling the requisite pieces together to create and operate programs, while minimizing the drain on individual group resources.

CBI follows the principles of creating intentional community: all efforts, and particularly conferences, are designed to be living laboratories for creating and participating in deep, authentic community as a common ground of reference for exploring core themes and integrating formal learning. The conferences offer a dynamic microcosm of the larger, diverse global community and a first-hand, personal experience of moving beyond artificial barriers to the reality of what is both possible and practical. The purposeful use of intentional community is a central element of CBI's work. It assumes the basic drive/need for integration through interconnectedness and belonging that can be nurtured to develop conscious intent toward harmony and peace in our relationships.

PROGRAMS AND ACTIVITIES

CBI organizes and sponsors international conferences, professional training programs, humanitarian relief projects, and professional exchanges; has assisted in establishing and developing locally based professional schools in human services; and actively provides consultation, networking, coordination support, and professional materials to assist newly emerging human service and civil society organizations in post-communist and developing countries that are regions of conflict. The focus is on improving local capacity for peace and healing through increasing skills and services, exploring human relationship dynamics, and expanding public dialogue and awareness of critical issues.

Conferences

Over the last sixteen years, CBI has organized a number of international, multicultural, and multidisciplinary conferences, many in collaboration with HARMONY Institute for Psychotherapy and Counseling in Russia and the International Humanistic Psychology Association (IHPA), and some in cooperation with other organizations, such as the Jane Goodall Institute. CBI maintains an extensive international network through its programs. Examples of conferences include

The annual International Conference on Conflict Resolution (ICR), which has been held each year in Russia since 1993, is a major international event that has received support over the years from the presidents of the United States and Russia, is endorsed by over ninety organizations internationally, and is open to participants globally. It brings together hundreds of presenters and participants from around the world for skills training in conflict resolution and for exploration of the essential elements of conflict, transformation, and healing. The ICR conference also serves as a major networking and recruiting source for training projects.

The annual International Conference on "Engaging The Other": The Power of Compassion (ETO) was first established in 2006 and quickly became an annual event. It examines concepts of "The Other" from a universal, cross-cultural perspective to promote wider public dialogue about images of "Us and Them." The conference addresses the roots of negative belief systems, stereotyping, prejudice, polarization, and enemy images; how to move past artificial barriers of misunderstanding and distrust to cultivate compassion and capacity for appreciation of diversity, reconciliation, and peace; and how to apply the results to the current state of world relationships. It is held in conjunction with the development of an edited book (in progress) addressing psychosocial concepts of "The Other" in a cross-cultural forum. The ETO conference, like the edited book and training project in progress, is an integrated collaboration to examine this fundamentally subjective phenomenon with an inclusive, multicultural eye.

The International Youth Conference on the Ecology of War and Peace was established in 2004 for participants from various societies around the world fourteen to eighteen years of age to address negative stereotypes, prejudice, and the demonizing and dehumanizing of "The Other." Working in cooperation with the Jane Goodall Institute, the theme of ecology has been integrated as a common link that resonates with all parties as they delve into personal interactions and, as a community, explore these relationship dynamics.

CBI has also organized and cooperated on a number of international conferences in Russia, Spain, Germany, and the United States. Conferences serve multiple purposes, including offering a highly charged milieu for engaging with others on a personal and professional level to share perspectives, information, and experiences; receive skills training; network; and develop cooperative action plans for putting principles to work in the world. The conferences are forums for teachers and learners alike, and they invite teachers to become learners and learners to become teachers.

Each year, important partnerships emerge from these conferences. Some directly involve CBI and its partners in organizing and operating programs, such as the projects described later in this chapter. Others involve individuals and organizations that meet at the conferences and pursue their own collaborations, and where CBI may simply play an initial role in facilitating these connections for a time. This supporting match-maker role has come to be a valuable service that CBI offers.

Integrated International Conference Series

In 2004 CBI initiated an experiment in coordinating an integrated series of five international conferences in three countries that shared a focus on exploring and advancing the consciousness of peace, forgiveness, and reconciliation. Although each was independent with variations in partners, content, and goals, all events in this series were programmatically linked to build on each other for an energetic flow and larger impact. Following the success of this model, CBI has continued the process, inviting other conferences to join the network to maximize the energy and products of each event and promote an expanding, proactive network of social activists and healers for greater mutual benefit.

Training Projects

As direct products of these conferences, CBI has organized a number of professional training projects in trauma recovery, conflict transformation, and civil society for professional and paraprofessional groups intended to raise the skill level of local colleagues in underserved regions of conflict. Among recipient groups are local mental health and relief workers, peace activists, school and university faculty and staff, and civil society service providers.

Catastrophic Trauma Recovery Project (CTR)

As a result of working with colleagues from Balkan countries during the Balkan Wars in the late 1990s to assist them in accessing treatment services for trauma victims, it soon became evident that there was little available to adequately meet the massive need. It was also determined that direct services offered by outside providers were sorely limited and short term at best, and that a far more effective route lay in increasing the treatment capacity of local relief workers and counselors—those who were already involved in assisting the large populations of victims within their communities. In response, CBI developed the Catastrophic Trauma Recovery (CTR) training model, a comprehensive, integrated training/treatment model for working with large populations of catastrophic trauma victims that is simple, standardized, repeatable, time sensitive, easily taught, and culturally sensitive. The CTR model, which is included in a contributed chapter to the book *Psychological Impact of War Trauma on Civilians,* edited by Dr. Stanley Krippner, became the design for CBI's trauma training efforts. In 1998 it established a humanitarian relief effort tailored to provide intensive train-the-trainer initiatives in catastrophic trauma recovery skills, provided by expert teams of mental health specialists to local professionals and relief workers in regions of conflict where services are underdeveloped and the society's infrastructure have broken down.

Since then, CBI has organized trauma trainings in cooperation with HARMONY Institute for Psychotherapy and Counseling in Russia, the EMDR-Humanitarian Assistance Program, and other professional training organizations serving communities in the Balkans, Middle East, Caucasus, and Russia. The relief effort is endorsed and supported by nongovernmental organizations (NGOs) within the regions served. As part of the training structure, CTR trainings are also typically attached to the ICR conference and conducted immediately after.

Current Training Projects under Development

1. Bait Al Hayat/House of Life: a project to establish a children's trauma treatment center in Nablus, West Bank, Palestine, to assist children suffering from trauma as a result of war and violence. Currently, there are no such trauma treatment services available, particularly for children, in the Nablus region.
2. "Engaging The Other": a training program growing out of the annual International Conference on "Engaging The Other," intended to promote increased public awareness, understanding, and sensitivity to the dynamics of negative stereotyping, prejudice, and fear-based belief systems. It is geared to the lay public (schools, community centers, universities, etc.). Like the conference, the goal is to promote a wider dialogue on these dynamics within communities and to address local issues.
3. Capacity For Peace and Democracy—Palestine: a collaborative project with Palestinian universities in Gaza and the West Bank to establish a Center for Conflict Resolution and Human Rights that would support visiting professors and provide a curriculum in human services (psychology, social work, health science, education) and civil society (democratic studies, conflict resolution/mediation, government, political science, economics/business). The purpose is to help prepare future Palestine leaders and local professionals to be skilled in providing critical human services to the population, all to increase capacity for a viable, peaceful Palestinian nation. Another aspect is to create opportunities for NGOs and universities in Palestine and Israel to cooperate on issues that promote understanding, reconciliation, and forgiveness.

Publications in Development

"Engaging The Other": an edited book project in conjunction with the international conference, "Engaging The Other." The book will include contributions by authors representing a diversity of cultures and societies around the world, exploring the fundamentally subjective phenomenon of "The Other," each through a unique cultural eye.

"Engaging The Other": a documentary film project of in-depth interviews, presentation excerpts, and community experiences compiled from the ETO conferences.

Journal of Conflict Transformation: a virtual, web-based journal compiling conference proceedings and articles addressing conflict transformation and healing.

Professional Exchanges

Early in CBI's development, when restricted travel created greater barriers to personal encounter, a number of professional exchanges were operated to promote this invaluable contact, primarily between post-communist or Middle Eastern societies and the United States. As a result of easier access and the presence of a number of available conferences and programs, today travel is more related to direct participation in these planned activities rather than separate exchanges.

Other Projects and Efforts Growing out of Conferences

A number of collaborations, projects, and even organizations initiated by participants have grown out of CBI's conferences over the years. A new project is underway to archive these various efforts to better track the conference products and to promote cooperative networking links between them.

THE POWER OF VISION

Sharing a vision is seen as essential to the purpose of CBI, because vision instills us with both hope and power, and a fortitude beyond ourselves that guides and moves us to action, particularly action for a better world. At the same time, one of the central accomplishments of CBI that has come to be appreciated is providing itself as a concrete example of putting legs on vision, and providing the reality of individual, grassroots empowerment and initiative in creating positive change in the world around us.

It is the kind of idea we all have the capacity to create and possess at some time and to some degree, and then bring into the world if we choose. The essential element is in taking the step of believing the possibility is real, and then the next step of acting as though it is real, until there is no difference. When vision is imbued with belief and presence in our day-to-day life, our actions serve to confirm and root it in reality.

CBI's first and lasting achievement, then, has come to be its own existence and presence as a creative change agent among a rapidly growing number of similarly creative agents in large and small examples around the globe that share a common characteristic: personal empowerment expressed through empowering others.

ORGANIZATIONAL SNAPSHOT

Organization: Common Bond Institute

Founder and/or Executive Director: Steve Olweean

Mission/Description: Common Bond Institute (CBI) is a U.S.-based, non-governmental organization that grew out of the Association for Humanistic Psychology's International (Soviet-American) Professional Exchange. The Professional Exchange was initiated in 1982 as one of the first Soviet-American nongovernmental human service exchanges. CBI organizes and sponsors international conferences, professional training programs, relief efforts, and professional exchanges, and actively provides networking and coordination support to assist newly emerging human service and civil society organizations in developing countries that are regions of conflict.

In its mission, cultivating the fundamental elements of a consciousness of peace and local capacity building are seen as natural, effective antidotes to small-group, radical extremism and large-group despair, as well as to the hardships and suffering of the human condition. To this end, enabling each society to effectively resolve and transform conflicts, satisfy core human needs within their communities, and construct effective, holistic mechanisms for self determination, self esteem, and fundamental human dignity and worth is the purpose of CBI's work.

Common Bond Institute is grounded in the application of humanistic psychology's principles in its commitment to capacity building at both the grassroots and social institutional level. It works to actively form strategic alliances and partnerships with organizations, groups, and individuals dedicated to nurturing global relationships while creating and promoting an authentic world culture of peace.

Website: www.cbiworld.org

Address: 12170 South Pine Ayr Drive

Climax, MI 49034 USA

Phone: +1.269.665.9393

Fax: +1.269.665.9393

E-mail: SOlweean@aol.com

5

The Social Work Education in Ethiopia Partnership

Alice K. Johnson Butterfield,
Abye Tasse, and Nathan Linsk

Our story is about the development of social work education in Ethiopia. It is about the power of our shared vision, leadership, and collaboration. It is about global networking and our efforts to capitalize on available and plentiful human resources from around the world and use them in an environment of scarce resources in Ethiopia. Our story is about the power of one person connecting with another to develop new programs to meet human needs, establish international partnerships in higher education, and bring about social change.

ONE PERSON CONNECTING WITH ANOTHER

Long before any of us thought about working in the development of social work education in Ethiopia, the seed for our involvement began with the adoption of three children from Ethiopia by Richard and Kay McChesney of St. Louis, Missouri. When taking their son, Leul, to the Ethiopian Orthodox Church for services, Kay met Dr. Enagaw Mehari, a medical doctor, who at the time was a visiting professor at Washington University in St. Louis. Through the People2People organization, Dr. Mehari was organizing a delegation of medical experts in HIV/AIDS from universities around the United States to travel to Ethiopia. The purpose of the visit was to meet with university, government, and health care officials in Ethiopia with the objective of identifying potential areas of collaboration in HIV/AIDS prevention and research between universities. In discussing the planned visit by medical faculty, Dr. McChesney asked a simple question: "What about the children—the orphan victims of HIV/AIDS?" Dr. Mehari responded quickly and invited Kay, a sociologist and family therapist, to join the delegation. Kay declined because of work, the newness of the adoption, and family responsibilities; she suggested that Alice Butterfield would be someone to substitute in her place. Alice had worked as a social work faculty member in child welfare projects in Romania, and also had personal experience in international adoption. Kay had first met Alice at a public health conference, and later, they worked together on a family homelessness project in St. Louis and became friends.

Alice received an e-mail inviting her to go to Ethiopia for seventeen days in May 2001 as a member of a delegation led by former ambassador to Ethiopia, David H. Shinn (2001). A decision had to be made quickly. Dean Creasie Finney Hairston of the University of Illinois–Chicago approved her trip. Upon accepting the invitation, Alice clarified that her participation with the People2People delegation would be to represent the Jane Addams School of Social Work, where she was a professor.

From her perspective, Alice was particularly interested in the role of social work in Ethiopia. What was the need for social work? Did the profession exist? Searching the academic literature, she found articles from the 1960s with reference to social work in Ethiopia (Sedler, 1968a; 1986b; Stein, 1969). There was a School of Social Work at Haile Selassie I University, which offered a bachelor's degree beginning in the late 1950s (Sedler, 1968c). During that time, the school was recognized in Ethiopia and throughout Africa as a center of excellence. Three young faculty were sent to the United States to obtain doctorates in social work as part of a plan to build the capacity of Ethiopian faculty. The next reference to social work in Ethiopia was in an article written by Katherine Kendall (1986), which noted the closing of the School of Social Work and its replacement by a degree in applied sociology:

> The social theory is heavily Marxist. . . . In addition to a course on Marxist thought and practice, students take courses on Marxist sociology and anthropology. . . . While there are no methodological courses in the social work sense, research and statistics are given considerable emphasis. . . . There is one course on the history of social welfare which is explored within the context of class struggle. Study visits have replaced field work. (p. 18)

Now the facts were evident. When the Derge military regime came to power in 1974, the school was closed. By definition, social problems did not exist within a socialist state; it was the purpose of government to meet all human needs. Social work was bourgeois—and did not have a place in Ethiopia.[1] "All reference to social work was discouraged on the grounds that it was reformist and represented a bourgeois machination to keep the working classes in a perpetual state of dependence" (Gebre-Selassie, 1999, p. 7).

But who were the doctoral students who came to the United States to study social work? Would it be still possible to find them? Searching the Internet gave no clue, so Alice turned to a network of colleagues who are members of the Association for Community Organization and Social Administration (ACOSA) (http://www.acosa.org). She sent out an e-mail that asked if anyone knew about social work education in Ethiopia or knew any social workers in Ethiopia. She got one reply—an e-mail from Dr. Rosemary Sarri, an emeritus faculty from the University of Michigan. Her former doctoral student, Seyoum Gebre-Selassie, had gotten his doctorate in sociology and social work in 1976, obtained a teaching position at the University of Wisconsin, and then went back to Ethiopia in 1979. Although the School of Social Work there had been closed, he had been a dean and also had served in university administration. She had lost contact with him over the years, but Rosemary was sure he was still in Ethiopia. Alice should contact Seyoum.

Finding Professor Seyoum was not difficult. It seemed that "everyone" she met in visits to the community or in meetings at Addis Ababa University knew him. Alice met Professor Seyoum Gebre-Selassie in May 2001. He confirmed the 1960s accounts about social work in Ethiopia written in the *International Social Work* journal. He and his longtime friend and colleague, Professor Andargatchew Tesfaye, were two of the three students sent for doctoral study to the United States. With his country reeling from the takeover by the military regime, Seyoum made a decision to return. "I did not want to be asked by someone in the United States as to what I did about it when my country was in deep peril. . . . I was ridden with doubt whether I was right in deciding to come back. But, in hindsight, I knew I made the right decision" (Surafel, 2001).

Back at their university, now named Addis Ababa University, the two professors were successful in "hiding" six courses in macro social work in the sociology and anthropology curriculum at Addis Ababa University. Some thirty years later in 2001, only this remnant of social work education remained. Professor Seyoum estimated that fewer than fifty social workers with baccalaureate degrees from Haile Selassie I University were still practicing in Ethiopia. Many had left Ethiopia, and most of those who remained were nearing the end of their careers. Nonetheless, these senior social workers were leaders in nongovernmental organizations (NGOs), and had mentored many applied sociology graduates who had followed them in the ways of social work. Also, within the Department of Sociology and Social Anthropology (SOSA), professors Seyoum, Andargatchew, and younger colleagues such as Tefari Abate, Ayalu Gebre, and Melese Getu had successfully placed the goal of developing a master's degree in social work in the university's five-year strategic plan. Later, this official statement in university documents became important in convincing an external funding agency to support a planning process for a graduate degree in social work. In just a few sentences over coffee at the Dessalgn Hotel, Professor Seyoum set the objectives for the next several years:

> We need to start the profession of social work in Ethiopia. We *should* start a School of Social Work—because that is the history here. Social work and law were the two strongest schools at Haile Selassie I University. But, first, we'll start with a master's degree.

SOCIAL WORK EDUCATION IN ETHIOPIA PARTNERSHIP (PROJECT SWEEP)

Together, Addis Ababa University and the University of Illinois–Chicago wrote a proposal for seed funds to Higher Education for Development (HED), the intermediary organization established in 1992 as the Association Liaison Office for

University Cooperation in Development (ALO). HED assists the nation's six major higher education associations in partnering with the U.S. Agency for International Development (USAID). HED has funded over 250 university-to-university partnerships since its inception, from education, law, agriculture, and other disciplines. The proposal submitted by the Jane Addams College of Social Work and Addis Ababa University was the first social work program to receive funding. The college received $99,000 to partner with Addis Ababa University to establish Ethiopia's first ever master's degree in social work. A five-year Memorandum of Agreement was signed by the two universities to collaborate in teaching, research, and service.

This small amount of seed funding and the higher education partnership it represented were essential in providing the funds and mechanism for the first part of realizing our partnership's dream of graduate social work education in Ethiopia. Beginning in 2002, a planning committee from Addis Ababa University (AAU) and the University of Illinois–Chicago (UIC) met several times in each country. We named our partnership the Social Work Education in Ethiopia Partnership (Project SWEEP). We worked together using a strategic planning approach with several phases, including an in-country needs assessment followed by curriculum development, faculty exchange, and program planning. We set up an advisory committee in Ethiopia, which consisted of social workers with BSW degrees from the previous program in social work and some with later degrees in applied sociology from the program that had replaced social work. A second advisory committee of local social work leaders in Chicago, including representatives from the Ethiopia Community Association, provided guidance, responded to requests for material goods, and assisted in exchanges of Ethiopian faculty to Chicago (for a complete report, see Johnson Butterfield & Linsk, 2005).

LEADERSHIP AT ADDIS ABABA UNIVERSITY

The planning and curriculum development process that began through Project SWEEP was at the grassroots level. As our small planning committee of UIC and AAU faculty worked to develop the MSW program, the AAU members of the team, particularly Professor Seyoum Gebre-Selassie, brought the project to the attention of the new president of Addis Ababa University, Professor Andreas Eshete, UNESCO Chair for Human Rights and Democracy. President Andreas put his power behind social work education. He valued the future degree and its potential role as part of the country's effort to reduce poverty through social and economic development. By the second year of our planning process in 2003, decision makers at the highest level of university administration had decided that social work would be started at Addis Ababa University as an independent school, not as a department-based program. In part, this decision revolved around the difficulty of "grafting" a graduate degree in social work into the Department of Sociology and Social Anthropology (SOSA). After professors Seyoum and Andargatchew retired, no SOSA faculty had been trained in social work. The brain drain also had had its effect: SOSA had sent three young staff to the United States and Canada to study social work, but none had returned. In addition, the department was already accepting many students, and to add a third discipline at the graduate level without an undergraduate degree in place would be difficult.

With this change of auspices, the work of the Project SWEEP partnership, and its plan for graduate social work education, gained the full support of AAU officials. At this time, the power shifted from a grassroots effort, driven by a small group of people and a planning grant, to ownership of the initiative by Addis Ababa University. From this point onward, the involvement of President Andreas was a major reason why Project SWEEP was successful. He championed the development of social work education, noting its relevance to affirmative action; the rights of women and children, including areas that intersect law and social work; and the need for counseling for students in their transition to urban, college life. President Andreas has continued to affirm the importance of social work as a profession, including its expansion to the baccalaureate and doctoral levels at Addis Ababa University, and in the future, its replication in regional colleges and emerging universities in Ethiopia.

In assessing the importance of leadership at Addis Ababa University, we doubt that starting a new School of Social Work from scratch would have become reality if it were not for the synergistic involvement of Dr. Abye Tasse, former dean of the Institut du Développement Social (IDS) in France, and an international leader of social work education. Abye's migration back to his native country is quite remarkable. He fled Ethiopia at sixteen when the Derge military regime came to power. He was in refugee camps in Sudan for two years, then migrated to Egypt and finally to France, where he got a scholarship to study political science. He was in need of a job to help support himself, and so he began his career in social work as a youth worker in a poor community. He eventually went on to obtain his master's degree and doctorate, and served at all levels of the university—from lecturer to dean of one of the top three schools in France. Returning to Ethiopia for the first time in thirty-three years, Abye visited Addis Ababa University, initially just to see what was happening in higher education. He met President Andreas, and soon thereafter, became involved bringing about university reforms.

In 2004 Abye took what was to be a two-year sabbatical. President Andreas appointed Abye as dean of social work and associate vice president for International Affairs. Abye brought leadership in international social work to Ethiopia. In October 2004, he was elected president of the International Association of Schools of Social Work (IASSW). Prior to that, he chaired the Katherine Kendall Award, given to an international social work educator by IASSW and the International Federation of Social Workers (IFSW). Thus, in just two years—from planning to the start of a graduate degree—Ethiopia went from a country *without* an educational program in social work to a country *with a School of Social Work* led by a dean who was the president of the International Association of Schools of Social Work (IASSW).

Dr. Abye brought reality to the vision of social work education in Ethiopia. His leadership style espoused a "can do" attitude. In practical terms, this meant starting the new school without anything—without a faculty, computers, office space, budget, or even approval for the degree through Addis Ababa University processes. Abye went to work immediately. Over a six-month period in early 2004, the curriculum was approved by the Graduate Council at AAU. Admissions criteria were developed, and exams were given and graded by the UIC-AAU faculty team. Forty students were admitted. With the leadership of President Andreas Eshete' and Dean Abye Tasse, the school had secured computers, office equipment, and classroom and library space for the School of Social Work in a new building on the university's main campus by the start of classes in September 2004. However, since university budgets must be approved more than a year in advance, the school opened without budgeted funds for the first year of operation.

How did Addis Ababa University move so quickly to start a new School of Social Work in a resource-poor environment without faculty lines or budgets in place? As noted previously, the commitment of leaders at the top administrative level of Addis Ababa University was principally important. Secondly, a small part of this answer is that Project SWEEP grant funds were extended for an additional year. UIC took no overhead or administrative costs for managing Project SWEEP, so all the $99,000 grant was used for program development and implementation. Grant funds were conserved throughout the two-year planning process by not paying salaries for the time team members worked on Project SWEEP, and by providing only hotel and travel costs, plus $12 per day per diem for UIC faculty. Initial activities included community visits; a needs assessment of graduating seniors, agency staff, and possible employers; as well as assistance in developing a field education manual by Faith Bonecutter, the director of field education at the Jane Addams College. In 2004 HED allowed the remaining funds to be used for travel for UIC professors Nathan Linsk, Donna Petras, and Alice Johnson Butterfield to teach intensive courses in the first year of offering the MSW degree at AAU. AAU dean Abye Tasse and associate dean Melese Getu taught courses above their regular workload in the new MSW program. Resident international faculty included Dr. James Rollin, an assistant professor at UIC, who was recruited by Teachers for Africa and joined the AAU faculty in 2004, followed by Dr. Deborah Zinn, in 2008. AAU hired two additional faculty, Dr. Sandhya Joshi from India in 2004 and Dr. Charlla Allen from Cleveland, Ohio, in 2006, to staff the new program.

LACK OF CLARITY AND CHANGES IN HIGHER EDUCATION

Two other factors were also essential in advancing the rapid development of social work education in Ethiopia: a lack of clarity about what social work was in the Ethiopian context and how it should be developed, and the rapidly changing context of higher education in Ethiopia. These factors intertwined to create an advantageous setting for the immediate development of social work education. First, the environment that we began working in certainly could be described as one that lacked clarity about social work education and how it should be developed. This confusion led to an open situation that allowed for innovation, often bypassing the formal system of organizational change, based on the vision of restarting social work education in Ethiopia.

> This lack of clarity combined with the felt need of something else. We felt a call for this new "thing" but nobody knew what it was really was or what it was supposed to be. Then, the idea clicked. As we started to work with the idea of social work, we realized that our "new idea" was reminiscent of the past history of social work education in Ethiopia. It drew on the reputation and accomplishments of the previous graduates of social work and applied sociology who served the country for many years in high positions of authority. The idea also developed as a response to the NGO reference to social work—calling it "social work" as what they were doing—but not really knowing social work. In this vacuum and confusion, all were ready to find ways to help. (Tasse, Johnson Butterfield, & Linsk, 2007, p. 8)

Second, this lack of clarity existed within a larger policy environment of change rapidly taking place in higher education. Historically, Ethiopia's 1 percent participation rate in higher education was one of the lowest in the world. Beginning in the 1990s, higher education became a national priority through strategic planning, national conferences, and new initiatives. "In addition to its traditional role of educating, creating knowledge and developing the mind, it is increasingly asked to train, be student-centered, practice-oriented, society-focused, and to teach professions that require skills and hands-on training" (Yizengaw, 2003, p. 7). The University Capacity Building Program (UCBP), a joint venture of the Ministry of Capacity Building and the Ministry of Education, began constructing thirteen new/extended universities throughout Ethiopia. By 2002, the larger environment of the university system in Ethiopia was rapidly expanding from its base of six universities and five colleges/institutes to nineteen public universities. When completed in 2009, the new universities will enroll more than 121,000 new students. In addition, a Higher Education Proclamation approved by the Ethiopian parliament initiated new reforms, including increased autonomy for institutions of higher education, a priority for developing new degree programs, and expanding graduate education to increase the number of Ethiopian academics (UCBP, 2008).

The government's priority of higher education positively influenced our ability to start two new graduate degrees—the master's in social work (MSW) in 2004 and a PhD in social work and social development in 2006—within the larger university system. Innovation and creativity were valued over bureaucracy and red tape. During planning and the start-up of the new graduate degree, our challenge was to figure out how to offer the classes or design the exam, or develop admissions criteria, or prepare a new student orientation—all the tasks associated with new program development and educational administration—and then do it. Much leeway was allowed for the AAU-UIC team to design new and innovative ways of delivering graduate education. When university approvals were required—such as in senate approval for the curriculum, or for the admissions criteria and processes—the university administration was prompt, professional, and attentive to urgent deadlines. All in all, our experience within the university environment was one of innovation and development. In this environment, the UIC-AAU partnership served as a catalyst that influenced the larger university by example through new ways of doing things related to graduate education. In the next section, we discuss some of the innovations that were part and parcel of the new MSW degree that were different ways of doing things from the traditional educational processes at Addis Ababa University.

THE PARADOX OF THE POOR AND EDUCATIONAL INNOVATIONS

As noted above, the establishment of the new Graduate School of Social Work (GSSW) fit well within the overall policy goals of higher education in Ethiopia. In addition to this alignment with the context of higher education is what we call the paradox of the poor: "the poor who have nothing, yet we have everything" (Tasse, 2007, p. 1). What does "the paradox of the poor" mean? We learned a lot about what this meant from watching Professor Seyoum at work. On short notice, he could make a few phone calls and pull key players together for an important meeting "before the Jane Addams group left town." It was he who identified many members of the advisory group, and all those he invited got involved and stayed involved over the years. His network was expansive and extensive. As we met people in Ethiopia and sought to introduce ourselves, we could not count the number of times that just the mention of Seyoum Gebre-Selassie's name elicited the following response: "He is my professor." He brought the UIC team into his network of colleagues—a network that he built in a resource-poor environment through his inspiration, work, and service.

It was Professor Seyoum who worked diligently behind the scenes at AAU as the champion of social work education. Our core UIC-AAU team has often reflected on the fact that Addis Ababa University's decision to start the social work program as an independent school was a blessing in disguise. We did not have to navigate our way through the processes of integrating a new program into a department's existing policies and procedures. Innovation could occur more rapidly because there was no need to deal with the typical turf issues and professional dispositions that make up academia in any part of the world. The challenge was to figure out what we needed and strategize how to obtain it. Since it would be impossible to start a new graduate program without teaching faculty, this was our partnership's first strategic concern.

Thus without "anything," we turned to what we had—a network of professional colleagues and organizations around the world that might have interest in contributing to the development of social work education in Ethiopia. We imagined mobilizing a diverse network of social work faculty from around the world to contribute their time and expertise to the school. Dean Abye sent an e-mail invitation letter to our colleagues in our UIC and IASSW networks (see Figure 5.1). In a few candid sentences, this was the dean's offer: "Come to Ethiopia. Pay your own way. Give a seminar. Teach. Live in my guest house and share my food." Over

Rouen/Addis Ababa March 2004

Dear colleagues and friends,

First of all, I would like to thank you all personally and on behalf of Addis Ababa University, for the spontaneous and generous help you offered to my request of participation in seminars that my colleagues of Addis Ababa University and myself, intend to organise at the new Graduate School of Social Work, which will start in September 2004. I know that all of you have many activities and large engagements in different areas, and I appreciate your commitment to contribute and enrich our seminars with your experience.

As I have mentioned with each of you in our previous exchanges, the Addis Ababa University has decided to open a new School of Social Work; and I have been nominated to be the first Dean of this School. The mobilisation of the entire university administration to give a high profile for this new school is, as I can see it, tremendous. This project elaborated by Addis Ababa University in co-operation with Jane Addams College of the University of Illinois at Chicago, is the first graduate school of social work ever in Ethiopia.

I would like to take this opportunity to thank the dedication of the faculty of Addis Ababa University, (particularly Seyoum Gebre-Selassie, Andargatchew Tesfaye, and Melese Getu) and of the University of Illinois at Chicago (especially Alice K. Johnson and Nathan L. Linsk) for their tireless engagement in this venture.

It is in this context that we wish to organise several seminars. The main objective of the seminars (12 seminars a year of a maximum of a week) is to give a wide opportunity for our graduate students, faculty members and partners from multiples agencies (public and private) a high level of input by distinguished social work educators and specialists on issues related to social work education from around the world.

Each seminar organised under this program will be in relation to the courses that we are going to teach in this new school. Based on an interactive method of teaching, the seminars will provide a unique opportunity for our students and faculty members to elaborate knowledge on social work education in the country. Beyond the direct interest to build a school with a high standing, this will also help, I am sure, to form deep relations among social work educators around the world with colleagues from Ethiopia teaching in this new school, will also develop institutional relations between the Addis Ababa University and your institutions.

I know your dedication for international solidarity in the field of Social Work Education and beyond, and I thank you again for agreeing to contribute to the development of a new school of Social Work in Africa and to build a new and unique kind of partnership.

Best wishes,

Abye Tasse

P.S. As I have mentioned to you, there is no problem on accommodation for your venue in Addis. If you need a letter of support from the Addis Ababa University in order to find funding for your travel, please feel free to contact me.

Figure 5.1   Letter Inviting Colleagues to Give Seminars and Secure Their Own Funding

sixty people from around the world answered the invitation. Many have come to Ethiopia at their own expense—exactly as they were invited—and provided a workshop or taught a course at no charge. International seminars were integrated with regular courses, and students were expected to attend. Table 5.1 shows the international faculty who went to Ethiopia to share their expertise.

We also used our network to fill the gaps in teaching that could not be covered by faculty in Ethiopia. One of the major innovations was the use of a block teaching model for offering MSW and PhD courses at Addis Ababa University. Courses

Table 5.1 International Seminars

International Trainer	Title of Seminar	Linked with MSW Course
Dorothy Faller, MSW, Faller International Training LLC, Cleveland, Ohio, USA.	Organizational Management, September 27–Oct 5, 2004.	SSWA 601 Integrated Practice Methods I.
Prof. Ralph Brody, Cleveland State University, Cleveland, Ohio, USA.	Seminar in Management, October 18–22, 2004.	SSWA 621 Management & Leadership.
Prof. Ariella Fridman and Dr. Miriam Golan, University of Tel-Aviv, Israel.	Seminar on Psychology of Women and Gender, December 6–10, 2004.	SSWA 611 Social Problems & Community Health.
Prof. Lena Dominelli, Past President of the International Association of School of Social work, Director, Center for International Social and Community Development, University of Southampton, United Kingdom.	Seminar on Social Policy & Ethics, January 10–14, 2005.	SSWA 631 Social Policy & Ethics.
Prof. Shimon Peres, Tel-Aviv University, Israel.	Seminar on Evaluation Research, May 16–20, 2005.	SSWA 642 Research Methods.
Asst. Prof. Gurid Aga Askeland, Diakonhjemment College, Norway.	Seminar on Reflexive Research Methods, May 9–13, 2005.	SSWA 642 Research Methods.
Senior Lecturer Greta Bradley, The University of Hull School of Nursing, Social Work and Applied Health Studies, England.	Seminar on Reflexive Research Methods, May 9–13, 2005.	SSWA 642 Research Methods.
Professor of International Social Work Karen Lyons, Department of Applied Social Sciences, London Metropolitan University.	Lectures on Globalization, Regionalism, and Social Work; Migration and Social Work; Child Care in an International Context—October 2005.	
Dr. Rena Feigin, Bob Shapell School of Social Work, Tel Aviv University, Israel.	Seminar on Breaking Through: Family Coping with Illness and Disability: An Integrative Treatment Concept. February 3, 2006.	
Prof. Nancy L. Green, École des Hautes Études en Sciences Sociales (Paris), France.	Seminar on Comparative Migration History, February 2006.	SSWA-672 Social Mobilization: Food Security & Refugee Resettlement.
Prof. Richard Kordesh, College of Urban Planning and Public Affairs, University of Illinois–Chicago.	Seminar on Family-Based and Asset-Based Approaches to Community Development, Dec. 17–21, 2007.	

typically feature an intensive, adult-learning block approach, which allows students to focus on the content of one course for one month at a time, four days a week. The format allows faculty from outside of Ethiopia to teach a complete course over a three- to-four-week period. This has been an important innovation because support from international faculty is necessary until the capacity of Ethiopian faculty is built. Overall, the use of international faculty also led to innovations in teaching pedagogy through the use of interactive teaching methods in the classroom. Methods include working in groups, role plays, simulations, community projects, group exercises, guest speakers, and so on. These pedagogical methods are different from the usual didactic lecture and exam format typical of teaching at AAU (see, for example, Askeland & Bradley, 2007).

With the start of the PhD in social work and social development in 2006, we expanded our network to include expert social work faculty from other universities in the United States. Those who taught courses at the School of Social Work at AAU include Robert Miller, University of Albany, *Qualitative Methods*; Valerie Chang, Indiana University, *Teaching and Pedagogy in Social Work*; Margaret Adamek, Indiana University, *Writing for Publication*; Richard Kordesh, University of Illinois–Chicago, *Program Evaluation and Policy Analysis*; Rosemary Sarri, University of Michigan, *Advanced Assessment for Action Research*; Larry Kreuger, University of Missouri, *Quantitative Methods*; Klaus Serr, Australian Catholic University, *Community Practice & Capacity Building*; Donna Petras, *Practice with Children & Families*; Nathan Linsk, University of Illinois–Chicago, *Social Problems and Community Health, Advanced Counseling Skills*, and *Meta Evaluation & Dissemination*; and Alice Johnson Butterfield, University of Illinois–Chicago, *Integrated Practice I: Groups and Communities, Action Research & Models of Social Change* and *Knowledge Building in Social Work and Social Development.*

Some colleagues on the list above were granted release time by their deans for teaching in Ethiopia. Some sandwiched teaching courses in Ethiopia between teaching semesters in the U.S. system, or used their summer vacation for teaching. Others were retired from formal academic positions and had more flexibility to teach during regular semesters in Ethiopia. Two from UIC fielded their sabbatical research in Ethiopia. Nathan was awarded a Fulbright African AIDS Research Program Award in 2006–7, and Alice carried out research on eight HED-funded higher education partnerships in Ethiopia during her sabbatical in 2007–8.

In fact, the development of research, especially action research, has been a hallmark of the program. Linsk was able to use the Fulbright award to conduct a study of the initial scale-up of HIV/AIDS antiretroviral drugs made possible by funding from the President's Emergency Plan for AIDS Relief (PEPFAR) and the Global Fund for Tuberculosis, Malaria and HIV. Although funds were coming quickly, it remained unknown whether people with HIV could use the treatments and adhere to care regimens. The study, made possible through a team of MSW students and volunteers, demonstrated that rates of adherence were high, but that the cultural context of adherence required redefinition to improve antiretroviral treatment (Linsk, Gosha, Getu, Aklilu, & Prabhughate, 2007). In addition, the

Figure 5.2   Field visit to rural Ethiopia. Courtesy of Alice K. Johnson Butterfield.

thesis requirement of the MSW provided a range of research products in diverse areas including HIV/AIDS, adolescent issues, homelessness, social networks, divorce consequences, water use, and a range of community development approaches, to name a few. Butterfield's continuing research on single women and their needs, strengths-based approaches, and university partnerships is providing vital data on community needs and ways to address them. The PhD program (see below) augments research productivity, creating a whole field of social work research that did not exist previously.

Other educational innovations also occurred. The School of Social Work was the first to include field education (internships) as part of its academic program. A Memorandum of Agreement was signed by AAU and the Christian Relief & Development Association (CRDA), a nonsectarian umbrella organization of over 200 NGOs. CRDA played an active role in developing field placements for AAU students. Three social work students were also placed on the standing committees of Parliament: Committee on Social Affairs, Committee on Finance and Community Development, and the Committee on Rural Development. The placements were so successful that the idea has now expanded to include other schools and colleges of AAU, such as economics and gender studies, with twenty-six interns placed in 2007. Future plans include developing a part-time program specifically for members of Parliament. Sixty-seven Parliament officials have registered to take the exam for admission to the master's in social work program. Thirty Parliament members representing all political parties will be accepted.

The School of Social Work requires a different admissions process than is usual at AAU. It includes a personal statement and a résumé in addition to the usual information about the applicant; three letters of reference (a form for writing a short paragraph about the applicant and signing it); sponsorship through government, NGOs, or self; bank statement; GPA; and exam. The process of admission includes a two-part point system: (1) pre-screening using the personal statement and other applicant information, and (2) blind review of the exams by the AAU-UIC faculty team. Efforts are made to assure that disadvantaged groups are represented among students in the MSW program, including women, those working in public welfare, those working in NGOs in rural areas, persons with disabilities, and persons with an interest in preparing for roles as social work faculty in Ethiopia. Admission requirements have been broadened to include the BA degree in social and/or health sciences or other disciplines, with weight given to work experience in NGOs or public welfare organizations. Another new admissions policy was a three-day student orientation and assessment program, which we called the Privileged Method of Learning. Sessions included the privileged process of learning, student and faculty expectations, methods of personal organization, and preferred modes of assessment for student learning. Students spend the weekend preparing an individual assessment, and then meet with their faculty advisor to discuss their learning plan. Overall, this intensive orientation has been valuable in dialoguing with students, establishing a culture of learning and mutual support, and sharing the development of the school, our vision of social work, and the future of the profession in Ethiopia. These sessions were also designed to orient students to the "different ways of doing things at the School of Social Work" when compared, perhaps, to the traditional type of educational experiences with which they were familiar.

Efforts were also made to take the university to the community and bring the community into the university. Field trips took students and faculty to rural communities, and ordinary people who had established local NGOs and their own microenterprise associations were invited to come to the classroom to share their expertise. For example, women from the Kechene Potters Association participated in a community assessment project in 2005; they presented their pottery products and the work of their association to students and professors. The benefits of this type of collaboration were mutual. In the case of the Kechene Potters, their engagement with the university resulted in a thesis project (Yeneabat, 2006), which in turn brought the potters' situation to the attention of a businessman from Cleveland, Ohio, who was participating in the Ethiopian Workforce Entrepreneurship Training Program. In 2007 he donated $5,000 to purchase grinding and clay mixing machines that will vastly improve the number and quality of pots the women can produce.

In just two years, eighty students with MSW degrees have graduated from AAU, with seventy students currently enrolled in the two-year, full-time program.

Graduates are highly sought by government, international NGOs, and local NGOs. Some graduates are now working with embassies and international aid organizations throughout Ethiopia. In recognition of the work of the UIC-AAU partnership, Addis Ababa University's School of Social Work and UIC's Jane Addams College of Social Work received the Partners in International Education Award from the Global Commission on Social Work Education, Council on Social Work Education in 2006. In 2007 the Council of International Programs USA received the same award for their more than fifty years of international training and exchange programs, including their collaborative role with Addis Ababa University in Ethiopia.

A DOCTORAL PROGRAM IN SOCIAL WORK
AND SOCIAL DEVELOPMENT

In retrospect, much of the work of the partnership has rested on the good will and voluntary service of many people from around the world. This type of project is sustainable as long as the vision of social work education holds, and people are able to stay involved. From the first planning meeting through Project SWEEP, the issue of sustainability was discussed. The words of Professor Seyoum still ring true: "Sustainability is built on the capacity of the faculty." We knew from then on that ultimately there must be a doctoral program in place to prepare faculty for positions at Addis Ababa University and other universities in Ethiopia that may develop social work programs. This idea became our vision of sustainability. In 2006 Addis Ababa University decided to start a doctoral program in social work and social development.

David Moxley, formerly of Wayne State University and now on the faculty of the University of Oklahoma, Alice, Abye, and Melese collaborated on a grant proposal to the Ministry of Education for funds to start the PhD program. Addis Ababa University was successful in obtaining US$141,000 for the new doctoral program from the Development Innovation Fund of the Ministry of Education, through funds from the World Bank. In 2006 eight of the first MSW graduates were admitted to doctoral study. In 2007 seven additional students were admitted, including three with MA degrees in fields other than social work. These doctoral students represent faculties at Awassa University, Bahir Dar University, and Addis Ababa University's Department of Psychology. They plan to return to their home universities upon completion of their degrees. In this way, the doctoral program is attempting to build faculty capacity in social work and related fields at other public universities in Ethiopia. Typically, doctoral students are appointed as lecturers, so their roles will include coordinating field education, advising students, serving as assistant deans, participating in strategic planning, and co-teaching courses with international faculty.

The curriculum plan for the PhD program combines ideas brought by the Ethiopian and international faculty who were involved in its development. According to Johnson Butterfield (2007, p. 6),

A challenge faced by the international team which developed the doctoral curriculum was combining their various views about what doctoral education should entail. The two Ethiopian members of our team had received doctorates in France and England; another professor obtained her doctorate in India; I had obtained mine in the United States. The British experience leaned toward individual work with a faculty chairperson and extensive individualized readings; the French experience included lively "discussion and debate" seminars with the great minds of the university; the program in India focused on applied research. My experience at Washington University in St. Louis involved interdisciplinary courses and research practicum. As we sought to create a plan for doctoral education in Ethiopia, each of us brought our biases to the table. . . . We also knew that the new doctoral program had to address the difficult problems of Ethiopia and the urgent need for faculty. . . . we sought a way to streamline the doctoral educational process without compromising quality. Our work together became synergistic.

The doctoral program at Addis Ababa University is a year-round program. Students complete all required courses over the first calendar year, so they are eligible to teach in the second and third years of study. A qualifying assessment based on the portfolio approach and an oral presentation to a faculty committee replaces the typical written exam. The dissertation can follow a traditional monograph format, or a set of three published articles that document the student's research and scholarship on a social issue of local, regional, or national importance. AAU faculty and its international team may design team-based or action-research projects that may include undergraduate and master's degree students who are participating directly in research. Based on faculty expertise and existing national priorities within Ethiopia, the doctoral program outlines four potential project areas:

- **Capacity Building:** augmenting the capacity of local communities to reduce poverty through comprehensive community development involving literacy, microenterprise, youth development, housing, rural development, and soil and water conservation, and using best practices from social development and participatory approaches
- **Child Welfare:** fostering improvements in child welfare, including orphan care, international and in-country adoption, nonformal education, gender equity, the reduction of harmful traditional practices, juvenile justice, divorce, and child custody
- **Health:** abating the transmission of HIV and addressing other public health issues (e.g., malaria, TB, blindness, polio, birth defects, water-born diarrhea diseases, malnourishment) by using best practices in outreach, prevention, treatment, and medication adherence (especially for antiretroviral therapies), community collaboration, and awareness building
- **Refugees and Migration:** improving humanitarian responses to displacement, migration, and refugee resettlement; conflict resolution; decreasing stigma and marginalization among vulnerable groups, including persons with disabilities, women, homeless persons; and so on.

SOCIAL WORK AS A COMPONENT OF CHANGE

From the beginning planning phase of Project SWEEP, the general situation of poverty in Ethiopia resulted in a very quick acknowledgement that social work was not a solution in and of itself. The needs of the country of Ethiopia are very great. As one of the poorest countries in the world, an estimated 80 percent of its 70 million people live on less than $2.00 a day. Most of Ethiopia's people are farmers in a country where droughts and famine recur. The literacy rate for adults over age seventeen is approximately 42 percent. Malaria, tuberculosis, HIV/AIDS, and other diseases contribute to a life expectancy at birth of about forty-eight years. Approximately 1.3 million persons (3.5 percent of the population) are living with HIV/AIDS. An estimated 870,000 children have been orphaned by the virus (UNAIDS, 2008), and the total number of children orphaned because of all causes is 4,800,000 (UNICEF, 2005).

These problems require interdisciplinary, comprehensive, and multifaceted approaches and solutions. Our vision was that social work alone was not sufficient. Rather, social work should be a component of change—a catalyst for mobilizing other systems to respond to Ethiopia's wide-ranging needs in community development, child welfare, health, food security, and so on. Our efforts to make social work a catalyst for change include a variety of collaborative efforts with other groups and organizations working in Ethiopia. Our collaboration

Figure 5.3   Primary-school children in Ethiopia. Courtesy of Richard Kordesh.

takes varied forms. In simple terms, what makes our partnership work is an ongoing effort to communicate and build synergy among and between various projects and activities taking place in Ethiopia. The next section discusses social work as a component of social change in Ethiopia through collaboration with other organizations.

COLLABORATION WITH OTHER ORGANIZATIONS

Our efforts at making social work a catalyst for change often took the form of collaboration with other groups and organizations with similar interests or work in Ethiopia. These efforts were not preplanned or strategically decided. They occurred through the opportunities and synergies that were created as a result of the overall process of bring people representing organizations from around the world to contribute to the development of social work education in Ethiopia. In addition, as we drew on our network, and as that network expanded, there were new opportunities for collaboration and partnerships. Without staff to keep all of these efforts organized, the connections between various people and projects were sometimes open and very visible, and at other times, not everyone was informed of the connections and opportunities that various members of our core group of UIC-AAU faculty were pursuing or developing. However, through e-mail, phone calls, and face-to-face meetings at international conferences, we tried to keep everyone informed.

Collaboration is subject to the availability of at least some resources. UIC's main resource was faculty with a continuing interest in building the social work and educational capacity of Ethiopian institutions. So, one of the major foci of the UIC faculty involvement has been the identification of other organizations with in-kind resources to help build the capacity of the Ethiopian institutions. All of the collaborative relationships described below share a similar goal, which is to help build the capacity of Ethiopian institutions. The list below briefly summarizes how various organizations collaborated over the six-year period between 2002 and 2008. Additional information is available on the SWEEP website at http://www.aboutsweep.org.

- **Books For Africa** collects, sorts, ships and distributes books to Africa. Books for Africa shipped forty-two boxes of books to Addis Ababa University in 2007. In February 2008, a forty-foot container (approximately 35,000 books) was shipped to Ethiopia for our partnership work with Addis Ababa University, Bahir Dar University, Gedam Sefer, schools, and other projects (http://www.booksforafrica.org).
- **Council of International Programs USA (CIPUSA)** is a nonprofit international exchange organization that brings well-qualified professionals to the United States for practical training experiences. CIPUSA hosted Ethiopian faculty that came to the United States through Project SWEEP, and received two grants from the U.S. Department of State for starting the Community Work

and Life Center at AAU, and the Ethiopian Workforce Entrepreneurship and Training Program (http://www.cipusa.org).

- **Christian Relief and Development Association (CRDA)** is a nonpartisan organization of more than 200 indigenous and international NGOs and faith-based agencies operating in Ethiopia. CRDA provides technical support, training, information, and capacity building support to NGOs. CRDA has played a major role in the field placement of social work students (http://www.crdaethiopia.org).
- **Community Work & Life Center (CWLC) at Addis Ababa University** provides career development and counseling for students at AAU. This grant expanded the SWEEP partnership to involve the Career Center at Cleveland State University, a comprehensive career development center that provides educational and career development opportunities in collaboration with university and community partners (http://www.aau.edu.et/communityworks/index/home.htm).
- **Ethiopian Workforce Entrepreneurship and Training Program.** Based on the success of the Community Work and Life Center, CIPUSA received U.S. State Department funds for entrepreneurship training with the Ethiopian Employers Federation (EEF). This project was linked with the CWLC at AAU. Two interns from the School of Social Work worked on the project, and many social work students participated in the week-long training. EEF signed a Memorandum of Agreement with AAU to provide linkages for student internships with the business community (http://www.cipusa.org).
- **Ethiopian North American Health Professionals Association (ENAHPA)** is a nonprofit organization established in 1999 by Ethiopian-born professionals now living and working in the United States and Canada. In 2005 ENAPHA shipped about 3,000 books and journal sets to Addis Ababa University for the School of Social Work (http://www.enahpa.org).
- **Higher Education for Development (HED)** promotes the involvement of U.S. higher education in global development. In 2007 HED provided funds to support a doctoral research assistant for research on eight higher education partnerships in Ethiopia (http://www.hedprogram.org).
- **Teachers for Africa Program of the International Foundation for Education and Self Help (IFESH)** is a nongovernmental, nonprofit, charitable organization that permits teachers, school administrators, and professors from the United States to spend an academic year in Africa to improve the educational systems. IFESH's Teachers for Africa (TFA) program has provided faculty for the School of Social Work at Addis Ababa University for four years (http://www.ifesh.org).
- **Linking Lives.** Anna Hovde, MSW, a social worker who participated with Alice in the original visit to Ethiopia, was integrally involved in developing SWEEP and guest lecturing in the MSW program. She has established an NGO that focuses on mental health and substance abuse issues at two hospitals and one community site in Addis Ababa, and has been a catalyst for the newly established Alcoholics Anonymous group.

NEXT STEPS AND DIRECTIONS

Our attempts to link the development of social work education in Ethiopia with the work of other organizations or projects in Ethiopia have built the capacity of our loose network to a new level. We call this level the evolution of the UIC-AAU partnership to other endeavors. This phase of the UIC-AAU partnership is just beginning. It builds, however, on the same basic idea that social work should be a catalyst for change—and one among many other disciplines and players that are needed to bring about such change. Thus, this second area related to making social work a catalyst for change includes new projects that build from the original partnership base, but extend to new areas or partners. This next section provides a brief overview of two emerging outreach projects: the development of an international university-community partnership with the Gedam Sefer community in Ethiopia and a tri-partnership linking Addis Ababa University, the University of Illinois–Chicago, and the Institute of Social Work in Tanzania. Looking to the future, we have also reconceptualized the meaning of the Social Work Education in Ethiopia Partnership.

Evolution of the UIC-AAU Partnership to Other Endeavors

Gedam Sefer is an urban slum area of Addis Ababa, Ethiopia. In 2004 social work students at AAU conducted a community assessment in Gedam Sefer. A research project in the summer of 2005 assessed the skills and capacities of a random sample of 100 female-headed households living in slum housing (Johnson Butterfield & Kebede, 2007), followed by thesis research on social networks and livelihoods (Gessese, 2006; Kebede, 2006). In 2007 PhD students at AAU continued the engagement with the Gedam Sefer community through action-research miniprojects. Thus, the work with Gedam Sefer that first started as a class assignment, evolved to form the basis for an international university-community partnership with the community (see Figure 5.4).

Improving child and family outcomes is interwoven into the university-community partnership in Gedam Sefer and its intervention strategy in both process and outcomes. The ultimate goal of the new partnership with the community is to improve the lives of women and children, particularly those subject to abuse and sexual exploitation. To do this, the university-community partnership brings together the people of the Gedam Sefer community with AAU's School of Social Work, UIC's Jane Addams College of Social Work, and the Love for Children Organization in Ethiopia. Our partnership promotes and implements a strategy known as Asset-Based Community Development (ABCD) (c.f., Kretzmann & McKnight, 1993). This strategy does not bring predefined projects to the community for their acceptance and participation. Rather, we are working with residents to (1) understand, document, and organize the community's inherent strengths and capabilities; (2) prioritize issues, develop methods of planning, and organize "the community's own projects"; and (3) implement these projects and evaluate results using participatory, action-research methods. Thus, the university-community partnership is

This project establishes a new university-community partnership between the Gedam Sefer community, Addis Ababa University School of Social Work, the University of Illinois at Chicago—USA, and Love for Children Organization. It builds on action research projects that AAU students and faculty have undertaken in cooperation with leaders and residents in the Gedam Sefer community. It grows from innovative efforts already underway in Gedam Sefer that show great potential for strengthening the community. Through a partnership of residents, leaders, graduate students and faculty, this initiative will empower the community to set goals for its improvement and create its own projects to improve the lives of children, youth, and families.

Goals

1) To organize a stable, diverse core group of community leaders. This group will include local government leaders, men and women who have been active in solving community problems, youth who wish to become productive participants in improving the community, school leaders, business leaders, and others.

2) To build the community's capacity to develop and promote sound community revitalization plans in partnership with local government.

3) To document and communicate the community's many assets.

4) To promote productive roles for families in community building.

5) To establish a model university-community partnership that can be applied to other areas of Addis Ababa.

Structure

1) The core group of community residents and leaders will number between thirty and forty members. It will serve as the participatory body through which community priorities are established and projects will be selected for implementation.

2) A larger network of community residents will be invited to participate in the project at forums, planning meetings, in project teams, and in action research projects.

3) There will be three full-time staff: a project coordinator and two outreach workers. These staff will be hosted by the Love for Children Organization, the fiscal agent for the project's startup grant.

4) A team of AAU doctoral and graduate students will assist with the project's implementation while carrying out action research projects.

5) Faculty from Addis Ababa University and the University of Illinois at Chicago will be involved as trainers, advisors, and evaluators.

Areas of Focus

Capacity building for communities own projects such as micro-enterprise, development of a community library and community center, child protection projects, youth-led enterprises, and others as they emerge from the community.

> For more information, contact: Mulu Yeneabat, MSW, Project Coordinator
> korabageru@yahoo.com; or Alice K. Johnson Butterfield, PhD akj@uic.edu

Figure 5.4   Gedam Sefer Action Research and Development Project: A University-Community Partnership. Courtesy of Alice K. Butterfield and Mulu Yeneabat.

community owned in that the community identifies its strengths, prioritizes its needs, makes a plan, and implements it through the investment of its assets and its participation in every process of the project.

At this time, we are working with several groups, including women's and men's garbage collector associations, youth associations, car washer associations made up of former juvenile delinquents and street youth, and traditional community leaders. We expect leadership opportunities to become available for local residents, especially among poor, semi-illiterate women and unemployed youth living in the Gedam Sefer community. Microenterprise, housing, the development of home-based businesses, a community library, literacy, and school-linked educational projects are some areas of interest among the community groups. For example, citizens in the Gedam Sefer community formed an association and started a community library with only four books. Addis Ababa University, the British Consulate, and Christian Children's Fund provided 1,400 additional books. Approximately 300 children and youth use the library each day. Our project will be working with the library in a summer tutoring project and will provide approximately 4,000 additional books through the Books for Africa shipment in 2008.

The Gedam Sefer Community-University Partnership will be a central force in action-research education at Addis Ababa University. Students working in the Gedam Sefer community are being taught how to do action research, which not only leads to the development of knowledge and the writing of scholarly papers, but also focuses on empowerment and capacity building in partnership with the communities where the research is taking place. The ABCD effort promotes, recognizes, and honors the contribution of the community throughout all phases of the work, and we expect to show outcomes directly tied to improved social functioning among poor families in Gedam Sefer. With the action research component that underlies the project, the project has potential for scaling up the strengths-based approach for university-community engagement with poor communities.

Tri-Partnership: UIC-AAU-ISW in Tanzania

One spin-off of Nathan Linsk's sabbatical at AAU GSSW was the request by the American International Health Alliance Twinning Center to partner with the Institute of Social Work (ISW) in Dar es Salaam, Tanzania. The partnership focuses on developing capacity at ISW to provide continuing education as well as to help develop an MSW and a future PhD program at ISW. ISW's history is a mirror image of AAU's social work programs. At the same time that the previous social work program in Ethiopia was closing, ISW was established as a technical school to equip the country with social workers to work in the child welfare system. Over the next thirty years, several certificate and higher diploma programs emerged under the auspices of social work, but the school lacked qualified faculty to teach at higher levels as well as higher degree programs. However, in 2005, ISW began its bachelor's in social work degree program. Nathan Linsk was approached to try to use some of the lessons from Project SWEEP to help enhance the ISW program as well as help them provide a community-based, paraprofessional social work training program in Tanzania. The program is now operational in order to enhance curriculum offerings, resources, an HIV training and counseling center, and field instruction, as well as to provide training to the Department of Social Welfare.

In 2008 a three-way partnership is being established among AAU's School of Social Work, ISW's programs, and the Jane Addams College of Social Work. This partnership will allow ISW to use the AAU model to jump-start graduate social work in Tanzania, using the same visiting faculty model, as well as provide opportunities for ISW faculty to begin doctoral study in Ethiopia. In addition, AAU's School of Social Work PhD students may obtain teaching and research opportunities in Tanzania. Forming a South-South interaction to enhance social work education incubated by the resources of Jane Addams College is an unheard of effort, where Americans facilitate local collaboration rather than impose their own programs in-country, particularly with respect to orphans and vulnerable children as well as HIV/AIDS.

Reconceptualizing Project SWEEP

The development of social work education in Ethiopia that has occurred over the past six years has outgrown our original conceptualization of the Social Work Education in Ethiopia Partnership. Initially, SWEEP referred to a grant-funded planning project between the University of Illinois–Chicago and Addis Ababa University. Today, the concept of SWEEP is much more. From its base in social work and higher education, SWEEP has evolved into an informal network representing faculty and students from other universities, professionals from various disciplines, and NGOs—all of which are engaged with various institutions and organizations in Ethiopia for education, social work, capacity building, and development purposes. With this in mind, in 2008 we redesigned and restructured the SWEEP web page to capture the dynamic nature of our loosely organized network and reflect the synergy of a variety of collaborative efforts by people and organizations from around the world.

The revised SWEEP web page emphasizes two broadly defined focal areas: *education* and *social work*. Our definition of education particularly includes the role of higher education partnerships in Ethiopia and Africa. Our definition of social work is one that is based on partnership engagement with communities and organizations, and on organizing and community development. It encompasses work in areas of community health, orphans and vulnerable children, refugee resettlement, and poverty reduction. The SWEEP web page at http://www.aboutsweep.org provides reports of activities and projects, as well as resources for the advancement of education, research, training, and service delivery in Ethiopia and Africa.

MENTOR, INFLUENCER, AND INSPIRATION: PROFESSOR SEYOUM GEBRE-SELASSIE

Our story began with meeting Professor Seyoum Gebre-Selassie in Ethiopia, and this chapter closes with bidding him good-bye. He was our mentor, influencer, and inspiration. We wonder what the chance would have been for social work education to start at the professional level had it not been for the tireless and ongoing work of Seyoum over the many years that he served his country as a professor, researcher, and social worker. Of a surety, his role in restarting social work education in Ethiopia was central and essential. In some respects, his tireless work in Ethiopia kept the foundation for social work strong in Ethiopia. To honor him, those who knew him in Ethiopia and the United States are in the process of starting a fund for scholarships and community support for the poor in Ethiopia in collaboration with the Ethiopian Society of Sociologists, Social Workers and Social Anthropologists (ESSSWA; http://www.essswa.org). We share here a short listing of some of his accomplishments and contributions to social work in Ethiopia. (See Figure 5.5.)

In closing our story about SWEEP and the development of graduate social work education in Ethiopia, the words of Professor Seyoum are fitting. In 1969 he represented Ethiopia and Africa in a panel discussion on teaching and social work values at an international conference. The chair was Dr. Herman D. Stein, a social work pioneer, who had worked with the young Seyoum in Africa. The question raised was "whether social work educators should undertake a conscious effort to promote changes in the value system of their society" (Stein, 1969, p. 33). Seyoum's answer reflects his view of social work education at Haile Selassie I University:

Professor Seyoum Gebre-Selassie
June 5, 1936–February 10, 2007

Professor Seyoum Gebre-Selassie entered into rest after a short illness on February 10, 2007. He was born and lived for much of his life in Addis Ababa. He was a Professor Emeritus in the Department of Sociology and Social Anthropology (SOSA) at Addis Ababa University (AAU). He earned his BA in 1959 (Ethiopia), his 1st MA in 1961 (India), his 2nd MA in 1975 (USA), and his Ph.D. in 1976 (USA). Professor Seyoum had extensive teaching, research and administrative experiences. He served as a Director of the Awassa Community Development Training and Demonstration Center, a Registrar of AAU, a Dean of the School of Social Work (Haile Selassie I University), a Dean of the College of Social Sciences at AAU, and a Chairman of the Department of Sociology at AAU. Prof. Seyoum co-founded various professional organizations and played leadership roles in most. Some of the organizations in which he made noble contributions include the Family of Guidance Association of Ethiopia, the Association for Social Work Education in Africa, the Ethiopian Society of Sociologists, Social Workers, and Anthropologists (ESSSWA), the Pastoral and Environmental Network for the Horn of Africa, and the International Association of Schools of Social Work (http://www.essswa.org.et/professor_seyoum_gebreselassie_h.htm).

Professor Seyoum Gebre-Selassie (June 5, 1936–February 10, 2007). Adapted from the webpage of the Association of Sociologists, Social Workers, and Social Anthropologists.

Figure 5.5 Professor Seyoum Gebre-Selassie

In Ethiopia, we have made a start in exposing students to experiences which help him to learn by doing. . . . When the student is exposed to a situation where he is forced to interact with people outside his "class," he discovers that people are not after all as stupid as he thought. He discovers that useful ideas can come from them. It is interesting to note that it is after such exposures that students start demanding more rights for self-determination for the people and for themselves. . . . They often express strong feelings about the importance of involvement and participation of the clientele in problem identification, decision making and action. (Stein, 1969, p. 31)

Nearly forty years later, this is the vision that Seyoum Gebre-Selassie brought to the AAU-UIC partnership: "The social worker is not one who sits on a pedestal and pontificates. The social worker works *with* the people. Not for the people, *with* the people. This is the important distinction."[2]

ORGANIZATIONAL SNAPSHOT

Organization: Social Work Education in Ethiopia Partnership (SWEEP)

Founders/Executive Directors: Alice K. Johnson Butterfield and Nathan L. Linsk

Mission/Description: The Jane Addams College of Social Work, University of Illinois–Chicago (UIC), Addis Ababa University (AAU), the Council of International Programs USA (CIPUSA), and a network of nonprofit agencies are engaged in an exciting effort to develop the first-ever master's degree in social work in Ethiopia, through a project known as the Social Work Education in Ethiopia Partnership, or SWEEP. The undergraduate social work program at AAU was closed in 1976 when a military regime ruled the country. Now, with a democratic government in place since the early 1990s, the SWEEP project is working in collaboration with AAU's new School of Social Work and NGOs in Ethiopia to develop social work education and practice.

Website: www.aboutsweep.org

Address: Jane Addams College of Social Work

University of Illinois–Chicago

1040 West Harrison Street (M/C 309)

Chicago, IL 60607 USA

Phone: +1.312.996.0036

Fax: +1.312.996.2770

E-mail: akj@uic.edu; nlinsk@uic.edu

NOTES

1. In Karl Marx's theory of class struggle, the bourgeoisie (merchants and artisans) were originally viewed as a progressive force in overthrowing the feudal system. Later, however, the middle class becomes "a reactionary force as it tries to prevent the ascendancy of the proletariat (wage earners) in order to maintain its own position of predominance" (High Beam Encyclopedia, 2008).
2. From *Social Work Education in Ethiopia Partnership,* a documentary film produced by Moges Tafesse and co-produced by Alice K. Johnson Butterfield and Nathan Linsk (2004). Synergy Habesha Film Production: An Independent Social Media, Addis Ababa, Ethiopia.

REFERENCES

Askeland, G. A., & Bradley, G. (2007). Linking critical reflection and qualitative research on an African social work master's programme. *International Social Work, 50*(5), 671–685.

Gebre-Selassie, S. (1999). *The genesis and development of the Department of Sociology and Social Administration.* Proceedings of the Founding Conference of E.S.S.S.W.A.: The Ethiopian Society of Sociologists, Social Workers and Anthropologists (pp. 6–8). Addis Ababa, Ethiopia: Addis Ababa University, Sociology Department.

Gessese, A. (2006). *Human strengths approach for sustainable livelihood.* Unpublished MSW thesis, School of Social Work, Addis Ababa University, Ethiopia.

High Beam Encyclopedia. (2008). Bourgeoisie. In *Columbia Encyclopedia* (6th ed.), 2008. Retrieved February 2, 2008, from http://www.encyclopedia.com/doc/1E1-bourgeoi.html.

Johnson Butterfield, A. K. (2007). The internationalization of doctoral social work education: Learning from a partnership in Ethiopia. *Advances in Social Work, 8*(2), 1–15.

Johnson Butterfield, A. K., & Kebede, W. (2007). *Asset based community development: Assessing women's skills in slum households in Ethiopia.* Paper presented at the International Consortium for Social Development, 15th International Symposium, Hong Kong, China.

Johnson Butterfield, A. K., & Linsk, N. (2005, August). *Social Work Education in Ethiopia Partnership—Project SWEEP. Final Report.* Association Liaison Office for University Cooperation in Development. USAID. Retrieved May 30, 2008, from http://www.aboutsweep.org/ALOReport-Final-AKJ.pdf.

Kebede, W. (2006). *Social networks and communication among female householders.* Unpublished MSW thesis, School of Social Work, Addis Ababa University, Ethiopia.

Kendall, K. A. (1986). Social work education in the 1980s: Accent on change. *International Social Work, 29*(1), 15–28.

Kretzmann, J. P., & McKnight, J. L. (1993). *Building communities from the inside out: A path toward finding and mobilizing a community's assets.* Chicago: ACTA.

Linsk, N. L., Gosha, M., Getu, M., Aklilu, M., & Prabhughate, P. (2007). *Adherence and treatment support in Ethiopia,* Paper presented at 2nd Annual International Treatment Adherence Conference, Jersey City, NJ.

Sedler, R. F. (1968a). Social welfare in a developing country: The Ethiopian experience. *International Social Work, 10*(1), 1–12.

Sedler, R. F. (1968b). Social welfare in a developing country: The Ethiopian experience: Part II—Social welfare service. *International Social Work, 11*(1), 9–22.

Sedler, R. F. (1968c). Social welfare in a developing country: The Ethiopian experience: Part III—The role of social work education. *International Social Work, 11*(1), 36–44.

Shinn, David H. (2001, July). *HIV/AIDS in Ethiopia: The silence is broken; the stigma is not.* Center for Strategic and International Studies, Africa Program. Washington, DC. Retrieved February 9, 2008, from http://www.csis.org/media/csis/pubs/anotes_0107.pdf.

Stein, H. D. (1969). Teachability and application of social work values: A panel discussion. *International Social Work, 12*(1), 23–34.

Surafel, G. (2001). Professor Seyoum Gebre-Selassie: Of an age and its worries. *Addis Tribune* Archives. Retrieved February 7, 2008, from http://www.addistribune.com/Archives/2001/03-08-01/Professor.htm.

Tasse, A. (2007, July 17). *The role of social work education in facilitating social development.* Plenary Session, International Consortium for Social Development, 15th International Symposium. Hong Kong, China.

Tasse, A., Johnson Butterfield, A. K., & Linsk, N. (2007). *Higher education partnerships for global development: Social work as a development actor.* Paper presented at APM Council on Social Work Education, San Francisco, CA.

UNAIDS. (2008). *Ethiopia.* Retrieved February 2, 2008, from http://www.unaids.org/en/CountryResponses/Countries/ethiopia.asp.

UNICEF. (2005). Ethiopia Statistics. Retrieved February 2, 2008, from http://www.unicef.org/infobycountry/ethiopia_statistics.html#30.

University Capacity Building Program (UCBP). (2007). Ministry of Education & Ministry of Capacity Building, Addis Ababa, Ethiopia. Retrieved February 1, 2008, from http://www.ucbp-ethiopia.com/.

Yeneabat, M. (2006). *Pottery production: An asset for women livelihood: Case study on Kechene women potters in Addis Ababa.* Unpublished MSW thesis, School of Social Work, Addis Ababa University, Ethiopia.

Yizengaw, T. (2003). *Transformation in higher education: Experiences with reform and expansion in Ethiopian higher education.* Keynote paper prepared for Regional Training Conference on Improving Tertiary Education in Sub-Saharan Africa: Things that Work! Accra, Ghana, September 23–25, 2003. Retrieved on February 2, 2008, from http://siteresources.worldbank.org/INTAFRREGTOPTEIA/Resources/teshome_keynote.pdf.

CONNECTIONS

For more information about the Social Work Education in Ethiopia Partnership, visit the web page at http://www.aboutsweep.org. We welcome collaboration and networking with other individuals, groups, and organizations in education, social work, and other disciplines through training, research, and program development. Contacts in the United States and the Ethiopia are

Alice K. Johnson Butterfield
Professor
Jane Addams College of Social Work
University of Illinois–Chicago
1040 West Harrison Street (M/C 309)
Chicago, IL 60607
Email: akj@uic.edu

Abye Tasse
Associate Vice President for International Affairs
Dean of Social Work
Addis Ababa University
P.O. Box 1176
Addis Ababa, Ethiopia
Email: abeytas@aau.edu.et

Nathan Linsk
Professor
Jane Addams College of Social Work
University of Illinois–Chicago
1040 West Harrison Street (M/C 309)
Chicago, IL 60607
Email: nlinsk@uic.edu

Websites

Social Work Education in Ethiopia Partnership (Project SWEEP). This website provides a history of SWEEP and its accomplishments. It provides information and resources for those interested in the advancement of education, research, training and service delivery in Ethiopia and Africa. http://www.aboutsweep.org

Addis Ababa University (AAU) is the oldest institution of higher education in Ethiopia. AAU's mission is to develop and disseminate knowledge relevant to solving basic problems of development through teaching, research, scholarship, and services to the community. AAU started the first-ever MSW degree in social work in Ethiopia in 2004, and a doctoral program in social work and social development in 2006. http://www.aau.edu.et

African Child Policy Forum is an independent advocacy organization working on behalf of African children. http://www.africanchildforum.org

Ethiopian Society of Sociologists, Social Workers, and Anthropologists (ESSSWA) promotes professional competence and ethics through the professions of sociology, social work, and anthropology. http://www.essswa.org.et/

University of Illinois–Chicago is actively engaged in several projects linking social work, teacher education, training, research, and community development in Ethiopia.

- **The Jane Addams College of Social Work,** http://www.uic.edu/jaddams/college/
- **College of Education,** http://education.uic.edu/
- **Great Cities Institute,** http://www.uic.edu/cuppa/gci/
- **Midwest AIDS Training and Education Center,** http://www.matec.info/

6

Center for Urban Pedagogy

Myron Panchuk and
Patrick Savaiano

The Center for Urban Pedagogy (CUP) is a nonprofit organization that is interested in how social movement evolves and influences legislation concerned with urban development. Our mission is to create community education about places and how they change. One of CUP's first exhibits was held on the centenary of the promulgation of the first building code of the city of New York in 1901, which mandated an indoor bathroom for every two families. The exhibit was hosted by the Storefront for Architecture and Art, and presented a contemporary look at the relationship between civic government and the needs of the people it serves. This exhibit was not a traditional "retrospective," but rather a first-time look at the guiding principles, directions, needs, and concerns of the urban dweller and his/her habitat. The result was to create a new reference point, a framework that critically evaluates the intricate interplay of need and function, code and environment, and even urban decay and renewal. For the Center for Urban Pedagogy, the city itself is a school from which we learn; its citizens, policy makers, and diverse social groups the architects, who design, create, destroy, and build.

PHILOSOPHY

The work of CUP stems from a belief that the power of imagination is central to the practice of democracy, and that the work of governing must engage the dreams and visions of citizens. CUP believes in the legibility of the world around us. What can we learn by investigation? By learning how to investigate, we train ourselves to change what we see.

CUP creates educational projects about places and how they change. Projects bring together art and design professionals—artists, graphic designers, architects, urban planners—with community-based advocates and researchers—organizers, government officials, academics, service providers, and policymakers. These partners work with CUP staff to create projects ranging from high school curricula to educational exhibitions.

CUP also works with youth on collaborative projects that explore the urban environment. Educational projects build on the everyday experiences of young people and help them learn about democracy, civic participation, and social justice. Civic engagement requires a new kind of civic education, one that explores how decisions are made, what is at stake, and how residents can be involved in this critical process. By implementing the tools of art, design, and technology, we draw the connections that exist between everyday life and the decisions that give it form.

The approach of project-based learning brings youth face to face with the people who make the decisions that affect their lives: community advocates, government officials, and businesspeople. Students then work with our staff to create educational projects that integrate their knowledge and share their insights with the general public.

For example, at City-as-School High School, an alternative public school in lower Manhattan, CUP organized a semester-long investigation into how New York City deals with its garbage. Students visited garbage sites and conducted interviews with garbage experts, community activists, and government officials. As a result of this investigation, the class created a thirty-minute documentary and a series of educational posters to communicate what they had learned to the broader community. CUP works in school, after school, and outside of school to reach students where they are. Programs range from single-session workshops to semester-long projects.

HISTORY

The seed for this organization was planted during two of the earliest projects. The first project was about building codes. The purpose was to engage a wide cross section of people who were involved in building code issues, such as community activists, policy analysts, and even local artists. This included a diverse tapestry of people who were involved in the regulatory process that impacts code legislation: those who uphold codes, those who wish to change them, and even those who evade them. The fruit of this effort was a highly effective and successful exhibition in which the different social sectors concerned with this issue came together and were engaged in a creative process of dialogue, input, and reflection. This was a very exciting moment in the work of this group because it actually produced an opportunity for reflection that had never existed in our city. People who were interested in architecture and art began to think about the politics of design in a way that was not just didactic, but that also created a unique occasion for understanding the actual social impact of design itself.

The second project that was critical in CUP's development focused on garbage and waste. The city was shutting down its only garbage dump, and since there was no long-term resolution in sight, we began to wonder how we could address this growing problem. A group of fifteen students was engaged to start investigating this issue. After a semester of visiting recycling stations, waste transfer points, and dumps, a number of educational projects were crafted (including a video presentation, a model, and poster art) to communicate what had been learned. A video documentary was screened at a local theater, and the students moderated a panel discussion about the future of the city's trash problem. By investigating the infrastructure, students uncovered a variety of political issues, not only the issue of where the trash actually goes and how it is shipped, but even who pays the health costs incurred in having trash nearby. This approach to urban concerns became the method and basis of most of our youth programs. The focus was on a single urban concern about which little was known; through investigating the issue, students were able to uncover an entire civic, political, economic, and social reality. When one looks around a city and tries to investigate why things are the way they are, much is learned about all the persons involved in shaping the urban landscape.

In 1997 CUP published the results of its first project in a small booklet entitled *A How-To Guidebook for Urban Objects*. At that time, CUP was an informal group of people with diverse backgrounds but a shared interest in undertaking interpretive projects about the city. Since then, CUP has grown organically as a vehicle for collaboration. CUP received its nonprofit status in 2002 and hired its first full-time staff members in 2005.

CUP has organized or participated in exhibitions at Storefront for Art and Architecture, Anthology Film Archives, Apex Art Curatorial Program, City University of New York Graduate Center, and PS 1 Contemporary Art Center in New York; Mess Hall and the Chicago Architecture Foundation in Chicago; and Kunsthalle Exnergasse in Vienna.

CUP has partnered with other nonprofits such as Sustainable South Bronx, Place in History, the Municipal Arts Society, the Fifth Avenue Committee, REPO History, Temporary Services, the Lower East Side Tenement Museum, Global Kids, the Good Old Lower East Side (GOLES), the Public Housing Residents of the Lower East Side (PHROLES), the Legal Aid Society, the Community Service Society of New York, the New York City Environmental Justice Alliance, the Fiscal Policy Institute, the Met Council on Housing, and the New York City Public Housing Residents Alliance.

Since 2001 CUP has worked with over 700 students from institutions and organizations such as the city-run Tier-II shelters, City-As-School, the Academy of Urban Planning, Math and Science Upward Bound, the Heritage School, Monroe High School, Parsons the New School of Design, the Cooper-Hewitt National Design Museum, the Wyckoff Houses, and PS 164.

FOUNDER AND STAFF
Damon Rich is the founder of CUP. There are three other individuals centrally involved with the organization: Rosten Woo, Valeria Mogilevich, and Lize Mogel. Each provides connections to other organizations with which CUP is involved

and plans long-term goals with them. CUP also provides the staff for the projects, creates the best teams possible to make a projects happen, and works with volunteers to implement them.

CUP engages an extensive network of volunteers. At any given time, there are probably about thirty individuals engaged with some aspect of the organization. These volunteers are involved in a diversity of tasks, including proofreading, writing e-mails, creating informative pamphlets, providing art direction, conducting TV shoots, and researching. Some get involved maybe once or twice a year; others work on projects for weeks and months at a time.

What makes CUP interesting is the variety of backgrounds represented, and the many talents volunteers bring to the collaborative efforts. Some have backgrounds in architecture and design, some in public policy, and others in media studies. Everyone benefits from a wealth of talent, a diversity of skills, and a multiplicity of influence.

SUCCESSFUL PROJECTS: A SAMPLER OF THE WORK OF CUP THROUGH THE YEARS
Mapping the Concourse

The Grand Concourse, a central thoroughfare in the Bronx designed to be the Park Avenue of the Bronx, turns 100 years old in 2009. In anticipation of this centennial, the Bronx Museum of Art asked CUP to design a charrette for high school students to study the Grand Concourse. In April 2007, CUP trained eight high school students from the Bronx High School for the Visual Arts to lead an all-day charrette for their peers. The charrette's goal was to produce a portrait of the neighborhood around the museum and brainstorm visions for its future. The project is ongoing and will continue through 2009.

This series of workshops will introduce young people in the Bronx to urban planning and urban design concepts as well as democratic participation schemes such as the connecting of physical design with the politics of implementation. The workshops will build on one another to produce a thorough, compelling, and adaptive vision of the concourse, the neighborhood, and the future.

Knoxville: Building Communities

The Art Gallery of Knoxville, Tennessee, invited CUP to explore the urbanism of its hometown. CUP's resulting installation drew upon various plans to re-energize Knoxville and included a sculpture of Knoxville's odd shape, which is the result of annexing smaller municipalities in order to raise tax revenues. Wall text and photographs documented these development plans with archival material from the city library and the Beck Cultural Exchange Center, which is dedicated to preserving African American history in Knoxville.

Schoolyard Visions

Planning should not be stale and monotonous. It should sound like a captivating beat over which other sounds, rhymes, and melodies can be played. In this class, we examined the exterior spaces that surround the Academy of Urban Planning. Our job is not to take things for granted, but to question why things are the way they are and propose new directions. This is a theoretical project: it probably will not be built, so participants can dream a little, and make outrageous and new proposals.

Green Information Center

"When is recycling day?"
"Where can I get a bike map?"
"What kind of trees are on my street?"
All of these questions and many more can be answered by visiting the Green Information Center, a roaming booth made by youth at the New Settlement Apartments in New York City. Students in the Bronx Helpers summer program created a mobile recycling information center out of recycled materials. The information center was packed with bicycle route maps, recycling and sorting information from the NYC Department of Sanitation, proposals for local tree planters, and green zines that catalogue the students' experiences during an entire summer of investigating tree-related environmental issues.

The Connection between Abandoned Buildings and Homeless People

Ecologists study the environment and how it changes. This class decided to look at environmental problems in New York City, such as abandoned buildings and homeless people—buildings without people and people without buildings.

Participants in this project interviewed four people who work with abandoned structures and homeless people in New York City. To understand housing issues and how old buildings can be remodeled, they then spoke with Carmen Vasquez at Hope Community and Nellie Hester Bailey at the Harlem Tenants Council. Kristen Simpson of the NYC Department of Homeless Services and Lindsay Davis at the Coalition for the Homeless were also interviewed.

After that, the group transcribed the interviews, took pictures, made collages, drew maps, studied what had been found, and discussed their thoughts. The project provided vital information for those who want to make a difference in this critical area of social justice.

Abuse of Power: The SPURA Story

The story of Manhattan is not only the story of the powerful crushing the weak, or sometimes the weak beating all odds to defeat the powerful. It is also the story of the weak becoming strong enough to screw the weaker.

Since the 1950s, the Seward Park Urban Renewal Area (SPURA), bounded by East Broadway, Willett, Essex, Delancey, and Grand streets, has been the center of divisive land-use politics. Today, it contains the largest publicly owned undeveloped site in Manhattan below 96th Street, locked in a fight between the partisans of low-income housing and the champions of economic development. Taking advantage of a fifty-year-old history of unrealized plans, CUP produced a booklet on SPURA's history.

In March 2006, for The Dimes of March exhibit at the Reena Spaulings Fine Art Gallery located in SPURA, Damon Rich created a set of pavement markings indicating surrounding sites of unrealized plans for housing, community spaces, and commercial facilities.

In March 2007, CUP installed elements of this project in Lost and Found City, an exhibition at the Storefront for Art and Architecture that was curated by students at the Bard Center for Curatorial Studies. In conjunction with the exhibit, Damon Rich led a walking tour of SPURA and its environs, featuring several guest guides who had been directly involved with the SPURA conflict.

What's Poppin' at Fulton Mall?

In partnership with the Cooper-Hewitt National Design Museum's Design Your 'Hood program, CUP's Damon Rich and Amber Yared worked with Alex Gilliam to develop and teach an eight-week course on architecture and design for New York City high school students at Brooklyn's Fulton Mall. This is an area that has been the target of city planning as well as constant efforts to try to improve this area. This course began as a public-history project to take a look at what was on this mall already, without considering what might be needed to improve it. Fulton Mall is actually one of the most commercially successful streets in New York City, but the quality of merchandise marketed and the types of consumers catered to are on the lower end of the economic spectrum. There was a discriminatory sense of the worth of this space in a statement made that "this low-class space needs to be improved."

Our project focused on the cultural significance of this area, and that if it were going to be revamped, it should be done in consultation with the people who live and do business there. This project consisted of stories and photographs. A year and a half later, a series of articles published in the *New York Times* and the *Daily News* addressed the unique cultural significance of the Fulton Mall area and created a needed perceptual shift in the consciousness of the public.

Students explored the area through sketches, drawings, photographs, interviews, and general social interaction. Back in the studio, they translated their observations into drawings, collages, skits, models, and a photocopied zine. These were displayed at the Brooklyn Historical Society.

Big Up, Jamaica!

What if information about the future of a community could be as sexy, alluring, and as much fun as shopping? In the Jamaica Food Court, a small bulletin board displays information about plans for Jamaica's future in a quiet, uninviting, and unexciting way. No alternative visions of the future were presented—only matter-of-fact architectural renderings of the plan as an established fact. The nearby retail shops of Jamaica Avenue, in marked contrast, celebrated the investigation of alternatives. You could get green with blue high-tops, Velcro, or lace-ups, or . . . ?

As part of the exhibition, Jamaica Flux, organized by the Jamaica Center for Arts and Culture, CUP built an experimental urban planning community outreach module using a pair of Nike Terminator high-tops with an embedded video screen, and installed it in the Sneaker Mart at the Gertz Mall. The screen displays thoughts from Jamaica residents on the past, present, and future of their neighborhood. On the street, a large poster announced the outreach initiative: Jamaica's Future.

Public Housing 101

Where did public housing come from? Who lives there? Who makes the decisions? What does it look like? What are some of the issues facing public housing today?

These questions guided three CUP educators and eight City-as-School students through a semester of collaborative learning. They first conducted interviews with a group of public housing stakeholders, including tenants, administrators, elected officials, researchers, architects, and organizers. A series of educational posters and a set of three video pieces were created to try to capture what had been learned.

CUP SERVICES
Educational Programming

CUP creates and implements project-based curricula for high school and college students. We love to work with inspired instructors and administrators to bring students face to face with issues that shape neighborhoods. We are excited by the challenge of working in different contexts, from afterschool math and science enrichment programs to Regents-based biology classes, in high school art classrooms and college architecture studios. Potential programs can range from semester-long, project-specific curricula to single-session workshops.

Professional Development

CUP provides workshops for teachers and administrators—helping educators connect students to their communities through art and design.

Exhibition Design and Development

Even in the Internet age, physical exhibitions retain a special power to bring together people and ideas. Working with historical museums, art institutions, professional organizations, and community groups, CUP curates, develops, and designs educational environments on a variety of scales, from kiosks to museums. Call or e-mail Damon Rich to discuss CUP's ability to help you bring your audience together with your ideals.

Video Production

CUP produces videos that bring clarity to complex questions, using techniques from documentary film and digital animation.

MEASURING SUCCESS

Because we work in the interpretive sphere and not in direct advocacy, or direct services, the success of our work is not directly measurable by standard metrics. Certainly, we measure success by the number of people who attend our events, complete our programs, and order/use our tools. We believe that we have built many coalitions and have had a positive effect on the politics of the city. Quite often our work is interpretive. Since we do not build buildings or create new structures, we attempt to help people understand the problems that exist within the urban environment where those structures might be built. This hopefully will lead to policy reassessment and to positive change. A prime example of this was the project we did in downtown New York City called What's Poppin' on Fulton Mall, profiled earlier in this chapter.

FUNDING

CUP is funded primarily through foundations and contracts with schools and organizations that hire its services. A smaller amount comes from private benefactors and donors. CUP's largest grants this year will be about $25,000. The annual budget is around $200,000.

When it started in 2002, CUP had a budget of $5,000. Its first project was funded by a gift from a local radio station, Hot 97, which donated a mixer we sold on eBay. Until about two years ago, all projects were worked on by volunteers.

NEXT STEPS, NEW OPPORTUNITIES

We are always trying to produce work that is geared to the specific needs of the local community. Our collaborative research teams are considering new ways of designing exhibits that are more durable and long lasting. At the same time, we keep trying to figure out how we can produce models and exhibitions that are nimble and can be easily assembled and disassembled. There is also a need for more Web design and media projects.

We would like to get more people involved in our efforts, and to be a resource for activists that want to do more design work. We are producing new programs that are specifically designed to attract such talent to our organization.

FOUNDER AND STAFF

Damon Rich is the **Founder and Chair** of CUP, a nonprofit organization that educates communities about design, planning, and politics. After training as an architect at Columbia University, Damon worked for New York City's Department of Parks and Recreation, eventually becoming the chief of staff for capital projects. Since leaving the department in 2000, in addition to running CUP, Damon has taught design at schools including Parsons the New School of Design, Heritage High School, the Brooklyn Museum, the Cooper Hewitt National Design Museum, and the Queens Library Adult Learning Center. He also writes regularly about architecture and politics for publications including the *Village Voice, Nation, Metropolis,* and *Architecture.* Recently, Damon was awarded a New York State Council on the Arts award for his work with adult literacy and architecture, as well as a fellowship from the MacDowell Colony for his work on the history of urban renewal. From 2007, Damon has served as a Loeb Fellow at the Harvard Graduate School of Design.

Rosten Woo, Executive Director, has been producing public educational projects with CUP since 1999. He teaches design history and theory at Parsons the New School for Design and produces historical research and writing on history, design, and public policy for Place Matters, the Municipal Arts Society, *Metropolis* magazine, and the *Village Voice.* He has also worked as a researcher and policy analyst for a variety of nonprofit organizations, including Common Ground Community and the Greenpoint Manufacturing and Design Center. He serves on the boards of like-minded nonprofits, Place in History and Groundswell Community Mural Project. He received his BA in government from Cornell University.

Valeria Mogilevich, Program Manager, a native New Yorker, coordinates the execution of design and education projects about the city's inner workings as CUP's Program Manager. She comes from a background in visual studies and film as well as architectural theory, with a degree from Brown University in modern culture and media (*magna cum laude,* 2004). In addition to working many years in the nonprofit sector, she is an independent film curator specializing in scientific films. Valeria is also on pest-control patrol in the CUP office.

Lize Mogel, Development, Associate/Artist, is an artist who makes maps, distributing and inserting her projects into urban public space. She has produced site-specific cartographic projects for transit shelters in Los Angeles and for former World's Fair sites in North America. Lize also has worked with the *Journal of Aesthetics and Protest* and the Center for Land Use Interpretation in Los Angeles. As a fundraiser, she was a grants officer at the Museum of Contemporary Art in Los Angeles from 2002–4, where she was responsible for foundation and government giving. She works as a grants consultant for the Center for Advanced Visual Studies at MIT and Good Old Lower East Side, among others.

ORGANIZATIONAL SNAPSHOT

Organization: Center for Urban Pedagogy (CUP)

Founder: Damon Rich

Mission/Description: The Center for Urban Pedagogy (CUP) creates educational projects about places and how they change. Their projects bring together art and design professionals—artists, graphic designers, architects, urban planners—with community-based advocates and researchers—organizers, government officials, academics, service providers, and policymakers. These partners work with CUP staff to create projects ranging from high school curricula to educational exhibitions. Their work grows from a belief that the power of imagination is central to the practice of democracy, and that the work of governing must engage the dreams and visions of citizens. CUP believes in the legibility of the world around us. It is the CUP philosophy that by learning how to investigate, we train ourselves to change what we see.

Website: anothercupdevelopment.org

Address: CUP

At the Old American Can Factory

232 Third Street #B402B

Brooklyn, NY 11215 USA

Phone: +1.718.596.7721

E-mail: info@anothercupdevelopment.org

7

Endeavor: High-Impact Entrepreneurs, High-Impact Change

Stephanie Benjamin, Teresa Barttrum, Annie Khan, and Valeria Levit

MISSION STATEMENT

Endeavor transforms the economies of emerging markets by identifying and supporting high-impact entrepreneurs. High-impact entrepreneurs have the biggest ideas and most ambitious plans. They have the potential to create thriving companies that employ hundreds, even thousands of people, and generate millions in wages and revenues. And they have the power to inspire countless others.

Endeavor targets only these high-impact entrepreneurs. Endeavor helps them to break down society's barriers to success, offers world-class strategic advice, and open doors to capital. With Endeavor's guidance, these entrepreneurs become role models, encourage others to innovate and take risks, and create sustainable economic growth.

Together, Endeavor and high-impact entrepreneurs change industries, communities, and entire countries.

HISTORY

Ten years ago in Latin America, economic interests were focused on the two extremes of the population: the poor and the very successful. Microfinancing helped the poor population get loans to start small businesses, which were needed to survive. At the other end of the spectrum, investors focused on large, national multiconglomerates. There was an overlooked segment of emerging markets made up of middle-sized companies that were not being offered any type of mentorship or guidance. Linda Rottenberg, a graduate of Harvard College and Yale Law School, saw there was opportunity in the emerging markets that was going unnoticed. In order to spur economic growth in emerging markets and bridge the gap between microcredit organizations and large-scale public-works projects, Linda Rottenberg co-founded Endeavor, along with fellow Yale Law

95

School graduate Peter Kellner, in 1997. They realized that if they configured a model that fused these segments of the emerging market economics together, a sizeable momentum for middle-sized businesses could be created. This momentum would enable the small- to middle-sized companies to expand, thereby enhancing private-sector development in Latin America and providing the opportunity for vast economic growth and expansion.

Endeavor grew around the goal of making an impact one entrepreneur at a time. The founders believed that if you inspired one entrepreneur, that person would inspire the next, and then each of these would inspire others, creating waves of change. Endeavor's founders were not looking at change on a national scale; rather, they were looking at change in human terms: human capital and the ability for human beings to change things.

To initiate the waves of change, Endeavor planned to go into Latin American countries and partner with the local business leaders where they would focus on two main goals. The first goal was to create jobs where employment was challenged. Endeavor wanted to scale companies in order to create a sizable number of jobs so that more people could work. Second, Endeavor wanted to alter the perception some of the cultures had when it came to taking risks. Entrepreneurship was not a viable option in many of these emergent market countries because of the cultural aversion to failure.

Initial funding for Endeavor came about from Linda Rottenberg knocking on investors' doors and presenting them with the issues facing entrepreneurs in Latin America. People called her crazy for doing this, but she stuck with it and continued to show people the value that Endeavor could bring to communities in these countries. She framed the proposition in this way: "You're a business leader and you're an Argentinean; you have an obligation to help bring your country to a level where the currency is not collapsing and the economy is sound." Her persistence with this argument eventually led to a couple of business leaders taking a risk on her dream, and funding was provided by an Argentine business leader and from the AVINA group. AVINA's mission, which can be found at www.avina.net, states, "We contribute to sustainable development in Latin America by encouraging productive alliances based on trust among social and business leaders and by brokering consensus around agendas for action." With this initial investment, Rottenberg and Kellner introduced Endeavor in Argentina and Chile.

THE ENDEAVOR APPROACH

Endeavor's plan for helping midsized companies followed this comprehensive, five-step approach: (1) identify high-growth, innovative entrepreneurs lacking systemic support; (2) support selected Endeavor Entrepreneurs by supplying mentoring, training, networks, and access to capital; (3) unite investors, mentors, and entrepreneurs in a network bound by shared values and goals; (4) disseminate best practices in entrepreneurship through conferences, media, case studies, and online tools; (5) promote local entrepreneurial role models to encourage belief that individuals living anywhere, from any background, can turn ideas into world-class ventures. Endeavor also identified five barriers to entrepreneurship that prevent ideas from becoming high-impact businesses. These include lack of role models, limited knowledge about new venture creation, limited access to smart capital, lack of trust, and lack of management expertise and contacts. Their five-step approach, explained in detail below, addresses each of these barriers.

The first part of Endeavor's plan required locating innovative, high-impact entrepreneurs. Rottenberg and Kellner sought out the ones who had the biggest ideas and most ambitious plans. They looked for candidates with the potential to create thriving companies that could employ hundreds, even thousands of people, and generate millions in wages and revenues. And they looked for entrepreneurs who would have the power to inspire countless others.

The process of locating the entrepreneurs who will become Endeavor Entrepreneurs currently takes six to eight months in each country. Rottenberg and Kellner analyze hundreds of entrepreneurs in search of the best emerging-market role models. Endeavor is not out to save companies that are struggling and rarely works with companies that are start-ups. They identify middle-sized companies that are between three and ten years old, are already generating a sizable amount of income, and appear to have the potential to expand exponentially. Each potential company goes through a very rigorous search and selection process. The guidelines for the search criteria include the categories of entrepreneurial initiative, business innovation, values and ethics, role model potential, development impact, and overall fit with Endeavor.

According to Endeavor, the criterion of entrepreneurial initiative focuses on whether the entrepreneur has demonstrated the vision, persistence, and drive to transform a new venture into a successful business. Readiness to take the business to the next level is also an essential component to the selection process. Exploring the likelihood of the business being able to change or improve a particular industry within the country or region is also an aspect of the criterion of business innovation. Each business must demonstrate its integrity and respect for the rule of the law, making their values and ethics clear to investors and consumers. The development impact criterion involves judging if the business has the potential to have substantial economic value through revenues, wages, and job creation. Finally, Endeavor must be able to see how its assistance can substantially increase the entrepreneur's chance for success. The entrepreneur needs to be able to accept input from and also give back to Endeavor in a mutually beneficial fashion.

Candidates are scouted by proactive research done by the Endeavor staff, from recommendations through the Endeavor network, or by nomination through the Endeavor website. The process of selection involves several levels of increasingly difficult interviews and reviews. The initial interview is conducted by the Endeavor staff to assess viability as a candidate. Then, a second opinion review takes place, during which senior-level VentureCorps advisors conduct multiple interviews with each candidate, probing business strategy, innovation, growth potential, and the entrepreneur's personal qualities. A local selection panel made up of ten to fifteen

VentureCorps and local board members interview candidates, deliberate, and select candidates for an international panel. The final review involves a managing director from another Endeavor office, who interviews the candidate, and a finance expert, who reviews the prospective company's financials. If an entrepreneur passes through all these levels, the company can then be presented to the International Selection Panel, made up of international business leaders. Only after the International Selection Panel interviews, deliberates, and unanimously votes on candidates can they then become Endeavor Entrepreneurs.

TAKING ENDEAVOR ENTREPRENEURS TO SCALE

Endeavor differentiates itself from others in the entrepreneurship-support sphere in two critical ways: *who* it identifies and *how* it supports them. At selection, Endeavor Entrepreneurs typically run young businesses with $0.5 million to $15 million in revenues and with high-growth potential. These businesses are caught in development's no-man's land. Endeavor steps in because these entrepreneurs need far more than a small loan from a microfinance institution, but they are not yet big enough or proven enough to attract the attention of multilateral institutions, such as the World Bank or private equity firms. As of 2005, 198 Endeavor Entrepreneurs from 140 companies have been certified through Endeavor's rigorous search and selection process, screened from a pool of 14,044 applicants.

The second part of Endeavor's approach is to establish a support system for the selected entrepreneurs. Endeavor provides them with the world-class resources they need to achieve the greatest impact. After designing a customized, eighteen-month assessment plan, Endeavor provides the specific tools and services these entrepreneurs will need to thrive. This means offering access to mentors and to strategic consulting, both on-site and off-site. To help these entrepreneurs confront their most serious business challenges, Endeavor matches them with business professionals in its network with relevant expertise, knowledge, and contacts. These VentureCorps advisors give critical feedback and guidance to the entrepreneurs on an ongoing basis. Endeavor's VentureCorps is made up of high-level consultants, investment bankers, lawyers, accountants, venture capitalists, entrepreneurs, and corporate executives.

Whether a company's need is raising capital, revamping a business model, or looking to franchise out a business plan, Endeavor identifies the tipping point that is preventing each company from going big. Endeavor gives the companies an entrée into a network of individuals they otherwise would not have had access to, including top business leaders both in their countries and from the United States.

Endeavor recruits top MBA students from leading U.S. business schools to spend their ten-week summers working on-site with the entrepreneurs to help them develop a business plan or market entry strategy. The projects include honed business plans, analyses of company growth options, and market feasibility studies. Endeavor also engages MBA students throughout the year in off-site consulting projects through partnerships with programs such as MIT's Global G-Lab and Harvard Business School's Field Studies, among others. In several Latin American countries, Endeavor has partnered with the Boston Consulting Group in order to provide further strategic guidance to the chosen Endeavor Entrepreneurs.

THE ENDEAVOR GLOBAL NETWORK

The third component of the model is another key to the success of the Endeavor Entrepreneurs, and it revolves around peer and professional networking. Endeavor unites their Endeavor Entrepreneurs with each other, creating a global community of peers. Each month, Endeavor countries arranges meetings for the Endeavor Entrepreneurs to share experiences, give each other advice, and discuss the challenges common to entrepreneurs in their country. For many emerging-market entrepreneurs, this is the first time they have met with others who understand their commitment and drive to create something new. One result of arranging these contacts between companies is that an entire community has developed where everyone involved is encouraged to think big and take risks. This has helped to circumvent certain barriers that have historically prevented local business from thriving in Latin American countries. Having access to an empathetic community of like-minded entrepreneurs is very important since there has traditionally been a marked stigma attached to failure; the aversion to risk has prevented other entrepreneurs from following through with original business ventures.

Other barriers have included a lack of mentors and a lack of readily available networking opportunities. Endeavor overcame these obstacles by setting up a local board of directors in each country, again with the top business people, and then by setting up a network of companies or other individuals who spend the time helping each company go to scale.

The fourth component of the model involves organizing exclusive workshops, seminars, individual presentations, and other special events for the selected entrepreneurs. These events occur locally on a monthly basis, and globally in Endeavor's annual New York City Leadership Forums and bi-annual Entrepreneur Immersion Tours. By directly assisting these selected entrepreneurs, Endeavor seeks to promote entrepreneurship on a broader local scale and also to bring Endeavor Entrepreneurs onto the international playing field. Endeavor works to increase local awareness about entrepreneurship and share best practices of the business creation process by partnering with local universities and the media, and by implementing policy reform. To encourage entrepreneurship among young people, Endeavor works with local business universities to develop entrepreneurship curricula. Endeavor convenes events for their entrepreneurs to present their companies to local university students. In addition, Endeavor works with professors at the top U.S. business schools to write case studies on Endeavor Entrepreneurs in order to share the lessons of the emerging-market entrepreneurship with a global academic community.

Through partnerships with major media publications, Endeavor promotes a culture of entrepreneurship to a mass audience. In Argentina, Endeavor produces a sixteen-page monthly newspaper section with *La Nacion*, the nation's most prestigious newspaper, which relates real histories of Argentine entrepreneurs. In Brazil, Endeavor and leading business magazine *Voce S.A.* sponsor the Entrepreneurs of the New Brazil award to recognize Brazilian entrepreneurs who have potential to become leaders in the Brazilian economy.

Endeavor is also working in partnership with the multilaterals to examine the policy and legislative changes that emerging-market governments can make to facilitate the development of incentives for new business creation and venture capital investing. In every country in which they operate, Endeavor and its entrepreneurs have met with government leaders to lobby for necessary infrastructure changes.

CONTRIBUTING TO WORLDWIDE SOLUTIONS

Endeavor saw the reality that it is not just one person or one solution to solve a problem. Issues such as global development or poverty are not going to be addressed just by issuing microfinance; there has to be a series of steps in thinking about how to get countries toward development, which is essentially one of the areas that Endeavor addresses. Endeavor offers alternative and additional solutions to other programs that are out there; it tries to ensure that the solutions being worked on compliment other organizations—not compete with them. Endeavor attempts to work in synchrony to make progress in global development. Private-sector solutions have become a priority in the world, and people are seeing the increased importance of creating jobs, helping to show how the growth of the private sector is a solution to getting people out of poverty. Endeavor ensures that its entrepreneurs are being connected with other corporations based on the prospective goal of having the companies work together to address global problems, such as poverty and a struggling economy, from a united front.

The last part of Endeavor's five-step model focuses on the goal that each Endeavor Entrepreneur will ultimately be able to give back to his or her community, and also inspire others in the community to become entrepreneurs. In the United States, entrepreneurs have become community leaders and philanthropists, donating time, money, and knowledge to their local communities. Endeavor aims to foster this same philanthropic tradition in emerging markets. In every Endeavor country, Endeavor Entrepreneurs have begun reinvesting in the local office through voluntary financial donations that help make the in-country operations self-sustainable. As community leaders and role models, these entrepreneurs also mentor other earlier-stage entrepreneurs, share their stories to inspire future generations, spearhead socially responsible business initiatives, and launch their own nonprofit organizations.

With Endeavor's guidance, the entrepreneurs become role models; they encourage others to innovate and take risks, and they create sustainable economic growth. The entrepreneurs do not just spend a year or two working with Endeavor, and then the relationship is over. Once an entrepreneur's company has achieved a certain level of growth, Endeavor's goal is that the company will continue giving back to the community and always being aware of and promoting further economic expansion well into the future. These may seem like lofty plans for midsized companies, but this model is hard to argue with when looking at Endeavor's record of success at helping entrepreneurs reach their potential.

ENDEAVOR'S VALUE PROPOSITION

Full potential, according to Endeavor, does not just mean accumulation of monetary capital for the company. Endeavor has created a "value proposition," demonstrating how stimulating entrepreneurship can transform entire emerging-market societies. The value proposition breaks down the combined effects of Endeavor working with a high-impact entrepreneur into five different categories of capital: financial, human, social, intellectual and cultural. Financial capital creates new jobs and wealth by unleashing new talent. With Endeavor's backing and active support, 55 percent of Endeavor Entrepreneur companies have collectively raised approximately $908.4 million in equity financing. Human capital develops leaders through hands-on training and advising. One measure of human capital is that 86 percent of Endeavor Companies provide in-house training and education to employees. Social capital mobilizes networks to attract investors and business mentors. An example of social capital is the 23,334 hours of one-on-one mentoring given by top professionals in Endeavor's VentureCorps. Intellectual capital produces cutting-edge research and sparks innovation. There have been 246 major entrepreneurship awards received by Endeavor and its entrepreneurs, illustrating how well their positive influences around the world have been recognized. Lastly, cultural capital showcases role models to generate opportunity and influence policy. Currently, 80.8 percent of Endeavor Entrepreneurs are financially giving back to Endeavor, promoting the program's continued expansion and growth.

Endeavor measures its own success by looking at the success of each the companies with which it works. Today, 96 percent of Endeavor Entrepreneur companies are still operating in countries where the vast majority of entrepreneurial ventures typically close within forty-two months. Sixty-eight percent of Endeavor Entrepreneurs were the first in their communities to receive outside financing or institutional support. Over 1,000 angel investors and venture capitalists recognize Endeavor's seal of approval. Endeavor's goal of expanding private sector development in emerging market economies is growing fast, especially if one looks at the fact that 380,593 people have already received entrepreneurial education directly through Endeavor. Aside from numbers, Endeavor also measures its success by observing how Endeavor Entrepreneurs continue to think big and creatively, and continue to expand and grow. They inspire others in their communities to open businesses and become entrepreneurs, thus continuing the cycle of economic expansion.

THE IMPACT OF ENDEAVOR ENTREPRENEURS

Endeavor offers evidence that high-impact entrepreneurs produce significantly more jobs than the average small-to-medium-sized (SME) companies. The average number of people employed by Endeavor Entrepreneurs is 263. High-impact entrepreneurs create high-value jobs that pay well, with benefits. Endeavor Entrepreneurs have created 79,386 jobs paying on average ten times the national minimum wage, generated US$1.9 billion in revenues during 2006 alone, and with Endeavor's support, secured close to US$1 billion in financing. Ninety-one percent of Endeavor Entrepreneurs provide more benefits than those required by law.

High-impact entrepreneurs develop innovations that improve the quality of life. Innovation has been proven to lead to increases in the minimum wage and other measures of the standard of living. Of Endeavor Entrepreneurs, 81 percent invest in research and development, with 50 percent having secured, or are in the process of securing, patents.

High-impact entrepreneurs attract investment capital, encouraging a virtuous cycle of growth. Even in the United States, fewer than half of new firms survive past the four-year mark. High-impact entrepreneurs are role models. Endeavor Entrepreneurs know approximately 5,800 people whom they have influenced to start high-impact businesses.

With Endeavor's ongoing support, Endeavor Entrepreneurs generated revenues of US$1.9 billion in 2006. Yet Endeavor operated in 2006 with a worldwide budget of only US$6.87 million. This 276 multiple illustrates how Endeavor effectively leverages its services and support to help entrepreneurs achieve success. Endeavor is in the top 2 percent of employers at Stanford's Graduate School of Business and is one of the most successful recruiters at the Harvard Business School. In 2007 alone, Endeavor screened over 350 MBA candidates, selecting 33 from ten top business schools to work for Endeavor Entrepreneurs and local Endeavor affiliates.

In the United States, access to professional support networks is commonplace. Endeavor Entrepreneurs cite lack of access to key networks as their number one obstacle prior to working with Endeavor. Millions of citizens have heard the stories of Endeavor Entrepreneurs in classrooms, conferences, and local media. Internationally, these entrepreneurs are writing books, becoming regular commentators on CNNenEspañol, and taking part in politics; Endeavor Entrepreneurs are becoming real leaders in their countries and are being recognized as role models around the world. There are 117 case studies on Endeavor Entrepreneurs being taught in universities around the world, and 3,497 youth in emerging markers have taken up the entrepreneurial path directly because of an Endeavor success story.

Endeavor Entrepreneur: OfficeNet

One example of a private-sector business that Endeavor helped catapult into being a large, multinational company is OfficeNet, an office supply company started in Argentina by Andres Freire and Santiago Bilinkis. Andres and Santiago finished their undergraduate studies at a top Argentine university and joined the majority of their peers as middle managers at Proctor & Gamble. Every Thursday night from 1995 to 1996, the twenty-four-year-old aspiring entrepreneurs met in a Buenos Aires bar to brainstorm ideas even though they had few local role models, no education on the entrepreneurial process, and little encouragement from family and friends.

One day, they hit upon the idea of creating the Staples of Latin America—taking advantage of the fragmented, inefficient office-supply industry and resolving to transform it through technology, reliable service, and modern marketing strategies. They spent months studying each aspect of the U.S. business and learning the Argentine market. They named their office supply company OfficeNet. Rather than launching retail stores, which had high capital requirements, Office Net was designed to be entirely delivery based. The concept of using telemarketers and catalogs was rarely employed in the Argentine market. Every time Andres and Santiago approached an investor, they were immediately refused. Finally, in the spring of 1997, they convinced a wealthy businessman to give them $50,000 in exchange for 100 percent ownership of the firm. Andres and Santiago seized the deal. Six months later, in 1998, when Endeavor first discovered the young entrepreneurs, OfficeNet had twenty-two employees and annual sales projections of $2 million.

With the help of Endeavor's network of venture capitalists, Andres and Santiago renegotiated a deal with their investors and went from zero ownership to 35 percent equity participation. Endeavor provided mentoring on financing, growth, and leadership development. Endeavor sent a Stanford MBA to develop a business model for regional expansion. Endeavor introduced the entrepreneurs to investors in Brazil, opening doors for OfficeNet's expansion into that country as well.

Today, OfficeNet is the largest and fastest-growing office supply company in Latin America. In 2004 Andres and Santiago sold the business to Staples. They have won numerous awards and are frequently featured in newspapers and television. They have shared their story with thousands of people at Endeavor conferences and university-sponsored events. Andres and Santiago were the first Endeavor Entrepreneurs to take active roles in giving back to Endeavor. Santiago became the first Endeavor Entrepreneur to join the board of Endeavor Argentina, and Andres recently joined Endeavor's Global Advisory Board. OfficeNet currently serves 40,000 companies in Argentina and Brazil; there are currently 520 employees and annual revenues total US$57.4 million.

OfficeNet is good example for how Endeavor chooses and works with companies. OfficeNet had a fairly well-established business, but it was only with the help of Endeavor that it was able to expand into another country, and the owners were able to gain 35 percent equity in their company.

THE LEARNING CURVE

Endeavor is the only nonprofit of its kind, and it has not been without its failures and lessons. It has had huge learning experiences, especially when Endeavor first started selecting entrepreneurs. Endeavor recognized different categories of entrepreneurs; some were considered to be diamonds in the rough, and others were seen as sure-fire successes. The big lesson Endeavor learned was that some of the entrepreneurs selected as sure-fire successes did not necessarily need help to become successful. Endeavor began to hone its search to focus on those entrepreneurs who really needed Endeavor in order to reach their maximum growth potential. Endeavor is not just looking to join up with a company because it is going to become successful; rather, the goal is for there to be a mutually beneficial relationship.

Fundamentally, Endeavor operates on the belief that there are entrepreneurs in every corner of the world and opportunity for great growth in all emerging-market countries. Endeavor operates in countries where it believes it will have the cooperation and support of the people who are going to be responsible for helping to take the middle-sized companies to scale. This includes identifying countries with stable economic growth and low corruption levels. Endeavor works with top business leaders, who not only provide the financial means for Endeavor to establish presence, but also agree to work and identify the entrepreneurs that are selected and helped to become the success stories that their countries really need.

Endeavor Entrepreneur: Geomar

Another example of an Endeavor Entrepreneur going from a midsized company to a large-scale success can be seen by looking at the story of Javier Donoso from Chile, who now exports seafood products to Asia, Europe, and the United States through his company, Geomar. Javier had taken over his family's clothes manufacturing company to pay for his college tuition, and he significantly increased revenues and employees by 400 percent and 7,000 percent, respectively. Years later, after visiting Asia, he saw an opportunity to export nontraditional seafood products from Chile; this vision soon became transformed into Geomar. Geomar produces gourmet, canned seafood products. The company purchases fresh seafood from the local fishing industry along Chile's 3,000 miles of coast and immediately processes the products in its Conception-based plant. Within twelve hours of arrival, the products are de-shelled; cut to market specifications; classified by color, size and type; and sterilized and packaged. The company has invested heavily in intense quality control, close interaction with clients, and value-added processes to build long-term brand loyalty in its target markets. Despite initial resistance from distributors to promoting a foreign brand, Geomar had established a strong presence throughout Asia when Endeavor met Javier.

An Endeavor MBA student and the G-Lab teams from MIT researched international expansion opportunities for Geomar. Endeavor Chile's board of directors and VentureCorps mentors helped Javier raise capital and negotiate with shareholders. Endeavor mentors provided guidance on internationalization, including currency transactions and capital structure. Endeavor mentors also helped develop a market penetration strategy and then forged business leads for the U.S. market.

Endeavor's financial restructuring enabled Geomar to experience 225 percent sales growth and 193 percent job growth. Javier subsequently received financing from a large Chilean investment group. He has had successful expansion into Spain and into the United States. He presented at the New York Fancy Food Show in 2004–6. Today, Javier is a local leader in the Entrepreneur Network and a great role model; he has been spearheading Endeavor Chile's Entrepreneur Reinvest Program. As evidenced by Javier's experience, local and international growth as well as increased numbers of jobs are all hallmarks of Endeavor Entrepreneurs.

LOCAL AND INTERNATIONAL GROWTH

Endeavor went from concept to reality based on the unfaltering belief held by the founders that entrepreneurs exist everywhere. Entrepreneurs inspire people to think big, and they also go out achieve results themselves. Endeavor is proactive about helping the entrepreneurs and also about recording and reporting results. Endeavor does this in order for the entrepreneurs to see how they have changed and grown, and also to illustrate how much more they can achieve. For a company to be able to see its recent growth in specific facts and figures and to be able to visualize its future potential is a motivating factor for each Endeavor Entrepreneur.

In terms of opportunities and obstacles, Endeavor is unique in that is sees them as being the same thing: both provide the chance to grow and thrive. When it comes to the cliché about the glass being half-empty or half-full, Endeavor always sees its glass as being half-full. It approaches challenges with a positive attitude, and by promoting a working environment where there is a lot of support available, Endeavor helps entrepreneurs treat their own obstacles as opportunities. Every problem that arises can be solved in an innovative matter, and Endeavor tries to inspire entrepreneurs to think in those terms as well. The entrepreneurs internalize this way of thinking, and then they can instill positive thinking in other people in their communities. Another way that Endeavor is unique is that its model can be easily molded to the individual needs of each client regardless of where the client is located. Endeavor's assistance is practical and useful since it encourages original thinking and adapts to the specific need faced by each individual entrepreneur.

Endeavor encourages innovative thinking, and it practices what it preaches. The CEO, Linda Rottenberg, is a leader who believes in listening to and being very supportive of her staff. She solicits advice from all those around her and believes that is a large reason for the success of Endeavor. When it comes to thinking about entrepreneurship in emerging markets, she cited Golda Meir as being one of her influences because Meir was a really strong woman who led Israel during a very precarious time.

Within these emerging-market countries, Endeavor is considered the "go to" organization for entrepreneurship: governments have approached Endeavor to draft policies; investors rely on Endeavor's seal of approval; universities partner with Endeavor to create case studies; and individuals attend Endeavor-sponsored conferences and download materials to learn concrete steps on the entrepreneurial process. The organization produces impact reports every year that contain a very extensive metrics page focused on measuring Endeavor's impact on these countries in terms of job creation and education received through entrepreneurial workshops. The numbers are measurements used to illustrate the continuing success of Endeavor and are a testament to the efforts of business leaders and government officials around the world.

Countries outside of Latin America have taken notice of these success stories, and Endeavor expansion plans are going to be at the heart of the organization's focus for the coming years. The organization has been approached by the president of Ghana, who said they need Endeavor in Ghana. Business leaders in Lebanon, Egypt, India, and throughout Asia and the Middle East have been clamoring for Endeavor to bring its model to their countries as well. Endeavor sees this as proof in and of itself that it is succeeding. After only ten years of operation, Endeavor currently operates in Argentina, Brazil, Chile, Colombia, Mexico, South Africa, Turkey, and Uruguay, and Endeavor India will be opening next. The ambitious expansion plan the organization is embarking upon has the goal of reaching twenty-five emerging markets, including countries in Asia, Africa and the Middle East, all within the next decade.

Endeavor Entrepreneur: Stitch Wise

One of the Endeavor Entrepreneurs who reflects Endeavor's growing global impact outside of Latin America is Natalie Killassy. She has been able to reduce the number of rock fatalities at AngloGoldAshanti's Mines in South Africa. Falling debris is a major cause of injuries and fatalities, and the stitching that Natalie designed prevents rocks from falling out of mining bags. In 1997, Natalie Killassy began a sewing company on the Western Deep Levels mine in the Gauteng Province of South Africa. Struck by the substantial number of men who were made paraplegics though mining accidents, and who no longer capable of mine work, she persuaded AngloGoldAshanti to provide machines and workspace for a new venture called Stitch Wise. After customizing sewing machines to suit disabled workers, she chose protective rainwear as the company's first product. Realizing that many of her workers' injuries stemmed from rock falls, Natalie spent eighteen months in a deep, underground mine test site to develop improved equipment to prevent roof collapse. Her solutions included improved backfill bags that support overhead rock. These products are now industry standard and are critical to the industry. "Without backfill bags, we'd be out of business," said one senior manager at AngloGoldAshanti on a National Geographic documentary. Made from woven polypropylene fabric, Stitch Wise backfill bags are more resilient and safer than the typical wooden supports used in mines. Endeavor first met Natalie in mid-2004 for her first screening interview. She attended the first panel in South Africa in Cape Town in December 2004.

Endeavor mentors helped Natalie hone her business strategy to stimulate new growth. Endeavor board members and mentors steered Natalie through critical negotiations with mining companies and the establishment of a new factory in Klersdrop. Endeavor sent three MBA interns: the first two MBAs helped simplify ownership structure, and the third MBA helped design an employee ownership plan.

Today, Natalie has 145 employees—nearly half of whom are paraplegics. With Endeavor's mentorship, she has redefined her business strategy and now has a profitable business with US$5.9 billion in revenues in 2007—proving that a socially conscious business can compete on price and quality. Natalie supplies 12,000 patented backfill bags a year to the mining industry—50 percent of the South African market. The South African Bureau of Standards recently retained Natalie to write the industry's specification for backfill and retention materials. Natalie was the first of Endeavor's South African Entrepreneurs' class to make a significant cash donation to Endeavor South Africa as part of the Entrepreneurship Reinvestment Program. With the recent registration of two new patents, Natalie and Stitch Wise are poised for new growth and broader impact with safety equipment, training, and the employment of differently abled workers.

Natalie Killassy provides a good example to highlight some of the multifaceted ways Endeavor chooses and helps its entrepreneurs. Natalie had started up her own company, which focused on helping those in her community by providing jobs that could be adapted for handicapped people, and she also recognized the market for safer products. This matched Endeavor's goal of increasing community production and revenue. Her story also provides examples of how Endeavor operates. It explains how Endeavor goes about improving a company's business and expansion plans. Natalie's company can continue to grow and create new products because of the help that Endeavor provided for Stitch Wise. The story of Stitch Wise shows that Endeavor is open to helping all different types of companies, in all different regions of the world, no matter how specific the entrepreneur's needs and goals may be. It also shows how Endeavor Entrepreneurs reinvest in their local Endeavor office, helping to ensure the program's continued success.

MEDIA MENTIONS AND AWARDS

Endeavor has attracted quite a lot of media attention. It is estimated that 381.6 million people have been reached through media content about Endeavor and Endeavor Entrepreneurs. In July 2007, in an updated and expanded paperback edition of *The World Is Flat* (pp. 495–496), the *New York Times* columnist Thomas L. Friedman called Endeavor's model for high-impact entrepreneurship "the best anti-poverty program of all." Friedman praises Endeavor's "mentor capitalist" model for helping midsize entrepreneurs expand and create jobs, and for supporting innovation in developing countries worldwide. "As important as it is to help make poor people into small business people," Friedman says, "it is just as important to make small business people in a developing country into big business people who can employ lots of their neighbors." Friedman goes in to explain that "it is precisely these sorts of middle-class start-ups and small businesses that create the most jobs and the greatest innovation in a society."

This is the "pro-entrepreneurship" example that Friedman says has the "inspirational power" to encourage individuals in the developing world, where role models are scarce, to think big. "There is no greater motivator for the poor than looking at one of their own who makes it big and saying: If she can do it, I can do it."

Endeavor's "mentor capitalist" model breaks down economic and cultural barriers through rigorous screening and strategic advising from its network of world-class business leaders. With their guidance, 266 Endeavor Entrepreneurs have created 79,000 jobs and generated $1.9 billion in revenues.

Endeavor is the only nonprofit that supports high-impact entrepreneurs in emerging markets. At the White House Conference on the Americas in July 2007, Secretary of Commerce Carlos M. Gutierrez stated, "We must work to ensure that there is equal opportunity for *everyone* in the Americas, not just those at the top of the economic ladder." He then cited Endeavor as being one of the top new companies working to help ensure equal opportunities for all people that "has hundreds of case studies of successful Latin pioneers."[1]

Endeavor has received numerous awards and notable recognitions for its work. For the fifth year in a row, Endeavor received the Social Capitalist Award, which recognizes it as one of the forty-five top-performing nonprofits in the world by Fast Company/Monitor Group. Some other recent awards include being named by NuWire Investor as one of the Top 15 Charities for Investors for 2007. Endeavor co-founder and CEO Linda Rottenberg won the 2007 Organization of Women in International Trade's Woman of the Year Award, which recognizes women around the world for their efforts in international trade and development. She also was honored among those receiving the 2007 Women of Worth Award from the Worth Collection LTD, which celebrates women who have achieved extraordinary success in their professional pursuits.

FUNDING

Linda Rottenberg started out with two businesses, and since then, Endeavor has grown exponentially. Endeavor's aim is to become a fully self-sustaining organization of, by, and for entrepreneurs. Currently, Endeavor has established an Entrepreneur Give-Back Program that asks Endeavor Entrepreneurs to donate a portion of equity or incremental revenues back to the organization in order to help the next generation of high-impact entrepreneurs succeed. The goal is to have each Endeavor office self-sustaining ten years after launch. In markets where there is not a strong tradition of philanthropy, Endeavor is changing the cultural mind-set and jump-starting a virtuous cycle of giving back.

Sustaining Endeavor financially, at both the local and global levels, involves a combination of several factors. This model requires an active board of directors and mentors. Each member on the board of directors pays to be on the board, which provides much of Endeavor's funding. Funding also comes from other places, including corporate donations. The mentors in Endeavor's VentureCorps are an essential part of the organization's entrepreneurial services; they contribute to Endeavor financially and through their time. Endeavor runs as a decentralized model: its global office operates separately from its affiliate offices in each country. This is similar to a franchise model, where each of the offices runs their own budgeting. This helps ensure that each office is able to focus on the individual needs of each company without having to conform to a greater global model.

Endeavor continually sets the bar incredibly high, ensuring that investors and other companies are able to trust the value of the entrepreneurs that Endeavor connects them to. Endeavor does not bend the rules when it comes to choosing their entrepreneurs; every entrepreneur must reach the very high threshold defining what qualifies as a high-impact Endeavor Entrepreneur.

ADVICE TO FUTURE ENTREPRENEURS

These high standards have helped Endeavor have an impressive first ten years, and the organization is grateful for all its success. However, it does not regret the mistakes and slipups along the way. Endeavor believes that becoming successful requires falling down a few times, being able to pick yourself back up, and learning from your mistakes. There is nothing in Endeavor's trajectory that the organization would have done differently, and it is willing to offer advice to others who are interested in learning about entrepreneurship. Although Endeavor's main headquarters in New York has only sixteen staff members, they are interested in answering questions about entrepreneurship and in collaborating any way that they can with all interested people. If someone is interested in becoming an entrepreneur and working with emerging markets, Endeavor highlights the importance of understanding what communities do and the importance of listening to people. It promotes getting out into the world and understanding the mechanics of different communities. Endeavor describes entrepreneurs as humans who are inspired by ideas, and says that ideas are the underlying point of any successful venture.

For further reading, Endeavor suggests two books. The first one is *The Business of Changing the World* by Marc Benioff and Carlye Adler. It talks about how cooperative efforts can engage corporations such as Starbucks with private-sector development and help emergent market countries get to where they need to be. Endeavor is also a big advocate of *The World Is Flat* by Thomas Friedman; quotations from the book were mentioned above, and in the book, Friedman talks further about the importance of Endeavor's current projects. Endeavor's website, www.Endeavor.org, has much more information, including a data bank of articles related to private-sector growth in emerging market communities.

Renowned institutions such as the World Economic Forum, World Bank, Harvard Business School, and the *Wall Street Journal,* as well as legendary entrepreneurs Michael Dell and Jerry Yang (Yahoo!), have all recognized Endeavor for its cutting-edge model for private-sector development. Endeavor is transforming the economies of emerging markets by identifying and supporting high-impact entrepreneurs. The rise of social entrepreneurship inspires people with business skills to solve social problems. This solution disrupts the status quo and leads to long-term, sustainable economic growth all throughout the world.

ORGANIZATIONAL SNAPSHOT

Organization: Endeavor

Founder: Linda Rottenberg

Mission/Description: Established in 1997, Endeavor is a global nonprofit organization that targets emerging-market countries transitioning from international aid to international investment. Endeavor helps transform the economies of emerging markets by identifying and supporting high-impact entrepreneurs.

High-impact entrepreneurs have the biggest ideas and most ambitious plans. They have the potential to create thriving companies that employ hundreds, even thousands, of people, and generate millions in wages and revenues. And they have the power to inspire countless others.

Endeavor targets only entrepreneurs with high-impact potential. They scour a country for these entrepreneurs, and they help them break down a society's barriers to success, offer world-class strategic advice, and open doors to capital. With Endeavor's guidance, these entrepreneurs become role models, encourage others to innovate and take risks, and create sustainable economic growth. Together, Endeavor and high-impact entrepreneurs are changing industries, communities, and entire countries.

Website: www.endeavor.org

Address: Endeavor Global

900 Broadway, Suite 600

New York, NY 10003 USA

Phone: +1.212.352.3200

Fax: +1.212.352.1892

E-mail: info@endeavor.org

NOTE

1. http://www.commerce.gov/NewsRoom/SecretarySpeeches/PROD01_003157

8

ACCION International

Teresa Barttrum

The mission of ACCION International is to give people the tools they need to work their way out of poverty. By providing "micro" loans, financial services, and business training to poor women and men who start their own businesses, ACCION's partner microfinance organizations help people work their own way up the economic ladder with dignity and pride. With capital, people can grow their own businesses. They can earn enough to afford basics such as running water, better food, and schooling for their children.

In a world where 3 billion people live on less than $2 a day, it is not enough to help 1,000 or even 100,000 individuals. ACCION's goal is to bring microfinance to tens of millions of people—enough to truly change the world. ACCION knows that there will never be enough donations to do this. That is why the organization has created an anti-poverty strategy that is permanent and self-sustaining.

ACCION was founded to address the desperate poverty in Latin America's cities. Begun as a student-run volunteer effort in the shantytowns of Caracas, ACCION today is one of the premier microfinance organizations in the world, with a network of lending partners that spans Latin America, the United States, Africa, and now Asia. Over the last four decades, it has built a tradition of developing innovative solutions to poverty. Although ACCION's approach has changed over the years, the driving force behind its mission remains the same: It is still the people served, the women and men of impoverished communities, who shape its work. It is their courage and ingenuity, and the tremendous power of their dreams, that continues to inspire ACCION and to renew its dedication to the search for new and better solutions to poverty.

HISTORY: A RETROSPECTIVE

ACCION International was founded in 1961 by an idealistic law student named Joseph Blatchford.

An amateur tennis player, Blatchford had just completed a goodwill tennis tour of thirty Latin American cities. He returned haunted by the images of Latin America's urban poor: the crowded shantytowns, the open sewers, the hungry and hopeless faces. Determined to help, Blatchford and his law school friends raised $90,000 from private companies to start a new kind of organization: a community development effort designed to help the poor help themselves.

In the summer of 1961, Blatchford and thirty volunteers flew to Venezuela and set to work. Initially greeted with skepticism, the fledgling "ACCIONistas" were soon working closely with local residents to identify the community's most pressing needs. Together, volunteers and residents installed electricity and sewer lines, started training and nutrition programs, and built schools and community centers.

Over the next ten years, ACCION started programs in three more countries: Brazil, Peru, and Colombia. During that time, the organization placed over 1,000 volunteers and contributed more than $9 million to development in some of the poorest communities of Latin America.

Microlending Begins

By the early 1970s, ACCION's leaders were becoming increasingly aware that their projects did not address the major cause of urban poverty in Latin America: lack of economic opportunity. "We began to sense that a school or a water system didn't necessarily have long-term impact. We were simply reorganizing the resources that a community already had within it, rather than increasing their resources," former ACCION director Terry Holcombe remembered.

The employment situation in the urban centers was dire. Drawn by the mirage of industrial employment, thousands of rural migrants were flocking to the cities each year. Once there, however, they found that jobs were scarce. The few that were available often did not pay a living wage. Unable to find work, and lacking a social safety net, many of these urban poor started their own small enterprises. They wove belts, banged out pots, and sold potatoes. But they had no way to grow their tiny businesses. To buy supplies, they often borrowed from local loan sharks at rates as high as 10 percent a day. Most of their profits went to interest payments, leaving them locked in a daily struggle for survival.

In 1973 ACCION staff in Recife, Brazil, noticed the prevalence of these informal businesses. If these small-scale entrepreneurs could borrow capital at commercial interest rates, they wondered, could they lift themselves out of poverty? ACCION's Recife program coined the term "microenterprise" and began issuing small loans. To ACCION's knowledge, these first loans helped launched the field of microcredit.

The experiment in Recife was a success. Within four years, the organization had provided 885 loans, helping to create or stabilize 1,386 new jobs. ACCION had found a way to generate new wealth for the working poor of Latin America.

Expanding Opportunity: Building a Model

Over the next decade, ACCION helped start microlending programs in fourteen countries in Latin America.

ACCION and its partners developed a lending method that met the distinct needs of microenterprises: small, short-term loans built confidence and a credit record; site visits replaced paperwork. With a loan repayment rate of 97 percent, ACCION's clients soon shattered the myth that the poor were bad credit risks. Given access to affordable capital, they could and would improve their lives.

ACCION soon found that microlending had another revolutionary quality: it paid for itself. The interest each borrower paid helped cover the cost of lending to another.

The ability to cover costs, augmented by ACCION's new loan guarantee fund, the Bridge Fund, enabled ACCION's partners to connect with the local banking sector and dramatically increase the number of microentrepreneurs they reached. Between 1989 and 1995, the amount of money loaned by ACCION's Latin American Network multiplied more than twenty times. Yet, all the while, ACCION knew that it was reaching less than 2 percent of the microentrepreneurs in need of its services.

The organization remained convinced that microlending had the potential to transform the economic landscape of Latin America. To do so, however, ACCION knew that microlenders would need access to a much larger pool of capital.

In response, ACCION helped create BancoSol, the first commercial bank in the world dedicated solely to microenterprise. Founded in Bolivia in 1992, BancoSol is a bank of the poor: its clients are market vendors, sandal makers, and seamstresses. Yet today, BancoSol offers its 82,000 active clients an impressive range of financial services, including savings accounts, credit cards, and housing loans—products that just five years ago were accessible only to Bolivia's upper classes.

In 1994 ACCION helped BancoSol sell certificates of deposit in the U.S. financial market, certificates backed by nothing more than the good word of a woman selling oranges on the streets of La Paz. For the first time, the world's premier financial institutions invested in microenterprise, not out of charity, but because it was good business.

BancoSol is no longer unique: more than fifteen ACCION-affiliated organizations are now regulated financial institutions, and others are on their way. With the power to access the financial markets, they have the potential to reach not just thousands, but millions, of the poor.

Bringing Microlending "Home": The U.S. Initiative

In 1991, concerned about growing income inequality and unemployment in the United States, ACCION brought its microlending model home, launching a program in Brooklyn, New York. Like the underprivileged microentrepreneurs helped by ACCION abroad, the diverse population of small business owners in the United States is faced with a specific set of barriers to accessing business financing: having no credit history, having damaged credit, or needing a loan that is too small for a bank to make. These are the people that ACCION aimed to help so that they, too, could work their way to economic success in a dignified manner.

Over the next five years, ACCION worked to adapt its lending model to the very different social and economic context of the United States. In 2000 ACCION's U.S. initiative was renamed ACCION USA, which today has offices in Atlanta, Miami, New England, and New York, as well as licensees in California, Illinois, New Mexico, and Texas. In 2005 the organization expanded its reach nationwide when it launched its Online Small Business Loan Application, enabling ACCION USA to offer its small business loans to entrepreneurs throughout the United States. Together, ACCION USA and its licensees make up the U.S. ACCION Network, the largest microlending network in the country. By year's end 2007, the U.S. ACCION Network had loaned more than $206 million to more than 21,000 low-income entrepreneurs in forty states and Puerto Rico.

A nonprofit subsidiary of ACCION International, ACCION USA is a community-based organization whose mission is to make access to credit a permanent resource for small business owners. To reach even more low-income business owners in need of credit, ACCION USA is centralizing loan processing, deploying Internet-based lending and call centers, and opening new lending offices. ACCION USA also capitalizes on innovative partnerships to provide credit and training to support small business development. ACCION USA has worked with banks such as Bank of America, Citizens Bank, and Wachovia to promote referrals of clients who do not meet standard bank requirements. In Miami, community partner AXA Financial provided funding for ACCION USA clients to receive one-on-one marketing and accounting training.

ACCION Expands to Africa

In October 2000, ACCION began working in partnership with microlending organizations in sub-Saharan Africa, marking its first initiative outside the Americas. Recognizing the vital need for microcredit throughout Africa, ACCION committed itself to reaching increasing numbers of the continent's poor, self-employed men and women in the years to come. Currently, ACCION is providing technical assistance to microlenders in Ghana, Nigeria, Tanzania, and Uganda, with plans to enter Cameroon and Senegal in 2009.

ACCION Expands to India

In 2005 ACCION reached further, to help even more working poor in one of the world's most populated countries, India, through the Unitus-ACCION Alliance for India. Since then it has also established partnerships with microfinance institutions YES Bank, Swadhaar Finaccess, and Grameen Koota.

ACCION'S MOTIVATION

According to William Burrus, president and CEO of ACCION USA and former executive director of ACCION International, "My inspiration comes directly from the people we serve. Their stories are full of courage, hard work, and dreams." These feelings are shared by each staff member at ACCION. ACCION remains a mission-driven organization, and the people they serve are the driving force behind its success. When introduced to staff members, one quickly realizes that ACCION's mission is the primary reason why people work here. They feel as if they are making a difference; they feel as if they are cultivating an important tool for global poverty alleviation.

WHY MICROFINANCE?

Most of the world's 3 billion poor people cannot find work. Few jobs are available where they live, and those that are often do not pay a living wage. To survive, they must create their own jobs by starting tiny businesses or microenterprises. They make and sell tortillas, sew clothes, or sell vegetables in the street—anything to put food on the table.

Microentrepreneurs work hard—sometimes eighteen hours a day. Yet with no capital to grow their businesses, they remain trapped in a cycle of poverty. To open their businesses each day, they are often forced to borrow from loan sharks, who charge as much as 10 percent a day, or they pay higher prices to buy goods on credit. Any profit they earn goes to others, leaving them locked in a daily struggle for survival. What they need to break free is working capital: a loan as small as $100 at a fair rate of interest. But most banks will not lend to them. The loans they need are often considered too small for banks to justify the time and expense to administer them, and microentrepreneurs lack the collateral and credit history required by traditional lenders.

That is why ACCION began issuing microloans over forty years ago. A small loan can cut the cost of raw goods or buy a sewing machine. Sales grow, and so do profits. With a growing income, people can work their way out of poverty.

In the United States, microfinance helps people move out of welfare, rebuilds inner city neighborhoods, and provides a viable alternative for those left behind by factory closings and corporate downsizing.

Microfinance is a smart strategy because it builds on the one asset found in even the poorest communities: the power and determination of the human spirit.

HOW ACCION WORKS

Historically, anti-poverty programs have not been able to help more than a tiny fraction of the world's poor. There simply is not enough charitable money in the world to adequately address the challenges, and there never will be. That is why ACCION is leading the effort to create a permanent answer to poverty. Unlike traditional charities and many other microlending efforts, ACCION's partner programs are designed to cover their own costs.

It works like this: borrowers pay interest on their loans, enough to cover the expense of making a loan. In this way, each borrower helps finance the cost of lending to the next. The more people the program reaches, the more resources it has to reach others.

This focus on financial sustainability has helped ACCION's partner programs increase the number of people served from 13,000 in 1988 to over 3 million at the end of 2007.

We now know that microfinance can help the poor and be profitable. In Mexico, ACCION's partner Banco Compartamos now serves over 838,000 poor and low-income entrepreneurs while making a profit. With profits, microfinance institutions can break free of the limitations of donor funds because they can attract private investment.

In other words, microfinance has the potential to access billions of dollars in the international financial markets to help the very people our system has traditionally left behind. ACCION's goal is to make this potential a reality.

WHO ARE THE BORROWERS ACCION'S WORK SERVES?

In Latin America, the Caribbean, Africa, and Asia, ACCION and its partner programs work with poor, self-employed men and women who rely on microenterprise as their main source of income. These individuals range from the very poor to those who have some assets but remain marginalized from the mainstream economy and society. ACCION's Latin American, Caribbean, African, and Asian borrowers

- Are among the regions' poorest people at the time of their first loan
- Usually have no collateral
- May not be able to read or write
- May not have enough capital to open for business every day
- Are 65 percent female

In the United States, ACCION USA works with low- and moderate-income borrowers who have their own businesses but are economically marginalized and have no access to commercial business loans. They are often unable to afford formal training and frequently have no forum for forming business contacts or receiving peer support. They are single mothers on public assistance and storefront owners with small but well-established businesses. Many are recent immigrants. ACCION USA borrowers

- Are 86 percent minority
- Are 42 percent female
- Own businesses such as restaurants, retail, computer services, beauty salons, and taxi services

- Often rely on their microbusiness for 50 percent or more of their family income
- Often have business assets of less than $5,000
- Often have no personal or business credit, or have bad credit prior to receiving an ACCION loan

THE ACCION MICROFINANCE MODEL

ACCION's partner programs provide small, short-term loans at interest rates that reflect the cost of lending. ACCION's loan methodology and range of financial services have been designed both to meet the needs of microentrepreneurs and to ensure that the microfinance organizations it works with are financially sustainable. Best of all, the model has enabled ACCION's partners' clients to work their own ways up the economic ladder, with dignity and pride.

ACCION considers microentrepreneurs skilled business people, not recipients of charity. Like traditional banks, ACCION partner programs evaluate potential borrowers using measurements such as business assets—which could be as small as a tin stall in the market—amount and cost of goods sold, cost of raw materials, and household expenses. But unlike traditional banks, the partner programs do not make loans based on revenue or collateral alone. Often, ACCION clients need only demonstrate a need for the loan and the will to achieve their goals.

Because of the poverty of its clients and their lack of credit history, ACCION sends loan officers to meet potential borrowers in their places of work, where they also weigh intangibles such as references from customers and neighbors, and the loan officer's own "gut feeling" about the microentrepreneur's drive to succeed. This character-based lending allows us to go "beyond the numbers" and develop a more complete picture of a potential borrower than a traditional credit score. The character-based lending involves traditional techniques, such as reviewing the business's prospects, examining any business plan that has been created, and determining if there is a market need. However, the model takes the lending process one step further. Loan officers working with ACCION will interview neighbors to see if the potential borrower pays his or her bills on time; check the potential borrower's character with neighbors, family, and business associates; and secure household items as collateral.

Borrowers either apply for loans individually, or if they lack physical collateral or a co-signer, they team up with a few other borrowers. Known as solidarity group lending, this method allows members to cross-guarantee one another's loans in lieu of collateral. This works well for those individuals who live in extremely poor or rural regions. It allows the group members to hold each other accountable for the loan repayment and provides additional support for each individual solidarity group member. Successful members of the solidarity group can then apply for further loans. For example, ten women might take out a $1,000 loan via solidarity group lending, and each individual woman would receive $100 of the total loan. The women may meet once a week to discuss business best practices and submit the loan payment that is due. If one group member is short on her payment that week, all the other members can pool funds to cover for that person, with the understanding that she will make it up to the group over time. ACCION spearheaded this approach in Latin America in the 1970s to help bring microlending to the poorest of the economically active population.

First loans start small—often as low as $100 in Latin America. Borrowers who repay their loans on time are eligible for increasingly larger loans. This process, called stepped lending, keeps initial risk at a minimum while allowing microentrepreneurs to carefully grow their businesses and increase their incomes.

THE ACCION APPROACH

ACCION's goal is to bring microloans to enough people to have a significant impact on poverty. There will never be enough charitable donations to accomplish this. It has been estimated that it would cost over $250 billion to reach 500 million poor people—a figure well beyond the reach of donor funds. That is why ACCION is leading the effort to make microlending financially self-sustaining. Although ACCION understands that this is only one of many solutions for addressing the problems of global poverty, its members remain motivated and driven toward this cause.

As mentioned, microlending programs have the potential to cover their own costs. The interest each borrower pays helps to finance the cost of lending to another. In most other poverty alleviation efforts, often driven by direct aid, every person helps bring the program closer to its financial limits. Successful microlending programs, on the other hand, generate more resources with each individual they help.

As a result, well-managed microlending programs generate more income than they spend, allowing them to expand and reach more marginalized microentrepreneurs. And, once they become economically viable financial institutions, they have the ability to access much broader sources of lending capital—the billions of dollars invested in the world's financial markets.

Several of ACCION's partners have already made the transition from non-profit, charity-dependent organizations to banks or other regulated financial institutions. The three largest (Banco Solidario of Ecuador, Banco Compartamos of Mexico, and Mibanco of Peru) each reach over 100,000 poor and low-income microentrepreneurs.

These pioneering microlending institutions have led the way for the microfinance industry, demonstrating that it is possible for a commercial lender to both serve the poor *and* be profitable. As a result, commercial banks that previously served only the upper class are increasingly opening their doors to microentrepreneurs. ACCION has helped five commercial banks—SOGEBANK (Haiti), Banco del Pichincha (Ecuador) and Banco ABN-AMRO Real (Brazil), YES Bank (India), and Ecobank (West Africa)—begin lending to the self-employed poor.

ACCION's emphasis on commercial viability and institutional growth—known as the commercial approach—has helped its partner microfinance institutions (MFIs) reach scale and financial self-sufficiency. To help its partners attain these goals, ACCION provides technical assistance to improve operations and efficiency, as well as loan guarantees to help access commercial capital.

This model has changed over time, and currently rests with the idea that ACCION acts as a technical consultant to those organizations they help establish as the initial source for microlending in each particular country. Typically, ACCION sets up a working relationship with one organization that then works with their own countrymen and women to establish microlending situations. At this point, ACCION will offer support and guidance and may make an investment in the company. This, in turn, allows the organization to further their investments in microentrepreneurs locally. ACCION continues to offer this support and assistance via assigned advisors in the designated countries. ACCION currently has thirty-five international partners, resulting in one of the most well-established microfinance networks in the world. In the United States, by contrast, loans are made directly by ACCION USA.

WHERE DOES ACCION WORK?

ACCION partners with more than thirty-five microfinance organizations throughout Latin America, the Caribbean, Asia, and Africa, as well as serving U.S. microentrepreneurs through the U.S. ACCION Network. For a more detailed description of locations see Table 8.1, and for regularly updated statistical information visit the ACCION website (www.accion.org).

ACCION KEY STATISTICS

ACCION's goal is to bring the full range of financial services to ever-increasing numbers of people, in order to have a significant impact on alleviating global poverty. ACCION's partners and affiliates operate in twenty-five countries in Latin America, the Caribbean, Asia, sub-Saharan Africa, and the United States. Since 1997 ACCION's affiliated programs have issued $12.3 billion in microloans to more than 4.94 million people, with a historical repayment rate of over 97 percent. (See Table 8.2.)

As part of ACCION's commitment to rigorous reporting standards and strong financial performance, the following reports are now available as PDFs on the organization's website. Some of the documents offered online include historical annual statistics of ACCION partners in Latin America and the Caribbean, Africa, Asia, and the United States since inception. They also include quarterly statistics by program of the ACCION Network in Latin America and the Caribbean, including data on new borrowers, active borrowers, amount disbursed, and active portfolios.

Table 8.1 ACCION Microfinance Partners

North America	South America	Peru
United States	**Argentina**	Mibanco
U.S. ACCION Network	Columbia Microcrédito	**Venezuela**
Mexico	(Banco Columbia)	BanGente
ADMIC	**Brazil**	**Africa**
Compartamos Banco	CrediAmigo (Banco do	**Ghana**
Central America	Nordeste)	EB-ACCION Savings & Loan
	Real Microcrédito (Banco	
El Salvador	ABN AMRO Real)	**Nigeria**
Apoyo Integral	**Bolivia**	ACCION Microfinance
Guatemala	BancoSol	Bank, Ltd
Génesis Empresarial	**Colombia**	**Tanzania**
Banrural	Cooperativa Emprender	Akiba Commercial Bank
Honduras	FINAMERICA	**Uganda**
Banco Popular Covelo	Fundación Mario Santo	Uganda Microfinance
(Bancovelo)	Domingo	Limited
FINSOL	**Ecuador**	**Asia**
Nicaragua	Banco Solidario	**China**
Financiera FAMA	CREDIFE (Banco del	Inner Mongolia Microcredit
Caribbean	Pichincha)	Company
	Fundación Ecuatoriana de	**India**
Dominican Republic	Desarrollo	Grameen Koota
Banco Ademi	**Paraguay**	Swadhaar
Haiti	El Comercio Financiera	YES SAMPANN (YES Bank)
SogeSol (SOGEBANK)	Fundación Paraguaya	

Source: ACCION International.

HOW IS ACCION SUSTAINED?

ACCION has been sustained in a variety of ways since its inception in 1961, and this remains true today. It is sustained through individual philanthropy, private foundation grants, public grants, and investments. It is reported that the bulk of revenue comes from private contributions but an approximate breakdown can be seen in Table 8.3.

Table 8.2 2007 Statistics for ACCION Partner Programs

	Latin America and the Caribbean	Africa	Asia	Totals
Active clients	3.03 million	88,538	1,976	3.12 million
Total amount disbursed	$5.01 billion	$123 million	$382,000	$5.14 billion
Active portfolio	$2.89 billion	$81.6 million	$169,000	$2.97 billion

Table 8.3 ACCION Revenue Sources, 2007

Source	Percentage of Operating Revenue
Private contributions	43%
Contracts and training fees	21%
Investments and fee income	29%
Dividends from investments	14%
AIMCO management fees	4%

ACCION is a 501(c)(3) nonprofit, and is committed to minimizing its administrative and fundraising expenses, consistently keeping these expenses at a level below 25 percent of total costs. For example, in 2007 ACCION (in terms of percentages of expenses) spent only 12 percent on administration and 12 percent on fundraising, while 76 percent was spent on program services.

HOW DOES ACCION MEASURE SUCCESS?

ACCION measures success in a variety of ways. One can measure success by looking at the number of clients the organization is reaching and by the growth in the number of clients served. Another measure of success is the active loan portfolio of the ACCION partner network. All of these numbers, regardless of which you choose to use as a benchmark, are increasing. ACCION admits it took a long time to get to this point—over thirty years—but now that the ball is rolling, growth has accelerated sharply. ACCION's website contains its annual report, which portrays the growth of the organization from its earliest days to the immediate past. For example, the report shows that it took ACCION three decades to reach its first 1 million clients. The second million were reached three years later, in mid-2006, and the third million in half that time, by the end of 2007.

ACCION also measures its success by going out to the communities, villages, and cities where their clients live and work, and asking them directly about the impact of microfinance on their lives. María Otero, ACCION president and CEO, tells a story of how one of ACCION's Central American clients responded when María asked her, "How has microfinance helped you?" The woman brought María into the next room. There, hanging proudly on the wall, were her children's diplomas from school. She replied, "This is how it's affected my life!" She had been able to pay the school fees and to sustain a reliable income over time to allow her children to finish school. She herself had never been able to finish school, and she had always prioritized education in her children's lives.

Yet another example is Jose Antonio Sanos of Villa de San Antonio, Honduras, a client of ACCION partner Banco Popular Covelo (Bancovelo). He and his family live in a small village just outside of Comayagua, about ninety minutes north of Tegucigalpa. Axel and Dana, ages 4 and 7, race around their backyard climbing on, over, and through stacks of cement blocks. Jose reflects on the business that will someday send them to college. "Like any businessman, I want to grow," he declares. "Like any father, I want to send my children to school."

Ten years ago, Jose started a cement block business with his brother and father. His father had mastered cement block making early in Jose's life and wanted to pass on the lessons of the trade to the next generation. For many years, they worked as a team, but sustained growth was hard to come by on a tight budget.

Nevertheless, consistent local demand for the blocks told Jose their business was a good one. Even when his father and brother left to work in construction in Comayagua, Jose carried on. His persistence paid off when he learned about ACCION partner Bancovelo's fixed asset loans for small businesses. After an enthusiastic conversation with the local Bancovelo loan officer, Jose knew that progress for his business was now within reach.

With a first loan of 10,000 limpiras, or US$550, Jose was able to buy updated tools and better quality sand and cement mix. Within a matter of months, he had paid the loan off and had taken out a second one for 30,000 limpiras, or US$1,600, to buy the shiny blue truck that he now uses to deliver orders.

With the right tools and materials, and a reliable vehicle, Jose is now surpassing his competition in quality and customer service, all thanks to access to capital through Bancovelo. He has more clients than ever and is employing two nephews to help him between their classes at the local high school. "Someday, when Dina and Axel are old enough," he promises me, "they will help me too, but only after they get their studies done!"

Juan Pirir, a client of ACCION partner Génesis in Guatemala City, Guatemala, has another story of success to share. When Juan was a boy, he had to work in the fields to help support his family instead of attending school. With little opportunity in his small village in rural Guatemala, he continued working the same fields into adulthood. But in order to support his six children, Juan needed to supplement his meager income. So he began to dabble in woodworking. Soon, he was spending his mornings on the farm, and his afternoons and nights building couches and chairs. He started selling them on the side, but the process was slow and the returns low. "I only had a couple of tools, and they were all manual." he recalls. "I would work for three days to build just one couch."

Then Juan heard about ACCION's partner, Génesis. With his first small loan, he invested in an electric saw. Sixteen loans later, he has a full workshop of tools, including a modern table saw. Employing several neighborhood boys part-time, he can now turn out one couch a day. Several nights a week, Juan travels two hours each way to sell his furniture in Guatemala City.

The profits from his business have enabled Juan to add a room and a tin roof to his concrete house. But most importantly, he is able to provide an education for his children. "When I was young, I had to work. Now all of my children are in school," he smiles. "It makes me happy to give them an opportunity I never had."

Alice Nkugwa is a client of ACCION partner Uganda Microfinance Limited (UML), and she can tell you that a successful business is not just about making enough money. "When the business is good, you don't get tired," she says with a smile. Alice, age 36, and her two employees work long hours, serving meat, beans, and chips at the carryout she opened three years ago. After working for seven years as a seamstress and dressmaker, Alice realized something critical: she would never "make enough money" in that line of work alone. Today, in addition to sewing shirts and dresses at home, she is dedicated to keeping her carryout open Monday through Saturday—and even some Sundays.

Alice received her first loan from UML in 2002, buying cooking oil, flour, and meat with the precious cash. Since then, she has received four other loans, the most recent for 1 million shillings, or approximately $550. The sum is more than she has ever handled, but she's not worried: "I have confidence in my business."

"We would be badly off without the loans," Alice says. "I'm not only running a business, I'm supporting my three children and four of my brother's, too." With a growing savings account and the experienced UML staff supporting her, Alice has peace of mind about her business—and ambitious plans for the children's futures. "I want them to learn so they can get a job to work." With business this good, Alice's energy is boundless. She is planning on opening another carryout soon. And her plans do not stop there: "Someday, I will build a house to rent out. You can make good money with that, too," she says proudly.

Yet another client eager to share her success story is Lucila Mendoza Moisin, a client of ACCION partner Fundacion Ecuatoriana de Desarrollo in Otavalo, Ecuador. Lucila wanted to give her children everything she never had: a decent house, an education, and the skills to land a good job. But Lucila knew she could never realize that dream on her maid's salary. So when she became pregnant with her first child, she opened a business of her own, a craft stand in Otavalo's famous market. To buy inventory, Lucila and her husband had to turn to a neighborhood loan shark. Soon they were spending most of their profits on interest payments. Lucila's dream began slipping away.

Then she found an alternative: Fundacion Ecuatoriana de Desarrollo. She borrowed US$100, paid off their debts, and stocked up on inventory. Today, after three loans, the couple has earned enough money to buy a small house of their own. Now Lucila is optimistic about her children's future. "My parents didn't have enough for me to study," she says. "With my children, it will be different."

You can find similar ACCION success stories around the globe. All of ACCION's microentrepreneurs have the same dreams and hopes: the chance for a better life for themselves and their families.

HOW HAS ACCION DEALT WITH CHALLENGES?

ACCION concedes that the road has not been without bumps. The organization has had to adjust—sometimes in a major way—how it operates several times over the forty-five years of its history. One major obstacle surfaced early in the life of the organization, and remains a challenge for it and all nonprofits. Then executive director John Hammock was on a fundraising trip to Pittsburgh as Bill Burrus visited New York, both attempting, on the same day—a day later referred to as

"Black Friday"—to secure significant and much-needed grants that would keep ACCION afloat. Both were turned down, and neither had any idea how they were going to make payroll the next week. Perseverance and determination gained the upper hand, though, and proved that ACCION was much more than an idea and that it would continue to prove viable.

After that day, Burrus and Hammock decided they needed to be more creative and experiment with different ways to help solve the funding problem. According to Bruce Tippet, another founding member, they began examining their work in Brazil, where they had begun experimenting with microlending. Although the business world did not believe poor clients had the resources or "moral fortitude," to quote Tippet, to pay back loans, ACCION had a different impression because the organization had had first-hand experience with members of the community, and believed in their integrity.

Within that first year of microlending, 1973–74, ACCION discovered something that has proven to be a cornerstone of microfinance and has made it an effective tool in helping to alleviate poverty: the poor can be good credit risks. When the numbers came in, ACCION found that its clients were repaying their loans at a rate of 99.9 percent.

Once the organization had proof that microlending could be effective, the next major obstacle to overcome involved expanding the model—to help more people. ACCION wanted to reach millions of people, not merely the hundreds their Brazilian pilot program had begun to assist. Over the years, ACCION persisted in its beliefs and practices, but remained flexible—ultimately achieving what many had previously thought to be impossible. More than forty years later, ACCION continues to grow and adapt to ever-changing times and world conditions, and successfully: at the close of 2007, the number of active clients served by its partners was over 3 million, in no fewer than twenty-five countries.

Until recently, ACCION had never had the financial reserves to be truly confident that it could build a sustainable organization over time. But one of the hallmarks of the organization has always been its adaptability, which has allowed it to change its approach time and again to suit needs and market conditions. ACCION has evolved from community developer, to microlender, to loan guarantee provider, to investor, and to more, and in so doing, it has grown independent of some of the major sources of funds that initially sustained it. Today, public funds account for only a tiny fraction of operating revenue. ACCION has increased private contributions, together with corporate philanthropy, enormously. For example, in September 2006, ACCION received a grant of over $5 million from insurance giant American International Group Inc. (AIG). As it expands, ACCION knows that developing and providing new financial tools for the poor, such as microinsurance, in order to allow microfinance to move beyond credit, is critical to help achieve scale. The AIG grant is assisting ACCION to realize that goal.

Perhaps even more significantly, ACCION has recently realized major assets from an investment in Mexican MFI partner Compartamos, which ACCION made through its Gateway Fund in 2000. Compartamos's enormously successful

IPO in April 2007, which underscored the viability of commercial microfinance and the deep interest of capital markets in the field, not only proved a seminal event for microfinance overall, but provided ACCION with a far, far stronger financial foundation.

ACCION today is growing exponentially, compared to the past. By the end of 2007, the organization had already expanded to over 200 employees, and microfinance had more than made its way into public awareness. One employee said recently that two and a half years ago, barely anyone was acquainted with the word "microfinance"; today, it is a term recognized by most individuals at the grocery store. With this growth rate, ACCION admits it will need to remain flexible as the pressures rise. Nonetheless, it admits there are things it could do, or could have done, better.

"If there was one thing I would have done differently, it would have been to change our name early on to something more 'marketable,'" says Bill Burrus. "We've suffered over the years because our name is not pronounceable by many people, and others just assume we're a Latin organization." Also, "I wish I had understood how to better raise the profile of ACCION for fundraising and recognition purposes," he concedes. "Over the years, we've been a well-kept secret that has often limited our ability to do our work. We've always been resource starved, in part, because we didn't market ourselves aggressively to the public."

WHAT'S NEXT FOR ACCION?

ACCION's approach is called the commercial model of microfinance. By ACCION's estimates, anywhere from 30–50 million people currently use microfinance to improve their lives, mostly through working capital loans. ACCION believes, however, that for microfinance to reach the billions of people that could benefit from it, a more scaleable and sustainable model of microfinance must be followed.

ACCION is expanding the parameters of microfinance by helping to engage commercial partners such as major banks and insurance companies, and helping its partner monetary financial institutions (MFIs) to tap capital markets. Now that the poor have proven to be credit worthy, ACCION's goal is to continue to demonstrate, as the Compartamos IPO has shown, that the industry is investment worthy. Microfinance as a viable asset class allows an MFI in a developing nation to issue bonds or equity to fund its growth and build its organization, reaching more and more of the entrepreneurial poor. ACCION believes that only through this commercial approach can microfinance truly scale to reach the hundreds of millions of people who could benefit from access to financial services.

ADDITIONAL COMMENTS BY ACCION

ACCION has published books, reports, and monographs that can be downloaded from the Publications section of their website. The topics range from predictions for microfinance in the next ten years to summaries of ACCION's conference series, Cracking the Capital Markets. ACCION says that the organiza-tion takes a great deal of pride in its thought leadership and industry expertise, and this manifests itself in the publications it produces.

MANAGEMENT AT ACCION
María Otero

María Otero is president and CEO of ACCION International, a leading global microfinance institution that seeks to open the financial systems in developing countries to reach the poor. Ms. Otero first joined ACCION in 1986 as director of its lending program in Honduras, where she lived for three years. She became the president of the organization in 2000.

Ms. Otero is a leading voice on sustainable microfinance and has published extensively on the subject, including as co-editor of *The New World of Microfi-nance* published by Kumarian Press. Ms. Otero chairs the board of ACCION Investments, a $20 million investment company for microfinance, and co-chairs the Microenterprise Coalition. She also serves on the boards of directors of micro-finance institutions in Latin America. Ms. Otero serves on several other boards as well, including that of the Calvert Foundation, the United States Institute of Peace, and BRAC Holding of Bangladesh, the largest nongovernmental organiza-tion (NGO) in the world.

From 1995 to 2005, Ms. Otero served as the chair of the MicroFinance Network, a global association of 30+ lending microfinance institutions. She chaired the board of Bread for the World from 1992–1997. In 1994 President Clinton appointed Ms. Otero to serve as chair of the board of directors of the Inter-American Foundation, a position she held until January 2000. She has also served in an advisory capacity to the World Bank's Consultative Group to Assist the Poorest (CGAP).

Since 1997, Ms. Otero has been an adjunct professor at the John Hopkins School for Advanced International Studies (SAIS). In 2000 she received *Hispanic* magazine's Latina Excellence Award, and was also featured in *Latina* magazine. In 2005 she was profiled in *Newsweek's* special report "How Women Lead" as one of twenty influential women in the United States.

María Otero has an MA in literature from the University of Maryland and an MA in international relations from John Hopkins SAIS. She was born and raised in La Paz, Bolivia, and resides in Washington, D.C.

William Burrus

In June 2000, William Burrus was named president and CEO of ACCION USA, a nonprofit organization created to fulfill ACCION's mission in the United States. Previously, Mr. Burrus had served as executive director of ACCION International from 1980–1994, a period of dramatic organizational development. In 1994 he agreed to lead ACCION's U.S. initiatives in the newly created position of senior vice-president of the U.S. division.

Mr. Burrus has dedicated most of his professional career to international development with a focus on Latin America. He began his career as a volunteer with the Peace Corps in the Dominican Republic. He and his wife later served as co-directors of an integrated rural development program in the state of Hidalgo, Mexico, sponsored by the American Friends Service Committee. In 1973 Mr. Burrus joined ACCION in Costa Rica as regional director for Central American and the Caribbean.

By the end of 1994, when Mr. Burrus began to focus his efforts on the United States, ACCION had developed a network of affiliated microenterprise programs in thirteen Latin American countries and five U.S. cities. By 2006, the U.S. ACCION Network had grown to five separate licensee organizations, three direct lending offices, and an Internet lending capability that, together, enabled the organization to lend nationwide.

Mr. Burrus holds an undergraduate degree in sociology from Arizona State University and a master's in international management from the Thunderbird Graduate School of International Management.

Mr. Burrus has received the Warren Award, Service to Humanity from Verde Valley School, and a Career Achievement Award from the Thunderbird Alumni Association.

ORGANIZATIONAL SNAPSHOT

Organization: ACCION

Executive Director: María Otero

Mission/Description: ACCION International is a private, nonprofit organization with the mission of giving people the financial tools they need—microenterprise loans, business training, and other financial services—to work their way out of poverty. A world pioneer in microfinance, ACCION was founded in 1961 and issued its first microloan in 1973 in Brazil. ACCION International's partner micro-finance institutions today are providing loans as low as $100 to poor men and women entrepreneurs in twenty-five countries in Latin America, the Caribbean, Asia, and sub-Saharan Africa as well as in the United States.

Website: www.accion.org

Address: ACCION International & ACCION USA Headquarters

56 Roland Street

Suite 300

Boston, MA 02129 USA

Phone: +1.617.625.7080

Fax: +1.617.625.7020

9

Invisible Conflicts/The Dwon Madiki Partnership

Evan Ledyard, Nathan Mustain,
Amy Nemeth, Katie Scranton,
Morgan Smith, David Thatcher,
Carolyn Ziembo, and
Diana Zurawski

INTRODUCTION
Evan Ledyard

Invisible Conflicts is a student organization at Loyola University in Chicago; it started out with only ten people, and within two years rapidly expanded to over 100 members. After uncovering heartbreaking atrocities in Northern Uganda, these students took the initiative to facilitate change in the lives of individuals living in zones of conflict worldwide. With limited resources, experience, time, and knowledge, the group did what it knew how to do best—build friendships. After creating personal relationships with the community in Gulu, Uganda, Invisible Conflicts launched the Dwon Madiki Partnership—a program that provides twenty war-torn orphans with an education, emotional support, health care, and more.

The following pages contain the personal stories of the individuals who created Invisible Conflicts and the Dwon Madiki Partnership, and the people who inspired them. It begins with the story of the cofounder, Nathan Mustain.

FOUNDER'S AUTOBIOGRAPHY
Nathan Mustain

I am a high-school dropout and recovering addict. But now, instead of cocaine and speed, I thrive on justice and love. On a Habitat for Humanity work trip, I found the reason to clean up my life: love. This encounter with love challenged me to become a better person. In this new life, I now have the pleasure and privilege of working with my friends to make the world a better place—one life at a time, through Invisible Conflicts.

HISTORY OF THE WAR
Nathan Mustain (research by Amy Nemeth)

In the fall of 2005, I read an article in *Smithsonian* titled "Uganda, the Horror." The piece described a twenty-year-long civil war in northern Uganda[1] that spawned a disaster that Jan Egeland, United Nations Undersecretary-General for Humanitarian Affairs in 2003, described as "the world's biggest neglected humanitarian crisis."[2] The war between the Ugandan government in the South and the rebel army, the Lord's Resistance Army (LRA) in the North, has persisted since 1986. This conflict has devastated the area in northern Uganda known as Acholiland[3] and created a horror for the children of this region.

With the people of northern Uganda growing weary of war, the rebels resorted to kidnapping children to fill their ranks. The LRA targeted children between the ages of five and fourteen. They did so because children are easily brainwashed and big enough to carry guns, but small enough to sneak into villages and schools to kidnap more children. Once they were taken into the bush, the children were immediately desensitized, forced to watch other abductees being tortured and brutally killed, and often forced to partake in the killings themselves.[4] Their victims were often mutilated, for example, left alive without toes, fingers, or lips. Vaginas and lips were punctured and padlocked shut. Children were forced to lick the spattered brains off their friends' cracked and crushed heads, which they were forced to beat to a pulp as they screamed and begged for mercy.[5] To ensure that the children did not escape, the LRA commanders sometimes forced them to kill their own parents, eliminating any possibility of returning home.[6] Since 1986 more than 30,000 children have been abducted.[7]

To escape nighttime abduction by the LRA and its brutal army of children, the children of Acholiland began to commute every night to Gulu, the main town in northern Uganda. Every night, thousands of children, called "night commuters," would flock to Gulu to sleep in the streets, under verandas, in the bus park, and in hospital corridors.[8] The war in northern Uganda created a generation of children too afraid to sleep in their own homes. At the same time, they have been robbed of a formal education.

As the war dragged on, the LRA's raids on villages and schools grew more gruesome. In an attempt to counter the insurgency in 1996, the Ugandan government forcibly displaced all northern Ugandans who lived in rural areas and moved them into internally displaced person camps (IDP) camps. According to the government, such extreme measures were necessary to protect the civilian population and to cut off the rebels' access to small farming villages, which were their main source of food and child soldiers.

The government gave the Ugandan people twenty-four hours to uproot their lives and move into these camps.[9] Anyone found outside the camps after the deadline would be treated as hostile rebel combatants. As of 2006, about 1.5 million Ugandans lived in the IDP camps where diseases, such as ringworm, malaria, and HIV/AIDS, run rampant as a result of the horrendous conditions in the camps.[10]

People living in camps rely completely on foreign aid, such as from the World Food Program, for survival since the Ugandan government provides almost nothing.[11]

After I first learned of the crisis, there were two things that especially horrified me. First, I was repulsed at the thought of children being brainwashed, mutilated, and forced to kill. Upon further reflection, what began to haunt me even more was the fact that I had never heard about this war. I had always made it a point to stay up with news. I read the *New York Times,* listened to NPR and the BBC, and considered myself relatively well informed. But this war had been going on for two decades, and I had never heard of it. Why was the world not outraged at this holocaust? It was not as if people didn't know. If *Smithsonian* could publish such a revealing article about it, the governments of the developed world must also have known. Why were the media reporting nothing? Why were the powerful governments of the world doing nothing? I decided I would make it my business to talk about this conflict. I would do my part to bring it into the public eye.

I made quite a nuisance of myself. At the gym, between classes, and at parties, I was constantly saying to my peers, "So, have you heard about what's going on in Northern Uganda?" I read everything I could find about the conflict and its history. I made it my personal mission to tell this story to anyone and everyone who would listen. And in contrast to the stereotype of the apathetic American student, people did care. My fellow students wanted to do something to stop these crimes against children, but they felt powerless. I constantly heard "Wow, I really want to help, but what can one person do?" My inevitable response was "Maybe one person can't do much, but if we work together, there's no limit to what we can accomplish."

Yet in order to gather crowds of like-minded people together, I needed a way to tell this story to many people at once. I discovered it by accident as I continued to bring up the topic of children soldiers at parties when people were having a good time. One time during spring break, at a University of Texas party, I made my usual comment, "You'll never believe what's going on in Northern Uganda . . . ," when someone replied, "Yeah, I know, I just saw this incredible documentary about it called *Invisible Children.*" He told me that his fraternity brothers had watched this movie together, and it had gotten them fired up to take action. As soon as I got home, I visited the Invisible Children website and ordered a copy of the DVD. When it came in the mail two weeks later, I watched it and was floored. It was more than a documentary. It was a call to action. I knew I had my medium for telling this story to my peers.

INVISIBLE CHILDREN
Amy Nemeth

Invisible Children is a youthful, grassroots organization that began in 2003 when three college-aged American men decided to travel to Africa. Originally, Laren, Jason, and Bobby set out to document the story of refugees from Darfur, Sudan. However, because of the war, they could not fly into southern Sudan, and ended up in northern Uganda instead. Gulu, the largest city in northern Uganda, is the center for the United Nations Peacemaking Mission to Sudan. The three filmmakers decided that this would be a good starting point for their story. One day, as they were traveling to Sudanese refugee camps, the truck in front of them was shot up by Ugandan rebels, members of the Lord's Resistance Army (LRA), and they were forced to turn back and stay in the town of Gulu for the night. The city was completely overrun by unsupervised children, sleeping in every place imaginable—under porches, in the bus park—and hundreds of them were packed like sardines on the floors of a local hospital. The three filmmakers began asking them questions, and realized that they had never heard of the civil war in Uganda. The story they discovered "shocked and inspired" them.[12]

These three filmmakers soon learned that northern Uganda's conflict had ravaged the region since 1986. The rebel LRA, led by Joseph Kony, aimed at overthrowing the Ugandan government to institute a government based on the Ten Commandments. Having little support from the people of northern Uganda, the LRA resorted to kidnapping children as young as five to fill their ranks. It is estimated that up to 90 percent of the LRA are children.[13] Laren, Jason, and Bobby made a documentary to tell the story of the "invisible children"[14] of northern Uganda, who have become both the weapons and the victims of this conflict.

After the filmmakers returned to the United States, they intended to share this documentary with their family and friends only. But soon they began screening it across the nation. At each screening event, people kept asking them, "What can we do?" Out of a need to do more, Jason, Laren, and Bobby created Invisible Children Inc. The mission of Invisible Children is "to improve the quality of life for war-affected children by providing access to quality education, enhanced learning environments, and innovative economic opportunities for the community."[15]

The film is exciting and entertaining, and helps audiences connect to the humanity of the children affected by the war in a way that our over-stimulated MTV generation can apprehend. I contacted the offices of Invisible Children in San Diego and asked them for promotional materials so I could hold a screening at Loyola University in Chicago, where I was a sophomore at that time. It turned out that *Invisible Children* was on a national tour, and they had a team visiting Chicago the following January. I thought that in the meantime, I would hold a screening myself.

THE FIRST SCREENING
Nathan Mustain

I tried to reserve a room on campus for the screening, but the office in charge of such matters informed me I could not do that unless I belonged to an officially recognized student organization. At that time, I was not part of any campus organization. I was a science geek. I spent all my free time holed up at the gym or with my nose in a book. I had not plugged into any of the campus clubs that were involved in social justice work. When I approached these campus groups, none of them showed interest, since they were all busy with their own projects. That was understandable, but very frustrating. How could I do it alone? So I tried being a little sneaky, and set a precedent for Invisible Conflicts' MO for the future: "It is easier to ask forgiveness than to ask permission."

I knew my friend Joey had started a campus club called Sangha before he graduated the previous year. So I called and asked him what I had to do in order to become a member. He said, "I hereby dub thee president." I now had authority to sign contracts with Invisible Children, reserve rooms, and put up promotional material on campus, all under the name of Sangha. Little did the university know, but Sangha had never held an official meeting or a single event.

I made banners and put up posters all over campus, on coffee shop bulletin boards, and in various spots in the local community. I e-mailed every professor on campus. I invited them and their classes to attend the screening, and explained why they should care, with different arguments for different disciplines. I wrote e-mails tailored specifically to political scientists, biologists, psychologists, and sociologists. I wanted everyone to know.

Although I put my phone number on all the posters with a note inviting people to help with the screening, only two people responded. One was Morgan Smith, a sophomore transfer student who had been in the process of organizing a screening of the film herself. We joined forces, and together we promoted the screening more effectively. Dr. David Kanis was the other person to call after seeing a poster at a local coffee shop. Dr. Kanis explained that he had been to Uganda several times, had in fact taught at a university in the heart of the conflict region, and knew the filmmakers of *Invisible Children* personally. He offered to come to the screening along with a couple of his Ugandan friends, and to respond to audience questions. On a cold night in January 2006, Morgan Smith, my friend Jeremy John, and I sat in Loyola's Galvin Auditorium (we had been joined by the crew of the *Invisible Children* national tour) and waited to see if our efforts had paid off. Morgan brilliantly thought to ask everyone for their e-mail addresses on the way in. It was her thinking that enabled the founders of Invisible Conflicts to come together. The auditorium filled to capacity, with nearly 300 people.

By the end of the screening, there was not a dry eye in the crowd. Then Dr. Kanis came to the front with his Ugandan friends, including a six-year-old boy named Joshua, recently from Gulu, and said, "This is the face of the war in Uganda. This child right here would be a prime target of the LRA rebels. It is children just like him who are being abducted every day and subjected to horror and brutality beyond anything we could imagine." At that point, the crying in the audience became audible. I was struck by how powerful it was to put a human face to the stories we had just heard. It was on this night also that I first met Caroline Akweyo, a beautiful and soft-spoken woman from Uganda who had been abducted by the LRA *three* times, suffered immensely, had her family sliced to pieces before her eyes, and finally made it to the United States where she received political asylum. Caroline shared her story in a very quiet and gentle way that demanded the attention of the audience. She further drove home the point that the people hurt by this war were just like the people in the audience, with real hopes and fears, people who feel pain and joy, and whose lives have been shattered by the bloody chaos of this war.

CAROLINE AKWEYO'S STORY
Interview conducted by Dave Thatcher; recorded by Amy Nemeth

In 1986, when the war began, I was nine years old. My first memory of the war was the killing of my uncle's wife. She was a local brewer, and one of the rebels accused my uncle's wife of poisoning him. The rebels came and cut her into pieces before the whole clan as I was forced to watch. The rebel movement was growing stronger in my village, so my father decided to construct a structure outside of the village where we went to sleep at night to avoid abduction. As time went on, abductions were more frequent, so my brothers were sent to a boarding school.

In 1988 my father was arrested and interrogated by government soldiers because we had a large farm in our village that had become the center for the village. They suspected my father of supporting the rebels. After they found him innocent, they warned him not to return to our village. My father then moved the rest of my family into Gulu-town, which was about thirty miles from our home.

We had no food in Gulu; so my mother, Grace, my sister, Florence, and I had to go back to our farm to collect food. The rebels ambushed us on our way and took Florence and me—they left my mother because she was older. Luckily, my mother was a school teacher, and one of the rebels was a former pupil who recognized her. My mother was able to arrange the release of Florence and me. I was eleven years old at the time of my first abduction.

When I finished primary school, I was sent to Aboke Girl's Secondary [high school] in the Lira District. The war had gotten a lot worse. The rebels were cutting off the legs, ears, and other limbs of civilians, and they were killing people for minor infractions. At Aboke, the rebels would go and abduct girls. While I was in school, there were three different abductions. The school was run by Catholic nuns who would follow the rebels into the bush and attempt to secure the release of the students by bribing the rebels with money. The girls from Aboke were valuable to the rebels because they were educated. Many of the rebels had very little or no schooling, but the abducted girls were still treated as property.

When I was sixteen, I was abducted from Aboke. The school had steel doors in [an] attempt to keep the rebels out. The rebels would shoot at the buildings and threaten to bomb them unless the doors were opened. Once the rebels got into the school, they would walk among us and choose the ones who were tall and slender. The rebels believed the tall and slender girls would be able to walk the longest distances and were also the smartest. I was abducted along with eighty-nine other girls.

For the first few days, we were forced to walk and run long distances. We had to resort to stealing food in order to survive. The rebels immediately attempted to interrogate and brainwash us—we were always under constant threat. The rebels would not let us [the Aboke girls] stay together because they feared that we would try and plot an escape. They paired us up with older girls who had already been in the bush for awhile and had already been brainwashed.

Once in the bush, I was given to a commander to be his fourth wife. While in the bush, I had to watch people being killed, and I was not allowed to show emotion. As a wife, I was treated as property and was expected to stay with the commander at all times. Because I was the wife of a commander, younger girls were given to me and my fellow wives to cook and clean for us.

I was able to escape while we were on the move between Kitgum and Lira. We were attacked by government soldiers and were commanded to lie in the grass until nightfall. After the fighting, everyone got up and continued on the road. I stayed hidden in the grass and did not move or speak for the whole night. The next day, I walked to the nearest village and found the local counselor, who got me in touch with the government. I returned home in 1997 and discovered I was pregnant. I was sixteen years old.

In 1999 I was invited to Chicago on a scholarship to learn how to become a Montessori teacher. When I arrived in the USA, I applied for political asylum and was granted asylum status.

INVISIBLE CONFLICTS BEGINS
Nathan Mustain

With Morgan's list of e-mail addresses from the first screening, we sent out an invitation for everyone to meet once again. Based on what we had heard and seen from the audience at the screening, and on what we had been thinking and discussing, I sent out this e-mail:

Dear Friends,

You are reading this email because like so many others, you have heard the cry of children living under the weight of terror, oppression and injustice, and you have decided to do something about it—i.e., you gave us your email address at the screening of *Invisible Children* last week. This is the call to action. This is an invitation to join the struggle for justice. This is our chance to live for something more.

Perhaps like me, when you watched that amazing film, several questions came to mind, such as

1. WHY didn't I hear about this before?
2. WHERE are the western media?
3. WHAT is our government's stance on the Ugandan conflict, and what is it doing to help bring about a just peace?
4. HOW can I help?

Of particular concern to us is question #4, and answering this question will be the focus of our endeavors. We want to know how we can help. In the near future, a group of people just like you (and including you) will join forces to found an alliance dedicated to answering this call to action we heard so powerfully last Monday night. This group will be dedicated to being part of the solution by attacking the problem in several ways:

1. Raising awareness—it is vital that people hear the stories that our media are ignoring. It is up to us to spread the word. If we are silent, these children will remain invisible, and the murder, rape and abduction will continue. If we tell their story, people will hear. People will act.
2. Raising support—as a group, we will explore ways in which we can raise financial, moral, and political support for those working on the ground both in Uganda, and here in the U.S. This is NOT a political group, but we WILL make it a point to tell our leaders that we want action. We will stand united, in solidarity with our brothers and sisters in Africa.
3. Answering the call—ultimately, we would like to provide opportunities for those who feel called to go to the areas of conflict and work "in the trenches." As Dr. David Kanis said last Monday, "I guarantee you that if 25 thousand American college students show up in Uganda over the next year, we will have MAJOR change." We believe in this vision, and we want to be a part of that first 25 thousand. We are also aware that Uganda is not the only sight of Invisible Conflict, and thus we will not limit ourselves to advocacy on behalf of that country. Rather, we will keep our minds, hearts, eyes and ears open to the cry of invisible conflicts and their invisible victims the world over. Uganda is where we begin.

As they say, "The only thing necessary for evil to triumph is for good men to do nothing." We will not stand by while evil men have their way. We have been inspired by the story told by Jason, Laren and Bobby, three regular guys about our age who decided to make a difference and use their talents to "be the change" they wanted to see in the world. This is our chance to do the same. We all have talents that were given to us for a reason. When we join forces and dedicate our skills and energy to making a difference, there is no end to what we can accomplish. Since this group has not yet formed, this is your chance to help shape it. We are open to suggestions and dependent on you to bring your ideas to the movement. You can make this your thing by bringing your unique talents to the table. Again, now is the time for creativity. Now is the time to educate ourselves and the world. Now is the time to start a movement.

Let's remember the boy at the end of the film who said, "Hopefully since you have a camera; you can't forget about us." We won't.

Earlier, I listed four questions I had after seeing this film. There has been, however, one other burning question that has been with me ever since I saw the film one year ago: WHEN DO WE START? I am very happy to say, that time is NOW.

Please let us know if you want to be removed from this list.

IMMEDIATE NEEDS

I. PHASE ONE: DIAGNOSIS: To hold an open forum open to all those who desire to help found this alliance. At our first meeting, we will work on the following:
A. Identify the problems we will attack
B. Outline our response to those problems

C. Determine how we'll execute our response
II. PROGNOSIS—the nasty details
    A. Discuss how we'll pay for the execution
    B. Brainstorm various roles, offices, administrative and procedural needs, i.e., the nitty gritty
    —(i.e. What's the problem, what're we gonna do about it, who's gonna do it, how're we gonna pay for it; recognize those experienced in dealing with university administration in order to get our club officially recognized by Loyola University.)
    C. Draft a constitution
    D. Elect officers
    E. Get university recognition
    F. Establish a schedule and timetable for the movement
III. EXECUTION—our movement hits the streets
    A. First official meeting as club
    B. First action
    C. First blood.

At our first meeting, about thirty people showed up and we spent a few hours sharing what was on our hearts and minds. During that time, and at the next two meetings, we laid down a few basic tenets we would follow as we formed the culture and structure of our organization. The following is a summary of the vision that took shape during those first meetings.

First, we had to decide whether to focus just on Uganda, or to expand our focus to include other conflicts that are ignored by wealthier and more well-developed countries. We quickly found that the room was charged with passion, and that people hungered both to learn more about other places where unreported conflicts ravaged people's lives and to take action to stop the violence. But we also wanted to focus our energy effectively on the conflicts we learned about. There was an intense desire in the room to know more, to expose the truth, and to fight evil, whether in Uganda or in our own backyards. We felt our generation was sleeping, and we wanted to help wake it up. In order to remain flexible so that we could expand our work to focus on other conflicts in the future, we named our new organization Invisible Conflicts: "Invisible," because we realized that the world was full of conflicts ignored by powerful governments, western media, and college campuses. It was also a tribute to the people of Invisible Children, whose "hip," fun, youthful, and positive approach to changing the world inspired us so much.

Next, we dedicated ourselves to learning all we could about the conflicts we would address. It was important to read history and current news from all perspectives, and especially to engage people from the conflict zones—to hear their stories, get to know them, and help them tell their stories. We believed that if our peers heard these stories, they would want to take action. Our organization would be an amplifier for the voices of victims. We would not speak for anyone, but rather empower people to speak for themselves. We would do this through art, film, public gatherings, political advocacy, and the establishment of personal relationships with people from conflict zones.

We did not want to stop at telling stories. We all felt a strong compulsion to take concrete action. Many of us were frustrated with abstract theoretical discussions about how to make the world a better place. We wanted to create a positive change in the world. Most of us were not from the typical "social justice" crowd. We were average college students from many different walks of life, faiths, political affiliations, and world views. We were united by a passion and a common desire to take action in order to change the world.

To encourage people to join us, we needed to overcome several obstacles. Lack of awareness was the first obstacle that we tackled by educating ourselves as much as possible. Next, we set out to overcome the feeling of powerlessness that infects our generation. To combat this sentiment, we worked out several strategies. First, we would tell these stories in a culturally relevant way. There can be no better example of a group that uses this approach than Invisible Children. Their documentary and other educational videos are done in a fast-paced, hip, and playful style that speaks to our MTV generation in its own language and urges viewers to take action. So we used their movie to help us tell the story of northern Uganda. Another obstacle to greater involvement among our peers was the existence of an "enlightened inner circle," a phenomenon that infects many groups. From the very beginning, the people of Invisible Conflicts made a commitment to reject a culture of exclusivity, and to foster an environment in which people from any socioeconomic, political, or religious background could come together to work for peace. We believed that if change is to happen, we needed to help our peers in making the quest for a better world a part of everyday life. We wanted to enable the future leaders of America, the lawyers, businessmen and women, and accountants to be a part of this movement without feeling ostracized for not selling all they owned and moving to Africa to live in a mud hut. This is why we seek to put the tools for making concrete change in people's hands, making it as simple as possible to make a difference. The earlier people see that their actions can change the world, the more likely they are to integrate the quest for justice into their everyday lives as they move on to build careers and raise families. We believe everyone can help. That is why we resolved to encourage creativity and even to get a little crazy if necessary. We would remain positive, but never deny the horrific nature of the conflicts we sought to end. We were a group of everyday optimists, realists, and idealists, and we knew we could change the world, one story at time.

But it was not enough to tell these stories. We wanted to be changed by them, and to become a part of them. We came to realize that it is one thing to fight for peace on behalf of "poor children" in Africa, but it was another to do so for one's friends. That is why we dedicated ourselves to establishing personal relationships between people in our own community and those in conflict regions. By using technology and art to communicate, we would build friendships with people in northern Uganda. We would also send people to the region to gain empathy and understanding, and to make friends.

Fostering relationships in conflict regions has been an extremely important part of our work. The things we have learned and gained through these friendships have transformed us and brought us both pain and joy. From the beginning, we agreed that our guiding principle would be humility. We were not anyone's "savior," and we rejected the hierarchy of paternalism. We have resources to share as wealthy Americans from a nation of power and privilege. Yet we were plagued by problems ourselves and, therefore, had much to learn from our friends in conflict regions. We were never under the illusion that we had the answers to all the world's problems. Rather, we wanted to make friends, to help them where we could, and to allow them to help us.

Once we established that we had much to learn, we agreed that we would not wait to act until we felt "qualified." We would take action whenever possible. All our actions were guided by our mission:

> We recognize that the world is full of invisible conflicts ignored by mainstream media and governments. We enable the victims of these conflicts to tell their stories, and we establish real and personal relationships between communities of power and privilege and those of poverty and oppression. Through the mutual exchange of values and knowledge, we find practical ways to help one another, and transform communities, both at home and in conflict regions. Committed to cultural relevance and positivity, we encourage everyday people to take action by giving them simple and concrete ways to make a difference. By taking action ourselves, we lead the way for our peers.

TAKING ACTION: ENDING A WAR
Nathan Mustain and Morgan Smith

We had identified the problem: There had been a war targeting children ravaging Uganda for twenty years, and most of the world did not know about it. The people of Uganda needed to tell their stories, and the world needed to help them stop the war and bring about a just and prosperous peace.

How could the problem be solved? The Sudanese government needed to stop funding and arming the LRA rebels. The people of America had to speak together and give our leaders the political capital they needed to take a stand for northern Uganda's children. If the United States pressured the Sudanese government to stop financing the war, and pressured the Ugandan government to take serious measures for peace, the war could be stopped. We needed to mobilize the American people and harness the power of the media.

Our first actions were to hold public screenings of the film *Invisible Children*. Afterwards, our new friend and advisor, Caroline Akweyo, shared with the audience about her life in Uganda. This was always a powerful experience that enabled the audience to connect with what they had just seen in a human way. To everyone who walked through the door, we gave a pamphlet listing simple things everyone could do to make a difference. With the pamphlet were blank sheets of paper and pens, with which we encouraged everyone to write a letter to the government representative of their choice—right then and there. We projected a sample letter onto the screen at the front of the auditorium, but encouraged people to speak from their hearts about what they had just learned from Caroline and the documentary. This tactic helped audiences see the power that individuals can have when they come together. Then we collected the letters as people left, stamped them, and mailed them. Since the first screening of *Invisible Children*, we have mailed nearly 1,000 letters to government officials.

In addition to a large letter-writing campaign, Invisible Conflicts began a campaign to ask Oprah Winfrey to cover the crisis on her show: we sent her sixty roses, with a note stating that each rose represented 500 children that had been abducted in northern Uganda. Naturally, we cannot take full credit for the segment about northern Uganda and Invisible Children on her show just months after our campaign began, but we did receive a call asking us to *stop* sending Oprah e-mails— they had gotten the picture.

Noting the success of our group at organizing large screenings, the Invisible Children organization asked us to arrange and promote a peace vigil in Chicago as part of a worldwide event they were planning called the Global Night Commute. We provided volunteers to run the event, and promoted it all over Illinois. Over 2,000 people showed up, and most stayed all night in Grant Park, despite a constant downpour of frigid rain. We also bombarded the media with press releases and got coverage by most major news outlets in Chicago. In cities throughout the world, nearly 100,000 people participated in the Global Night Commutes. That night, almost everyone wrote a personal letter to their state representatives and to President George W. Bush, asking for the promotion of peace in northern Uganda. It is said to be the largest demonstration concerning African issues in U.S. history. The Senate took note and issued a joint resolution calling for peace in Uganda. They promised to allocate more resources to peace efforts, to increase humanitarian aid, and to help the Ugandan government rebuild infrastructure once peace came. The rebels and the Ugandan army signed a cease-fire shortly thereafter, which, though tenuous, has held a fragile peace in place ever since.[16]

Aware that the work was not over when the guns fell silent, Invisible Conflicts has continued to work for a lasting and just peace in northern Uganda. In October 2006, we sent a delegation to Washington, D.C., for the northern Uganda lobby days. The weekend was packed with speakers, including Betty Bigombe, the ambassador from Uganda, and Ugandans who had been abducted by the LRA. The last day was spent talking to Illinois senators Barack Obama and Richard Durbin, as well as U.S. Representative Jan Schakowsky's (D–IL) representatives about supporting the peace talks that were taking place in Uganda. The trip revitalized our understanding of the importance of raising our voices and asking for change. The organizations sponsoring the lobby days held a symposium for the students so that they could get a better understanding of the war in Uganda. As informative and important as it was to comprehend the situation, we got frustrated with everyone trying to theorize why there is such chaos in Uganda. It reminded us why we love Invisible Conflicts: we want to *know* the kids that bear the stories of the country. We want to make relationships and partner with them so that they know they are not alone. Uganda lobby days reiterated for us the importance of (1) building a strong connection with the people of Uganda and (2) taking political action as often as possible. The weekend in Washington, D.C., showed us that both are valuable and needed in order to create change.

Our efforts to open the eyes of our community to the atrocities occurring in northern Uganda paid off. Since 2003, when Invisible Children made their documentary, night commuting and child abduction in northern Uganda have ceased. In 2006 a cease-fire was declared and peace talks have ensued between the Ugandan government and the LRA. Because of pressure from civil society, many international actors, including the United States, have sent envoys to Uganda to show their support for the peace talks.

One remarkable thing we learned from the many Ugandans we met through our advocacy work was what they wanted for their country. Whenever we met Ugandans, we made it a point to ask what they thought their country needed. Every single time they replied, "Education." If Ugandans wanted education, we would do our best to help them get it.

THE DWON MADIKI PARTNERSHIP
Dwon Madiki Beginnings

Katie Scranton

My first taste of Uganda was in the Chicago home of Caroline Akweyo. Caroline had been attending screenings of the documentary *Invisible Children* for months, willingly sharing her unfathomable stories of being abducted by the LRA in Uganda. Invisible Conflicts had invited Caroline numerous times to share her experiences, and she always humbly accepted. As in any relationship, it took time before we could all become friends with Caroline, our new Ugandan acquaintance. I spoke to her only briefly after screenings, filled with curiosity as to how a woman could survive war, cross an ocean, and so effortlessly speak to entire audiences of college students, professors, and locals. During the following summer, two of the founding members of Invisible Conflicts, Morgan Smith and Nathan Mustain, began meeting with Caroline in hopes of forming a personal connection between the Chicago-based college group and the children of Gulu, Uganda. Caroline told them that her mother, Grace, was a teacher in Gulu and had always dreamed of starting an orphanage for children affected by the war. Because of limited resources, Invisible Conflicts decided to put quality over quantity by supporting a small number of children instead of attempting to build a large orphanage. Providing about fifteen kids with an education at the primary level was, initially, the most realistic task for the group.

The next fall, Morgan and I often visited Caroline's home in Rogers Park, a north-side neighborhood of Chicago, to discuss the vague, unformed ideas of supporting the education of a few kids in Gulu. First, we had to narrow down which children we would sponsor. Ultimately, we decided to support those that were most vulnerable—children orphaned by the war or by the AIDS pandemic.

Our talks about the evolving partnership in Gulu were often interrupted by the smell of homemade Acholi food as Caroline would appear from the kitchen insisting that we eat dinner. We soon learned to show up at Caroline's without a tight schedule or a full stomach. The side conversations between Caroline and her family in Luo, the food we were eating, and the unhurried pace of our visits made Morgan and me feel as if we had left the United States for a few hours and landed in Gulu. We were becoming friends with a woman of shocking history and immeasurable strength. Even after all she had been through, Caroline did not stop sharing her story and cooking dinner for us.

On the day of the Gulu Walk, Caroline and members of Invisible Conflicts joined many others in solidarity with the people of Uganda by walking eight miles through the streets of Chicago. Morgan and I were strolling down the sidewalk casually talking to Caroline when an idea surged. We asked Caroline, "How do you say 'the voice of tomorrow' in the Acholi language?" She paused to think for a few moments. After searching the language of her childhood and her far-off home, she replied, "I guess that would be something like Dwon Madiki." A name for the growing project had been born. The naming of the Dwon Madiki Partnership was not simply the choosing of a few words—it was creation of a vision. Our hope increased as we realized that our efforts would amplify the voices of children who had been robbed of a say in their own futures. A year later, Caroline's daughter, Stella, said that in Gulu, the name Dwon Madiki "has a ring to it when people hear it there . . . the name is like poetry."

The first responsibilities of brainstorming for the Dwon Madiki Partnership were passed on to Morgan and to me. Who were we to design a framework for a program in a country we had never visited and for children we had never met? We did not speak their language. We did not know their names. We were not acquainted with the protocols and procedures of an international nongovernmental organization (NGO). We did not even know how to call Uganda, let alone start an educational partnership.

Later, Morgan and I arrived at a local café on Sheridan Road, ordered sandwiches, found a table, and let our minds wander. Our conversation was a whirlwind of ideas and theories and visions and themes we had each individually thought of for some time. *How do we support these kids . . . we should amplify their voices . . . we can't speak on their behalf . . . we need to let them do the talking . . . how can they express themselves to us . . . if they take pictures of their lives and do art, we could use it here somehow . . . we could do art exhibits . . . we could invite people and make it a fundraiser . . . how many kids can we support . . . what are we even doing . . . we've never done this before . . . how could we . . . we're only college students . . . what's the first step . . . how do we move from theory to reality?*

Without the chance to dialogue and build off of each other's inspiration, we would not have been able to piece it all together the way we did. And even then, our plan was not totally straightforward or even feasible.

At our next Invisible Conflicts meeting, Morgan and I felt as if we would burst. We had been filled with some indescribable sense of direction that I would attribute to no one more capable than God. We entered the room that Thursday night at eight o'clock with overwhelming anticipation. The development of it all had unfolded before our eyes, and it was now time to update the group on progress. Since both of us were somewhat hesitant to speak in front of everyone, we talked to each other before the meeting. *How much do we tell? Our ideas are not very well formed yet. Should we wait to update everyone until we have a more concrete vision?*

Our hesitancy was probably the result of more than just shyness or insecurity. When I asked myself why I would be apprehensive to tell such exciting news to the group, I had to confront a deeper, more personal possibility. The moment Morgan and I opened our mouths, the vision for the partnership would no longer be *ours.* In fact, it never was ours in the first place, but in that moment, we were reminded that this belongs to everyone. This indeed *is* a partnership because it is held together not just by Morgan and me, but by Caroline and Grace and everyone in Invisible Conflicts, and especially by the children in Gulu.

Morgan began that night, uninhibited. She shared the ideas of exchanging art and exhibits. She told of the new name, the Dwon Madiki Partnership, which even uses the Acholi's native language, Luo, to capture the vision of amplifying the voice of Ugandans. The secret was out. And to our relief, the responsibility was no longer on our shoulders alone. We were joining forces. Our excitement had spread to all corners of the room. Our ideas were not judged for their likelihood or perfection. Instead, they had been welcomed as the first steps toward the formation of a relationship with strangers across the world.

I heard the voice of Uganda for the first time late one night in a tiny Chicago apartment. I had never used an international phone card before. It was about midnight when I called because I was told it would be early morning in Uganda. The number was so long I almost forgot why I was calling, and the sound the phone made was so foreign to me that I was not sure if it was a ring or a busy signal. I heard the bright, accented voice of a woman answer while roosters sounded in the background. About a year before, I did not even know where Uganda was in Africa, and now I was calling to that distant country, trusting that there was actually a woman there named Grace, and that she would be expecting a call that morning before she left for school. We stumbled through the conversation because of the delay, but our delight to finally speak to each other dispelled any awkwardness.

Soon after, Grace began informing us of their needs and hopes for the partnership. They agreed on the name Dwon Madiki, and she said that the first move was to rent a small office across from Lacor Hospital in Gulu and buy a sign to put out front. The estimate was $30 a month to rent the office and about $10 to have a sign printed (see Photo 9.1). This was the first time that Invisible Conflicts had to be financially conscientious. Paying rent every month meant we were entering into a long-term commitment. There would be no turning back. Our first wire transfer to Grace was just enough for the rent, a sign, and a few office supplies, such as a stapler and a desk.

Photo 9.1 The Dwon Madiki Partnership office is located in the Labor Trading Center in Gulu-Town, Uganda. It serves as both office and center for the after-school program. Courtesy of David Thatcher.

I'll never forget the photograph Grace e-mailed to us of her in the office, with nothing but a stapler on the desk. Yet that simple photograph captured the determined spirit of a woman in circumstances we had never known. The photo captured the face of a new friend and the beginnings of our journey as a partnership.

We took the first step to get to know the kids. One afternoon, we invited Invisible Conflicts members to write and decorate short questionnaires for the kids. We brainstormed fun, innocent questions to ask the kids, and we let them know they could answer either in writing or in pictures or both. Our desire was to include all the kids, so we asked Grace to help those who were too young to write. That day, about seven of us finished more than a dozen colorful sheets of paper, full of questions for the children, and mailed them off, eager to hear back from the kids.

As a group, we felt that we could initially provide for fifteen kids at the primary school level. That fall semester, we started meeting with Caroline to narrow down the category of children we would sponsor, deciding that we would support those that were most vulnerable.

We regularly communicated by e-mail and occasionally by phone. Grace had chosen which kids would be included in the partnership based on criteria such as need, loss of parents, and trauma from experiences with the LRA. One day we got an e-mail with an attachment. All the little pictures and short biographies had been taped onto a sheet of paper, scanned, and e-mailed to us. There on a bright computer screen at Loyola University Chicago were fifteen beautiful faces with names. These were the faces of Dwon Madiki.

Weeks later, a thick package arrived in the mail filled with little drawings and our questionnaires—complete with answers to our questions in the delightful crayon scrawls of children. The drastic variety of their pictures stirred us. Some were of young girls cooking and boys playing soccer, while others were of soldiers, machetes, severed limbs, helicopters, bullets, blood, and death. The answers to our questions were just as varied. Some wrote that their favorite thing to do was eat or play, while others wrote that their favorite thing to do was fight. In response to the question, what makes you laugh, some had simply written "fighting," or had drawn two men with guns (see Photo 9.2). We all held their art in awe and could finally feel a bit of these kids' reality.

It was clear we could not simply stop at exchanging art. It was time to move forward with the children's education. Grace, as always, did work before we even asked her to. She had already found local schools for each child and had arranged their placements with the teachers. Now all that was lacking was money. It was early November; their school fees were due by January, or else the kids would miss out on an entire term of schooling.

While Grace was putting the program together in Uganda, the students here in the United States were working on fundraising. How would we make enough money to get these kids through the year? Most of our money had come from small donations from the screenings, bake sales, and T-shirt sales. We discussed increasing bake sales and T-shirt sales, but knew that these alone would not be enough. So, in keeping with the young, innovative, and certainly ridiculous approach of Invisible Conflicts, we figured out how to raise the $6,000 in less than two months.

Late one night at Morgan's apartment, about a dozen of us gathered to brainstorm over some take-out Mexican food. An idea appeared out of nowhere. Partly as a silly joke, and partly out of frustration for lack of a better idea, I shouted, "Why don't we just jump in the lake?" After a brief moment of silence, Nathan replied, "Why not?" Soon everyone was convinced that it was the best, most insane way we could raise $6,000 in two months.

We were now going to jump into freezing Lake Michigan in the dead of winter. The name I.C. Plunge was cleverly coined. We divided up tasks such as who would research the safety, who would contact lifeguards, who would begin drafting an I.C. Plunge information packet, and so on. Who would have thought that too much Mexican food, a joke of an idea, and a few inspired college students would add up to the birth of an educational partnership in Gulu, Uganda?

I.C. Plunge 2006

Morgan Smith

December 2, 2006, was the day of the first annual I.C. Plunge. After barely a month of planning the day's activities, creating art to reflect our goals and desires

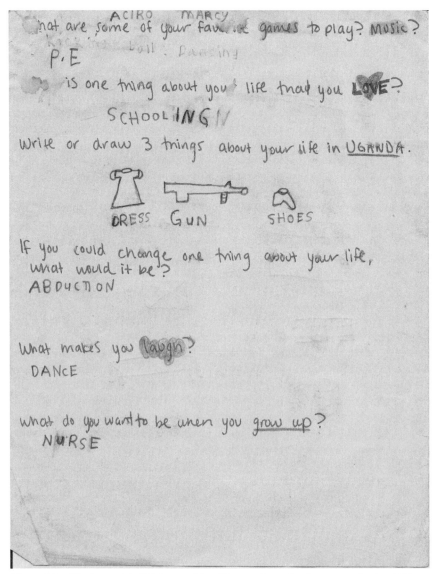

hat are some of your fav___ games to play? MUSIC?

ACIRO   MARCY

P.E   ___ Dancing

__ is one thing about you life that you LOVE?

SCHOOLING

Write or draw 3 things about your life in UGANDA.

DRESS   GUN   SHOES

If you could change one thing about your life, what would it be?
ABDUCTION

What makes you laugh?
DANCE

What do you want to be when you grow up?
NURSE

Photo 9.2 The Dwon Madiki Partnership offers an after-school program for the children of Dwon Madiki and the surrounding community. This artwork was made by Aciro Mercy, a child in the after-school program. Courtesy of the Dwon Madiki Partnership.

for Dwon Madiki, and raising capital, the I.C. Plunge came into existence. Over thirty-five people jumped, and two hundred showed up in support. Together, we raised over $7,000, exceeding our goal by $1,000. The level of collaboration between students, Chipotle Mexican Grill, Metropolis Coffee Company, and bagel shops that occurred in such a short period of time was humbling. Many people took action right away and pursued various avenues of creativity to assist in the dynamic production of the I.C plunge. Students from schools all over Illinois, including the University of Illinois at Urbana-Champaign and the University of Illinois–Chicago, showed up ready to jump into the cold water. Invisible Conflicts members facilitated the sign-in and money collection, and dispersed information about the Dwon Madiki partnership. At around one o'clock in the afternoon, all thirty-five plungers headed outside into the frigid December air to take part in an idea that started off as a joke and would end up transforming lives of twenty students in another country. The jump was exhilarating. That something so silly could change someone's life created an odd sensation. After we warmed up, ate some food, and drank hot chocolate, the amount of money raised was announced. It was shocking enough that we actually met our goal, but raising $1,000 above that opened our eyes to the possibilities that exist when we are courageous enough to be adventurous with our creativity.

The Establishment of Dwon Madiki

Dave Thatcher and Diana Zurawski

Before the plunge, the Dwon Madiki Partnership was little more than an idea. On December 2, after the participants had dried off, the costumes had been judged, and the money had been counted, the idea became a reality. By early January, Invisible Conflicts had deposited over $7,000 in the bank and had four members preparing for a summer trip to northern Uganda to set up the partnership.

During the months of January to May 2007, the foundations for the partnership were laid. Dwon Madiki evolved from the mere fiscal sponsorship of education to a holistic program with integrated after-school and holiday-break components. Equipped with little knowledge of how to set up such an organization and program, a couple of members spent long hours on the phone communicating with Grace Odonga, the director in Uganda, trying to evaluate the immediate logistical costs needed to get started.

We began by wiring money to pay for school uniforms, scholastic materials, and school fees, allowing the kids to begin their first trimester of the year. Next, money was sent for basic start-up costs. We purchased a computer, printer, desks, and other needed supplies for the office. Slowly, a legitimate office and program began to emerge. The kids started to come to the office after school, and Grace, along with four volunteers she had recruited, began to provide them with activities such as art, traditional music, and dance training. As the months went on, Invisible Conflicts continued to receive packages of the kids' artwork. They were beautiful, heartbreaking, and endearing. Drawings of guns and war were scattered in between sketches of children playing and families cooking. All twenty-one of the kids were victims of a war that had robbed them of a childhood and of the most basic human rights, such as adequate housing, nutrition, health, and security. This realization powerfully hit home when at some point, one of the children, Jimmy Komakech, mysteriously disappeared. To this day, we have no idea where he is or what happened to him.

With so many factors working against the kids' capacities to succeed in life, we realized that just paying for their school fees was not enough. How could they do well in school and in life beyond if they received only one meal a day? Could the children succeed if they were exposed to debilitating sicknesses and diseases? How could we deal with guardians who are never fully invested in their education?

It was these early insights that helped us to understand the need for a more comprehensive framework and a holistic program that would address the myriad issues affecting the kids. As this framework was developed with Grace and her volunteers, the mission and vision of the Dwon Madiki Partnership was born.

VISION
The Dwon Madiki Partnership (DMP) works for a world where orphan and vulnerable children of northern Uganda are provided the necessary resources, support and environment to succeed in school and achieve holistic development of self, family and community.

MISSION
The DMAP empowers children to succeed in school and life through

- provision of quality education
- engagement in & access to holistic development, activities, resources and mentorship
- fostering of personal relationships with students in Chicago through media, art and technology

In addition to the vision and mission, an ethos, or a set of guiding principles, also emerged regarding how we would accomplish the mission and operate a successful program. These guiding principles reflect that the program is a partnership, and not a charity. We call them The Four E's:

Guiding Principles—The Four E's

Educate ourselves and others
Engage in meaningful, concrete, and sustainable ways to be catalysts for change
Exchange ideas, stories, and wisdom to foster real and personal relationships
Empower ourselves and others through education, engagement, and exchange

Following the establishment of the framework, vision, and mission, another important expansion of the partnership occurred when Invisible Conflicts teamed up with the Gear Up Alliance—a federally funded program that works with failing inner-city schools to prepare kids for postsecondary education. Invisible Conflicts members spent time with kids from failing inner-city Chicago schools during a summer camp operated by Gear Up. Members of Invisible Conflicts, Diana Zurawski and Laura Morales, talked with the kids about conflict, violence, and conflict resolution in their own communities. The culmination of the program was a conference call between the Dwon Madiki children in Gulu and the Gear Up kids in Chicago, during which they dialogued and connected over common experiences, hopes, and appreciation of hip-hop star 50-Cent. The final question of the event was particularly poignant: a thirteen-year-old Chicago student inquired, "Do you ever get afraid to walk alone at night?" His voice had a certain sense of familiarity as though he, too, knew the fear he spoke of. The students on the other end of the line answered truthfully, explaining how war has affected their daily lives.

Because we felt it was not enough to carry on a distant relationship if the program was going to succeed, in the summer of 2007, we sent four members, Dave Thatcher, Amy Nemeth, Lauren Springstroh, and Monica Mormon, to finally meet our friends in Gulu, Uganda. As the departure for the summer trip drew closer, the group began to organize fundraising events, donation drives, and sensitization campaigns. Donations included cameras, art supplies, clothes, toys, a web cam for the office, vitamins, toothpaste and toothbrushes, soccer balls, and more school supplies. All together, the four traveling group members had a combined total of twelve bags (nine of which arrived in Uganda two weeks after the travelers did). The traveling team left on May 31 and arrived in Uganda on June 1. The kids in Gulu were extremely excited to meet the students, and wrote and sang this song for them: "I woke up in the morning and heard that my school fees were paid/For, that someone would care for my life so far away in the States/I wish, I wish that the angels, that the angels would never depart/And if it is possible to open our hearts, for you to see our love for you."

Seeing the program firsthand and witnessing the social, physical, and economic conditions within which the kids lived was a life-changing experience for the group. It was an experience of paradoxes: bubbling happiness arising from kids who lived in a sea of suffering. At the office, the kids seemed to play happily as if they had not a care in the world, but it was in talking to their guardians and in visiting their homes that the atrocities of the war and the dire needs it had created became apparent. Besides the horrible economic and physical conditions the war had created, every child in the program had a personal experience of violence. Many had been born in the bush to mothers who had been abducted. Some had been forcibly made to witness torturous killings. Others had friends or family members who had been abducted, never to be heard from again. It all constituted a trauma-ridden life, through which the kids were astoundingly resilient.

So how were college students, some just eighteen years old, supposed to understand and develop—in partnership with a school teacher a thousand miles away with her small cadre of young volunteers—a program that could address such issues? Was it even possible? During their stay, the team collected data from surveys conducted with the kids, their guardians, and their teachers. These interviews, supplemented by pictures and voice and video recordings, recorded the plight of children in northern Uganda. This documentation provided not only vital information as to how the program could be improved, but it also allowed the group to help the children by telling their stories in the United States and advocating on the kids' behalf.

The team was invited as guests on the main radio station in the North—Mega FM—to speak about the Dwon Madiki Partnership. The following day, the office was flooded with members of the community who had children they wanted to enroll in the program.

After a summer of listening to and documenting stories of the war, engaging the community, spending time with the kids and their guardians, and seeing firsthand the IDP camps, the team returned with a wealth of knowledge concerning what needed to be done to empower the kids in Uganda in order to make the partnership more effective. Four developmental categories were identified to structure the after-school activities. These activities would address a range of issues impeding the kids' ability to succeed in life, focusing on holistic development of self, family, and community. A specific vision and mission was created for each category:

Health
  Vision: The DMP works for a world where orphan children of northern Uganda will perform basic hygiene, have adequate nutrition, practice proper disease prevention, respond in a healthy manner to emotions, and acknowledge their self-worth.
  Mission: DMP will provide supplies, adequate meals, education of disease process and preventive measures, emotional explanation and support, and encouragement.

Social Values
  Vision: The DMP works to help children develop a positive self-image in order to encourage healthy social relationships with family, peers, and community.
  Mission: The DMP will help through multimedia activities, community events, and fun activities that encourage teamwork.
  Nurture and understand cultural values
  Develop a strong sense of self-worth
  Create modes of communication between children and community members

Life Skills
  Vision: DMP works to provide children in northern Uganda with the necessary resources to help them envision their goals and future aspirations.
  Mission: This will be achieved through motivation:
    Provide exciting learning and multimedia tools
    Encourage goal setting through steps
    Cultivate positive self-image
    Develop a self and community value system

Education
  Vision: The DMP strives for an environment in which children in northern Uganda would receive quality education, internalize its worth, and have access to the necessary support in order to achieve their academic goals.
  Mission: The DMP will
    Pay school and lunch fees
    Provide school supplies, uniforms, and tutoring
    Facilitate relationships with positive role models in the community
    Provide educational, interactive activities
    Cultivate the value of education with family and peers

Uganda Trip, Winter 2007

Amy Nemeth and Carolyn Ziembo

To build on this momentum, we knew that we needed to continue developing the program. In the fall of 2007, we began planning for another trip to Uganda. Three members volunteered to go during the month of December—Amanda Fuentes, Graci Willis, and Kate Reynolds. By assessing the situation in Uganda from the previous trip, we had determined the kids lacked proper health education. In order to give the children of Dwon Madiki the proper tools to be successful in life, we decided to prioritize a health initiative for the trip. The main goal was to implement a health program—which worked out well since Amanda and Kate were both pursuing nursing in school. The girls left with a mission to incorporate health instruction and health care into the children's after-school program. This was to help facilitate basic health skills, such as learning facts about germs and how to fight infection in everyday life circumstances. Other objectives of the trip were to re-evaluate the after-school program and progress of the kids, conduct more documentation and needs assessment surveys, and begin recording the kids singing, playing instruments, and reciting poems for a CD project.

I.C. Plunge 2007

Morgan Smith

To make the winter trip feasible and to sustain DMP for a second year, it was time for another chilly swim. Since group membership had more than quadrupled, and in light of the previous I.C. Plunge's astounding monetary result and the large number of plungers, we decided to challenge ourselves by raising our goal to $12,000. Unlike the previous year, we had time to prepare. During the entire fall semester, we vigorously encouraged college students, high school students, church congregations, and Loyola University faculty members to join in the I.C. Plunge. The teamwork that took place to prepare for the event was outstanding. We even involved local polar bear clubs, radio stations, and newspapers to help spread the word about the fundraiser. After all, the I.C. Plunge had been added to the "Top 100 Things to do at Loyola."

With the amount of time we had to organize the event, at the I.C. Plunge reception, we were able to demonstrate to the participants the significance of the partnership through artwork and our own video documentary. To demonstrate the four developmental categories of DMP (health, social values, life skills, and education), pictures of the children in their daily activities were displayed by each category throughout the entire room. But the artwork was not just there for show—it was interactive, allowing people to respond to the kids by sending them their thoughts, encouragement, and prayers. The kids in Uganda even gave the plungers some encouragement. One DMP orphan was asked, "How do you feel about all them jumping into a freezing lake for the I.C. Plunge?" He said, "To me they are doing it because they love us, like they are suffering for us."

Eventually it was time for the plunge, and roughly 300 people were waiting at the beach for support. The weather was terrible. It was snowy, icy, and incredibly windy. Braving the harsh conditions, sixty-five plungers stormed into Lake Michigan, shouting and laughing—and for the first time in her life, our dear friend Caroline Akweyo stepped into a body of water. Once all the donations were counted—the vast majority in $10s and $20s—we had surpassed our goal of $12,000 by raising over $15,000.

Amplifying Voices

Carolyn Ziembo

The artwork at the I.C. Plunge 2007 was an enormous success, and since we have made it a point to *empower* and *amplify* the voices of the unheard, Invisible Conflicts was given a unique opportunity to let the children of DMP tell their stories with an exhibit at the Push Pin Gallery in the Loyola University Museum of Art (LUMA) in the spring of 2008. This public exhibit featured drawings and poems by the children, photographs taken by and of them, and other media, including bracelets and banana leaf creations all crafted by the Dwon Madiki kids. The LUMA exhibit was a thrilling opportunity for the children to explain and illustrate their stories through their own work. One of Dwon Madiki's tenets remains to *engage*; thus, the exhibit asked viewers of the gallery how they felt about what they had seen, and explained what they could do to help and empower the children of the DMP. By allowing the children to tell their stories to people from across the world and by engaging these people in Invisible Conflicts' mission, the LUMA exhibit brought inspiration to many guests because of the children's spirit and faith against all odds.

VISION FOR THE FUTURE
The Dwon Madiki Partnership

Carolyn Ziembo

Invisible Conflicts and DMP plan to continue evolving and improving. In November 2007, we purchased a plot of land near our Gulu office. The land, in conjunction with a previously owned plot, will combine to create more free space for the children to play. On this land, Invisible Conflicts wants to build a soccer field, net-ball field, school, and eventually a new office. In addition to these improvements, we would like to move all the DMP children into top Ugandan schools in the area. With increased funding, the children will receive better education in private schools, and have better resources and more qualified teachers.

We have chosen to provide a sustainable means of education and empowerment, making sure each child successfully finishes his or her schooling. A quality and stable education prepares children to achieve and discover their goals in life. Thus, Dwon Madiki plans to make sure each child in the program completes secondary school.

The Dwon Madiki Partnership has become a positive force in the community of Acholi people. They come from around the area to watch the children dance and sing songs. The hopeful nature of the children has brought together all kinds of people, especially in difficult times. Eventually, we plan to increase the economic sustainability of Dwon Madiki in Gulu by fostering successful revenue-producing endeavors, therefore lessening the partnership's reliance on our financial assistance. We hope that our Ugandan partners will be able to sustain the program on their own in the future.

The Democratic Republic of Congo

Amy Nemeth

Another vision we have is to expand beyond Uganda and establish programs similar to the Dwon Madiki Partnership in other conflict regions. Since our establishment in 2005, we have been looking into other areas that have yet to be exposed to the Western world. In 2006, we were told the story of the Democratic Republic of Congo's (DRC) struggle and knew we could not turn our back on the DRC.

Four times larger than France, the Democratic Republic of Congo is situated in the Great Lakes region of Africa.[17] The DRC has vast mines of diamonds, gold, copper, cobalt, coltan,[18] and cassiterite.[19] Its history has been one of conflict and instability, influenced by the foreign policies of its neighbors and by policies of Western countries such as the United States. In 1998 it was the center of a war that involved six other African nations. The Second Congo War (1998–2002) also ushered in a period of foreign investment, during which many contracts made with Western or multinational corporations were done through third parties. Very little profit from these resources found its way back to the Congolese people.[20] It is estimated that three million people died during the Second Congo War.[21] Because the conflict that still plagues East Congo is an international one, we believe that the international community has the responsibility to bring peace to the DRC. Peace in the DRC would greatly facilitate the establishment of peace in the rest of Africa.[22]

At Invisible Conflicts, we believe that, with knowledge and the right tools, people have the power to make a difference in the world. On November 30, 2006, we hosted the investigative journalist Keith Harmon Snow at Loyola University–Chicago. Before an audience of Loyola students and faculty, Snow enlightened the community on the atrocities that are committed daily in the DRC, and he also gave us concrete ways to stop these atrocities.[23]

We firmly believe that a partnership between communities of power and privilege and communities of poverty and oppression is necessary to bring about positive change; thus, we strive as much as possible to listen and to partner with people from regions of conflict. In 2006 we partnered with Nugalula Kela, a member of Friends of the Congo,[24] and Jacques Bahati, a member of Africa Faith and Justice Network,[25] in order to better educate ourselves.

Invisible Conflicts also seeks to lead by example. In 2006 we participated in the Run for the Congo 5K walk and run event in Lincoln Park, Chicago. Through this event, we showed our solidarity for the Congolese and raised awareness among the Chicago community. In 2007 we formed a DRC committee that is dedicated to finding ways to educate ourselves and our community on the situation in the DRC. We hope to screen documentaries about the DRC to the Loyola community and to host more speakers to talk about the DRC. The DRC committee has also provided us with a sample letter and key contacts in the political and business communities that have the power to influence an end to the atrocities being committed in the DRC. In 2008 we are planning to participate in the DRC lobby days in Washington, D.C., to encourage our legislators to make the DRC a priority.

CONCLUSION
Evan Ledyard, Katie Scranton, and Dave Thatcher

As the partnership between the students at Loyola University–Chicago and the community in Gulu continues to grow, Invisible Conflicts has expanded to the University of Illinois at Urbana-Champaign (UIUC). The UIUC chapter of Invisible Conflicts, led by Nathan Mustain's brother, Patrick Mustain, in the United States and by Deacon Leonsyo in Uganda, has formed a partnership with the community of Pajule, Uganda; the group plans to create a program similar to the Dwon Madiki Partnership. Establishing more partnerships between other universities and communities around the world is what Invisible Conflicts hopes to witness in the future. By building more partnerships around the globe, more relationships will be formed and more lives impacted.

You may hear people say that some situations are hopeless. But it is never hopeless. With the relationships Invisible Conflicts has formed over the past three years, the group has seen the faces of real people in these situations staring back with hope. It is easy to just write off devastating situations as hopeless, but we find hope through our relationships with others—and that takes a lot of time, trust, openness, and commitment. Members of Invisible Conflicts have learned that creating change requires many small steps, and that the Dwon Madiki Partnership did not evolve without guidance or hard work. As Invisible Conflicts has demonstrated, doing big is not always the best way to foster change, but that big change can be found in the smallest of actions. However, the important thing is simply *to act*. Recognizing the importance of action, a member of Invisible Conflicts, Katie

Scranton, has said, "I know that I cannot touch everyone's life. I know that I am capable of so little. And yet in response to such a crisis, I have to make a decision. Either I love one person fully, or I love no one at all. Either I speak to one person with hope, or I speak not at all. Either I enter into service and uncertainty, or I move not at all. Either I become friends with a woman in Uganda that I've never met, or I come to know no one at all. Either I see hope in the foreground of despair, or I truly see nothing at all."

It is of this kind of belief and passion that the late Senator Robert Kennedy spoke in an address to the University of Cape Town. He said, "Few will have the greatness to bend history; but each of us can work to change a small portion of the events, and in the total of all these acts will be written the history of this generation. . . . It is from numberless diverse acts of courage and belief that human history is thus shaped. Each time a man stands up for an ideal, or acts to improve the lot of others, or strikes out against injustice, he sends forth a tiny ripple of hope, and crossing each other from a million different centers of energy and daring those ripples build a current which can sweep down the mightiest walls of oppression and resistance" (Day of Affirmation Address, June 6, 1966).

We are standing up. We are raising our idealistic voices against injustice. Tiny ripples of hope are emanating from bake sales, screenings, letters, and summer adventures, carrying themselves from the shores of Lake Michigan to the heart of war-torn Uganda. These ripples are traveling the thousands of miles between shores on currents of intimate, personal, and empowering relationships. And they are gaining momentum.

This is our story. It is a story of countless small actions and of the development of true friendships. This is a story in which a few hundred small donations opened a world of possibility, and where lives were changed on both sides of the Atlantic. Its success lies in the enduring, purposeful relationships that were established and that give so much meaning to life. In the very act of empowering others, in helping some to overcome the structures of poverty and oppression, we have in turn been empowered. The children of Dwon Madiki have empowered us with hope and with understanding. We have learned so much through our interactions with them. As they have recounted their stories of growing up in the midst of war, we have been able to glean what it means to embody courage and strength. This has carried over to all that we do and has given us the courage to continue forward.

As the kids' grades continue to improve and as three meals a day become a constant occurrence in their lives, the ripples continue to spread. Our first child graduated from middle school this past year and will be moving on to high school. Her name is Joan, and she wants to be a doctor. She has discovered empowerment for the first time, and her story is our story. To quote the social activist Margaret Mead, "Never doubt that a small group of thoughtful committed citizens can change the world; indeed, it is the only thing that ever does."[26]

APPENDIX: WHAT YOU CAN DO
Act with Invisible Conflicts–Loyola:

> Participate in the I.C. Plunge
> Donate to us online at www.invisibleconflicts.org
> Start a chapter of Invisible Conflicts at your church, high school, or college
> E-mail us to see how you can get involved at invisibleconflicts. loyola@gmail.com

Act on YOUR Issue/Passion: SMALL Ways to Make a Difference

Educate Yourself:

> Research the issue
> Google alerts
> Talk to people from the conflict regions (from local NGOs, etc.)

Gather People:

> Find others concerned about a similar issue
> Talk to local schools with likeminded groups
> Contact churches
> Send out e-mails
> Make Facebook groups
> Put up posters in café

Begin to Act:

> Screen documentaries
> Present at functions
> Meet people from conflict zones
> Ask them how to partner
> Contact local art stores for supplies
> Write to the government (go to http://www.congress.org/congressorg/home/ to find the contact information for your officials in Congress)

Links

Websites: Uganda

> www.invisibleconflicts.org
> www.invisiblechildren.com
> http://www.ugandarising.com/home.html
> http://www.ugandacan.org/
> http://www.enoughproject.org/uganda

Websites: Democratic Republic of Congo

http://www.afjn.org/d.r.congo/overview/
http://www.enoughproject.org/congo
http://www.friendsofthecongo.org/
http://www.runforcongowomen.org/

Sample Letter: Uganda

Dear _____,

I write to express my deep concern about the conflict in northern Uganda. For more than twenty years, the Lord's Resistance Army (LRA) has been fighting to overthrow the government of Uganda. The LRA rebels have captured more than 30,000 children to use as frontline soldiers and sex slaves.

Fear of abduction causes thousands of children to flee their rural homes each night. The conflict has uprooted at least 80 percent of northern Uganda's population, and up to 1.3 million people live in squalid camps that usually lack adequate clean water and sanitation.

Leadership from the United States can bring peace to this troubled region. I respectfully ask that you advocate for the following:

The U.S. must support and strengthen the Juba peace process.
Peace talks are at a critical time right now and need support from the U.S. and the international community to succeed.
Call the State Department, urging them to publicly support the peace talks.

- Increase humanitarian and development assistance for northern Uganda.
- More than 1.3 million people are displaced by this conflict and are dependent on international assistance. Please see that U.S. aid will not be decreased even though there is now relative peace in the region.
- Please call for and participate in public hearings to examine the crisis in northern Uganda.

Your attention to this urgent matter can drastically improve the lives of those in northern Uganda —especially those of children.

Sincerely,

_____

Sample Letter: Democratic Republic of Congo

Dear _____

Although in recent months peacekeeping efforts in Darfur and Northern Uganda have been gaining greater media attention, one conflict has remained under the radar. Violence in the Democratic Republic of Congo has reached a critical point.

According to the Enough! Project (www.enoughproject.org), 260,000 people have been displaced, and dozens of innocent bystanders have been injured or killed as a result of factionalized militant groups such as the Rasta militia. The relations between these many groups are incredibly complex; among the militias are groups led by Hutu rebels who were involved in the 1994 genocide in Rwanda. Many of these militias have been involved in brutal atrocities against villagers in the DRC. Adding to the complexity of the military operations are the UN peacekeeping missions, which have been reduced to barely more than an observer role.

The time to act is now. The United States, a leading player on the global stage, needs to work with our allies and the UN in order to press the Congolese government to neutralize these militant groups and develop an aid plan, including the stabilization of both the political and humanitarian crises in the DRC. More detailed information on this and other conflicts is available at www.enoughproject.org. As one of the wealthiest and most powerful nations in the world, the United States government needs to step up its awareness and aid of all conflicts, not just those gaining media attention.

Sincerely,

_____

Thank you!

Acknowledgments

All of us at Invisible Conflicts would like to express our thanks to

- Invisible Children, whose moving documentary inspired us at Loyola University–Chicago to take action. We have learned so much from your organization, and we thank you for your courage and insight.
- Dr. David Kanis, our exceptional resource for the conflict in northern Uganda. You have taught us so much, and we can not express our gratitude for your patience in our journey to establish our group.
- Caroline Akweyo, your strength has been an inspiration to us all. You have become a wonderful friend and advisor to our group. Without Caroline, the Dwon Madiki Partnership would not be in existence.
- Grace Odonga, our director in Uganda, who has dedicated countless hours and resources to helping us make the Dwon Madiki Partnership a reality. We cannot thank you enough for opening up your heart and home to the children of Dwon Madiki.
- The volunteers at the Dwon Madiki Partnership: Kevin Opira, Paul Onono, Lily, Robert Komakech, and Simon Ojara for your dedication to the success of the Dwon Madiki Partnership.
- Drew Tessler, our dear friend from the Gear-Up Alliance. Your kind heart and hard work is what has connected lives between students in Chicago and DMP.
- Jacques Bahati, our invaluable contact into the horrors of the conflict in the Democratic Republic of Congo. Your passion has aroused us all at Invisible

Conflicts to take action to help end the conflict in the DRC. Thank you for opening our eyes to another tragic conflict in the world.

- Dr. Patrick Boyle, who was our faculty advisor for the first two years. Thank you for putting your faith in our brand-new group.
- Dr. Chris E. Stout, a new friend to Invisible Conflicts. We thank you for giving us the opportunity to be a part of this project. We look forward to years of alliance and mentorship in the future.
- Dr. John Donoghue, our new friend and faculty advisor. Your encouragement and support has meant so much to us; it gives us hope for the future of Invisible Conflicts.
- Our families and friends of Invisible Conflicts. Your love, support, and prayers have made us who we are today. Thank you for your patience and understanding, despite our constant bombardments for things such as pledges to jump into Lake Michigan in December.

ORGANIZATIONAL SNAPSHOT

Organization: Invisible Conflicts/Dwon Madiki Partnership

Founder: Nathan Mustain

Mission/Description: Invisible Conflicts is a student organization that sponsors the education, mentorship, and empowerment of twenty Ugandan orphans and vulnerable children. A twenty-one-year civil war in northern Uganda, between the government and a rebel faction called the Lord's Resistance Army (LRA), has led to the forced displacement of over 1.7 million people into internal refugee camps. To support their rebellion, the LRA abducted over 30,000 Ugandan children, forcing them to be sex slaves and fight as soldiers. Because of these atrocities, all of the Dwon Madiki Partnership–sponsored children live in squalid conditions in and around the many displacement camps. Since life around these camps is marked by poverty, hunger, and little or no access to education, an entire generation of children find themselves denied a childhood and a chance to succeed in life. The Dwon Madiki Partnership, by funding the education of these children and addressing their developmental needs, offers them a chance to succeed and in turn give back to their communities, thus helping break the cycles of poverty and violence caused by the war.

Website: www.invisibleconflicts.org

Address: Invisible Conflicts

Crown Center

6525 North Sheridan Road

Room 546

Chicago, IL 60626 USA

Phone: (412) 5807284

E-mail: invisibleconflicts.loyola@gmail.com

NOTES

1. P. Raffaele, "Uganda: The Horror," *Smithsonian* (February 2005) (retrieved from http://www.smithsonianmag.com/people-places/uganda.html?c=y&page=1).

2. Uganda Conflict Action Network, "Religious Sign-On Letter for Peace in Northern Uganda" (2006) (retrieved December 22, 2007, from http://www.ugandacan.org/signonletter.php).

3. C. Mansour (writer), and L. Poole and J. Russell (directors), *Invisible Children* [motion picture], (USA, 2005). Acholi is an ethnic tribe from Uganda. Many Uganda simply call northern Uganda "Acholi-Land" because the majority of the population from northern Uganda are Acholis.

4. *Invisible Children*, 2005.

5. P. Raffaele, "Uganda: The Horror," *Smithsonian* (February 2005) (retrieved from http://www.smithsonianmag.com/people-places/uganda.html?c=y&page=1).

6. P. McCormack (writer), and P. McCormack and J. J. Miller (directors), *Uganda Rising* [motion picture] (Canada: Mindset Media, 2006).

7. Uganda Conflict Action Network, "The Conflict" (2006) (retrieved December 21, 2007, from http://www.ugandacan.org/history.php).

8. *Invisible Children*, 2005.

9. Invisible Children, History of the War (retrieved October 11, 2007, from http://www.invisiblechildren.com/about/history/).

10. K. Drews, "A Long Way Gone: Four LU Students Volunteer in Uganda." *Phoenix, closer look* (September 12, 2007).

11. D. Thatcher (producer/writer), *Freezin for a Reason* [motion picture] (USA, 2007).

12. *Invisible Children*, 2005.

13. Invisible Children, History of the War.

14. These children are "invisible" because "they roam distant battlefields away from public scrutiny, because no records are kept of their numbers or age, because their own armies deny they exist" (*Invisible Children*, 2005).

15. *Invisible Children* (retrieved October 11, 2007, from http://www.invisiblechildren.com/theMission).

16. *Invisible Children* (retrieved January 5, 2008, from http://www.invisiblechildren.com/theMovie/media/).

17. History of the War, *DR Congo's Life or Death Transition* [Motion picture] (USA: Catholic Relief Services 2006).

18. Coltan, or colombo-tantalite ore, is used to make pinhead capacitors and is an essential component used in all cell phones. Congo contains 80 percent of the world's reserves of coltan.

19. Cassiterite, or tin oxide, is a mineral used for electronic circuit boards. It is the most traded metal on the London Exchange.

20. Natural Resources in Conflict: Democratic Republic of Congo. (n.d.), *Global Witness* (retrieved January 2, 2008, from http://www.globalwitness.org/).

21. Country Profile: Democratic Republic of Congo (2007, October 13). *British Broadcasting Company* (retrieved January 2, 2008, from http://news.bbc.co.uk/2/hi/africa/country_profiles/1076399.stm).

22. J. Bahati (2007, November 3). Interview with Jacques Bahati. Interview presented at lunch with Invisible Conflicts.

23. W. Barrett (2006, December 6). Hidden Reality: Award-winning journalist Keith Harmon Snow visits Loyola to discuss. *Phoenix*, news (retrieved January 2, 2008, from

Loyola University Chicago website: http://media.www.loyolaphoenix.com/media/storage/ paper673/news/2006/12/06/News/Hidden.Reality-2523951.shtml).
24. http://www.friendsofthecongo.org/.
25. http://www.afjn.org/.
26. The Institute for Intercultural Studies (retrieved June 12, 2008, from http://www.inter culturalstudies.org/faq.html#quote).

10

Building Educated Leaders for Life (BELL)

Earl Martin Phalen
and Teresa Barttrum

Building Educated Leaders for Life (BELL) is a nonprofit educational organization that runs academically focused programs for children. The organization defines education broadly but divides it into three main categories: the mastering of the basic skills, the development of social skills (in terms of how people interact as a community), and the knowledge of self.

BELL recognizes the pathway to opportunity for children lies in education. BELL transforms children into scholars and leaders through the delivery of nationally recognized, high-impact summer and after-school educational programs. BELL exists to dramatically increase the academic achievements, self-esteem, and life opportunities of children living in low-income, urban communities. BELL pursues a goal that 100 percent of their scholars will achieve academic and social proficiency in their formative elementary school years. It is the organization's hope that BELL scholars will graduate from college and pursue meaningful career paths. They will, hopefully then, give back to their community. They will be great fathers and mothers, friends and mentors, leaders and citizens. BELL is one part of a larger movement of social entrepreneurs dedicated to the evolution of society and the achievement of a more equitable and just world.

BELL sees itself as a part of the civil and human rights movement. The organization's leaders believe in persistence, unyielding faith, and acknowledgment of past sacrifices. Earl Martin Phalen, BELL's cofounder and CEO, refers back to the days of the Montgomery, Alabama, bus boycott. Individuals risked their security and their children's security for something that was right. Therefore, Phalen believes that when individuals are able to step back and immerse themselves in history, in terms of recognizing the sacrifices others are making to achieve a particular goal, individuals quit complaining because they realize that what individuals do today does not even come close to the sacrifices that were made to open doors for us today. This recognition underlies the patience and drive for BELL's success today.

By helping children achieve academic and social proficiency during their formative elementary school years and embrace their rich cultural heritage, BELL is inspiring the next generation of great teachers, doctors, lawyers, artists, and community leaders. By mobilizing parents, teachers, and young adults, BELL is living the idea that "it takes a village to raise a child."

BELL was founded in 1992 by a group of black and Latino students from Harvard Law School as a community service project conducted at the Agassiz School in Cambridge, Massachusetts. Led by Earl Martin Phalen and Andrew L. Carter, the law students wanted to give back to the community in the same way others had given back to them or had opened opportunities for them in their lives.

The students began a small tutoring program in a local school in Roxbury, Massachusetts, where most children could not read, write, or do math at grade-level proficiency. The students quickly discovered it was easy to get their scholars' aspirations to rise, but most of the children in the program had not mastered the basic foundation of academic skills that would allow them to meet their heightened dreams.

After the first pilot program with its initial group of twenty scholars, Phalen and his colleagues were motivated by their results. They then partnered with a group of parents and decided a need existed to formalize a program. Phalen believed the mentoring portion of the program inspired children and helped them to believe in themselves, so this portion of the pilot program remained. A rigorous academic program was added to help make sure the scholars mastered the three Rs: reading, writing, and arithmetic.

BELL was able to follow this initial group of twenty scholars and discovered that every member had enrolled in or graduated from college, compared to only 30 percent of their peers.

In 1993 BELL partnered with both the Agassiz Elementary School in Cambridge and the Tobin Elementary School in Roxbury, and established itself as a nonprofit organization. Co-founder Earl Martin Phalen continues to lead BELL, and Phalen's mentor, Harvard Law professor Charles Ogletree Jr., served as board chair for thirteen years before transitioning to board chair emeritus.

BELL evolved and complemented its BELL After School Program with the BELL Summer Program in 1996 to achieve an even greater impact on children's lives. BELL soon began making partnerships, winning awards, and maintaining quality service as it evolved. It was not long before BELL found itself expanding to other cities. In 1997 BELL expanded to New York City and two years later began work to Washington, D.C.

As of 2007, BELL has 12,180 scholars in the summer and after-school programs. BELL now runs programs in Baltimore, Boston, Detroit, New York, and Springfield (MA). BELL's original group of twenty volunteers has expanded to approximately 1,200 employees; 1,000 of these are part-time positions. Of the 1,000 employees, 50 percent are teachers, and the other 50 percent are college and

Figure 10.1   BELL hopes, in pursuing its mission, that their impact on children is not limited to the reach of their programs, but that they also present models to be replicated and applied throughout the world to help thousands or even millions of children excel. Courtesy of BELL.

graduate student tutors. The remaining are full-time employees who handle administration and lead the school-based sites.

In pursuing its mission, BELL hopes the impact on children is not limited to the reach of the programs, but that the programs also present models to be replicated and applied throughout the world to help thousands, even millions, of children excel. There is no limit to the impact BELL can have on education; there is no limit to what a child can achieve with the support and guidance of caring tutors and mentors.

BELL's vision is centered on a belief in the limitless potential of all children. By providing the best after-school and summer educational programs, BELL is helping children develop the core reading, writing, and math skills children need to succeed in school and in life.

BELL does not limit its work to teaching children academic skills; rather, BELL seeks to instill, through mentorship and high expectations, a strong belief among all children that they can pursue their dreams. BELL also believes that engaging parents in the education process will strengthen schools, and engaging young adults in meaningful service experience will strengthen communities. BELL provides support for parents to engage as advocates and facilitators of their children's education. BELL celebrates the values of community and diversity, and helps children, families, and adults take ownership of their shared resources and vision for their communities.

BELL programs offer tutoring in literacy and math with research-based and multicultural curricula. The scholars are mentored by positive adult role models to build self-esteem and respect for others. BELL maintains a staff of committed, certified teachers and trained college-age tutors. The programs are run in small groups and consist of experiential learning through guest speakers, field trips, and service projects.

In BELL programs, scholars excel. In each of the last five years, every child entering BELL at the failing level in reading and math advanced to a higher academic level. More than 80 percent of BELL scholars achieved proficient or advanced levels in core skills, compared to 30 percent of their peers.

Originally, the BELL After School Program was a two-day-a-week program. Over time parents began voicing their desire to have the program offered more days a week. The summer program operates five days per week, eight hours per day; and now the after-school program operates three, four, or five days per week, based on the school system. With that schedule in place, BELL expanded and made the transition from volunteer staff to paid positions to allow the program to operate more days per week.

This transition to paid staff was made for two primary reasons. First, with BELL expanding, the organization realized that in order to make this commitment, it would need consistent staff. This would ensure the curriculum would be covered thoroughly and consistently, and would help provide quality services. In order to have this consistency in staff, BELL would have to create paid positions.

Second, BELL found it difficult to maintain mentors of color for the program. Phalen and others were approached by students of color who loved donating their time to mentor and tutor children, but they often found themselves needing paid part-time employment. They were forced to quit volunteering in order to find paying jobs. It was very important to BELL to maintain a majority of students of color as tutors so the BELL scholars can see role models, who may not be from Baltimore, Boston, Detroit, New York or Springfield (MA), but who may be from Chicago, Los Angeles, and Houston. These tutors grew up in tough communities, and they, too, aspired to attend college. They made this one of their goals and were living that goal. BELL wanted to make sure kids saw living, breathing examples that looked like them and who could inspire them to work hard.

To creatively overcome this obstacle, BELL applied to have mentors and tutors paid through work-study positions. As it continued to grow, BELL began to pay its tutors directly. BELL has continued to pay staff in order to ensure consistency of instruction and also to maintain a majority of role models of color.

When BELL first started, people thought the idea of using after-school time and summer hours for academics were ridiculous. Many voiced concerns that these hours were best used for art, music, and play because children had already worked hard in school. Phalen believes children need a holistic education, and BELL's summer program has that: morning is academics and afternoon is art, drama, field trips, guest speakers, music, and service projects. Phalen illustrates his point by the following example: If your child could not read, and you had the choice of helping him or her learn to read for two hours or play basketball for two hours, which would you rather the child do? Phalen responds to his own example by saying, "Quite frankly, I don't care what your answer is because these scholars are like my children, and I know when they are sixteen and seventeen, and I see them on the streets and they say, 'Mr. Phalen you didn't prepare me with what I needed to be successful.' I don't want to do that to them. We are going to teach them how to read and raise their self-esteem about who they can become and make sure they understand that when they move on to do great things, they better turn around and give back to others."

BELL AFTER SCHOOL

At BELL, learning does not stop when school is over for the day. The BELL After School Program is a supplemental educational program designed to boost children's academic and social achievements in a safe and supportive environment.

BELL After School meets on weekdays for 2.5 hours per day at school-based sites. In the program, scholars receive a nutritious snack before certified teachers and highly trained university students provide one hour of literacy tutoring to scholars in small groups (see Table 10.1). BELL staff use a skills-based, multicultural curriculum to help scholars learn core reading and writing skills. Literacy tutoring is followed by forty minutes of homework help, with an emphasis on math. Scholar-choice enrichment completes the day, and includes activities such as art, drama, dance, and physical education. Special activities such as guest speakers and cultural presentations contribute to scholars' healthy social development.

BELL SUMMER

BELL recognizes that one of the best strategies for impacting children's achievements is to provide educational opportunities when they are on summer vacation. That is why the organization developed the BELL Accelerated Learning Summer Program (BELL Summer).

Summer learning programs such as BELL Summer help children use the summer season to advance their academic performance and broaden their understanding of the world. Every year, BELL's summer outcomes show the impact the program has on the academic achievements and social development of the scholars. In the program, scholars gain an average of six months in grade-equivalent reading, writing, and math skills (see Figure 10.3).

Today, researchers have flocked to quantify the effectiveness of summer learning programs on the academic and social developments of children. Most recently, the Nellie Mae Education Foundation released a report titled *The Learning Season: The Untapped Power of Summer to Advance Student Achievement*. Among their key

Table 10.1 Typical Day in the BELL After School Program*

Daily Schedule		Description
3:00–3:30	Snack and Community Time	Community Time provides scholars the opportunity to develop positive, supportive peer relationships through group activities.
3:30–4:30	Literacy Activities	Literacy tutoring uses skills-based curricula and a leveled readers' library of more than 100 multicultural children's books. Literacy activities also include journal writing, independent reading, and guided reading.
4:30–5:10	Homework and Math	Math tutoring uses a skills-based curriculum and a variety of manipulatives to develop an understanding of basic math concepts and skills. BELL also provides individualized help with school-assigned homework.
5:10–5:30	Enrichment Activities	Scholars end the day engaged in educational games and team-building activities.
5:30	Session ends	Session ends, and parents pick up children.
Fridays	Mentor Fridays	Special activities, including cultural, athletic, or performing arts activities, art workshops, community service projects, and field trips.

*Schedule varies by location.
Source: BELL After School Program Description (2007).

findings, one is strongly aligned with BELL's own assessment of the impact of out-of-school-time educational opportunities:

> The summer months represent a unique slice of time, when children can learn and develop in myriad ways that will help them in school and far beyond. Summer learning is not just about retaining information; it is about problem-solving, analyzing and synthesizing information, generating new ideas and, working in teams, learning to be with all kinds of people—all skills that help building learning in a broad way, and can, at time when schools are narrowing their curriculum, lend breadth to student learning.

BELL's eleven-year experience with summer education has shown the unique and powerful opportunities the summer months provide for learning. On average, American students spend 180 days in school during the year, which is significantly less than their peers in Europe and Asia. For example, children in India and China attend school somewhere between forty to seventy additional days each year. Over twelve years, that amounts to *three to four additional years* of schooling.

BELL Summer is a full-day, five-day-per-week program. In the morning, scholars learn core reading, writing, and math skills from a highly trained staff of

Figure 10.2 Summer learning programs like BELL Summer help children use the summer season to advance their academic performance and broaden their understanding of the world. Courtesy of John Abbott.

professional teachers and teacher assistants (see Table 10.2). In the afternoon, scholars focus on strengthening social skills through daily enrichment activities such as art, music, drama, and dance. On Mentor Fridays, scholars learn from guest speakers and cultural presentations, visit museums and parks, and engage their community in service projects.

In 2007 BELL's summer program served nearly 4,000 scholars in the three regions of Baltimore, Boston, and New York City. This is double the number of scholars served the previous year. Most of this growth was in the newest region, Baltimore, which has been experiencing phenomenal success since 2005. BELL Summer in Baltimore had the distinct honor of being selected among six nationally recognized programs by the Baltimore City Public School System to implement a district-wide summer education initiative. This newly developed partnership with the city provided the opportunity for 2,000 children in twelve Baltimore public schools to experience the impact of BELL Summer's program.

The consistent endorsements of summer learning only validate the importance of supporting high-quality programs such as BELL Summer. BELL is delighted to announce that the STEP UP Act, in which BELL was cited in as a model for effective

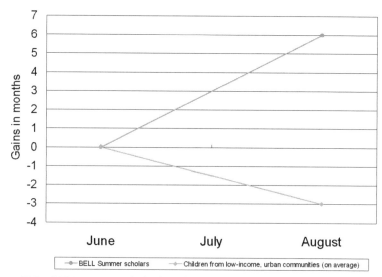

Figure 10.3 BELL summer scholars' academic gains, by month, all cities combined. Source: Tiffany M. Cooper (2003), "BELL Accelerated Learning Summer Program: 2003 Program Outcomes," 7; H. Cooper et al. (1996), "The Effects of Summer School Vacation on Achievement Test Scores," *Review of Educational Research* 66 (3):227–268.

summer learning programs, was signed into law by President Bush on August 9, 2007. As part of the America COMPETES Act, the legislation will provide nearly 70,000 children across the country with high-quality, summer learning programs similar to those offered by BELL and the Center for Summer Learning.

This triumph is a victory for BELL's scholars, parents, staff, and community supporters, whose passion for education has created greater opportunities for all children across the nation. They, too, will now have the chance to realize their potential through summer learning initiatives.

Phalen believes that in five years from now, summer learning will be the core cornerstone to American public education. He thinks BELL will be one of the quiet contributors to moving the country in that direction, and this makes him feel proud.

WHERE DOES PHALEN'S INSPIRATION COME FROM?

Earl Martin Phalen is proud to say he was adopted and was in foster care for two years. He calls his family amazing. He calls his mother and father role models and mentors. He is touched by how, even though they had seven children of their own, they chose to give yet another child a chance at a better life. He was deeply affected by how his parents chose to live their lives and the values that guided them. Phalen believes the love his parents taught him and had for each one of their children

Table 10.2 Typical Day in the BELL Summer Program*

Daily Schedule		Description
8:30–9:00	Breakfast Community Time	Community Time provides scholars the opportunity to develop positive, supportive peer relationships through group activities.
9:00–11:00	Literacy Instruction	Literacy tutoring uses skills-based curricula and a leveled readers' library of more than 100 multicultural children's books. Literacy activities also include journal writing, independent reading, and guided reading.
11:00–12:00	Math Instruction	Math tutoring uses a skills-based curriculum and a variety of manipulatives to develop an understanding of basic math concepts and skills. BELL also provides individualized help with school-assigned homework.
12:00–1:00	Lunch & Recess	
1:00–4:00	Enrichment Activities	Art, music, physical education, dance, and drama.
4:00–4:30	Community Time & Dismissal	Session ends, and parents pick up children.
Fridays	Mentor Fridays	Special activities, including cultural, athletic, or performing arts activities, art workshops, community service projects, and field trips.

*Schedule varies by location.
Source: BELL Summer Program Description (2007).

helped craft and shape him into the person he is, and that love has prepared him to be a good leader. He recognizes his opportunities in life have been because of the talent God bestowed upon him, but also because somebody cared enough to give back. Phalen feels his personal life journey is intimately linked to the organization's history and what it tries to provide for their scholars today.

The turning point in Phalen's life that motivated him to incite positive change for something he feels passionately about occurred during his first summer break from law school. He originally attended law school because he wanted to become involved in politics. Phalen mentioned that he always thought he would end up being a mayor somewhere and use his political status to promote social justice.

Typically, first year law students spend their first summer vacation working in a law firm and learning the basics of the profession. Phalen was encouraged by a mentor of his during this period to spend his summer doing something creative instead. He mentioned that Phalen could always pick up working in a law firm his second summer.

Phalen found himself in Kingston, Jamaica, that summer, working for the Jamaican Council for Human Rights. He and his colleagues were performing habeas corpus work. He liked the work and loved the people he worked with, but he told his supervisor that he really missed being around children. He is from a big family, has thirty nieces and nephews, and found himself missing their company. His supervisor encouraged him to volunteer at Maxfield Park Orphanage, a local orphanage in Kingston. On his first day volunteering there, Phalen found himself teaching a first grader how to add. He admits he struggled with it at first, but once she understood that if you took one pencil and one crayon and counted them, $1 + 1 = 2$. Phalen recalls seeing her eyes light up and knew, at that moment, this was his personal calling. He decided to use the rest of his experience in law school to build an organization that would help many more children's eyes to light up as that girl's did.

Along Earl Martin Phalen's path, others have helped mentor and shape the individual he is today. One such individual is Professor Charles Ogletree. He is considered one of the most influential lawyers in the country and has played a significant role in high-profile cases, such as the Anita Hill/Clarence Thomas hearings, and helped draft the South African Constitution. Phalen is inspired by Professor Ogletree's drive and motivation. As a leader and friend, Phalen believes Professor Ogletree had the greatest non-family member influence on him because Ogletree put his name behind BELL. His name allowed funding doors to open that would not otherwise have existed for BELL. Phalen believes Ogletree has constantly been there for BELL, helping the organization get bigger, stronger, and better. Phalen firmly believes BELL's association with Professor Ogletree has given BELL credibility in the eyes of others.

Dr. Robert Peterkin is another mentor of Earl's who had a great impact on BELL. Dr. Peterkin has been on the board of BELL since the beginning. Phalen stresses the importance of Dr. Peterkin's role in BELL's development because he was able to provide expert advice on creating strong educational programs. In the 1980s, Dr. Peterkin founded the first schools for African American boys in the Milwaukee, Wisconsin, school district, and he has been the superintendent of several school districts.

Another significant person in Earl's life was Ruth Batson. She was a civil rights leader whose importance and impact has her featured in the acclaimed television series *Eyes on the Prize*. Ms. Batson passed away two years ago. Phalen was touched by her passion toward children, fairness, equality, and justice. She was deeply committed to social justice, was uncompromising in her fight for justice and equality, and firmly believed in what this country has the potential to be. She informed Phalen that he was the next generation of leadership. She told him that somebody had helped her out and had given her opportunities when she began fighting for social justice, and her passing knowledge on was her way of continuing the united effort of struggling for equality.

She inspired Phalen to see the difference a small group of people—when united and willing to risk everything—can make. She inspired him on how to really be the kind of David in the David and Goliath fight and come out victorious.

A large amount of Phalen's inspiration comes from his belief in God and his spirituality. He credits his parents with instilling these values within him. He believes if you boil things down to good and evil or right and wrong, he is trying to be on the side of good. He is trying to live a life he believes God would look favorably upon. He admits he is not doing it perfectly but uses his spirituality as a daily guide. It continues to drive him forward and to help him remain committed.

His love of history has also been a source of inspiration. For example, while in St. Louis to present at the National Urban League's annual conference in July 2007, he visited the William J. Clinton Presidential Library in Little Rock, Arkansas. It had the Emancipation Proclamation on display. He feels seeing a piece of history like this and others help one better understand the struggles of our ancestors.

He also listens to Martin Luther King Jr.'s tapes and Malcolm X's tapes. He tries to stay connected. He feels individuals can easily "fall asleep" in regard to others' plight. The things that keep him "awake" are history, time with his family, and time with scholars. Last year he was only able to visit program sites for fundraising visits. This year he made a point to return to several schools and be a mentor for scholars because spending time with scholars and seeing their eyes light up inspire him to work harder to find ways to create communities that are safe and allow everyone to pursue the best this country has to offer.

BELL'S OUTCOME INITIATIVES

From the beginning, BELL has aggressively pursued ways of measuring its services for quality and impact. Phalen states BELL wanted to know what was working for their scholars. The staff wanted access to immediate feedback so they could change their program if it was not working. BELL recognized it had made a commitment to the children and wanted to ensure the program had the ability to fulfill that commitment.

Phalen fears we live in a society where a vast majority of the nation does not believe the children BELL serves have any intellectual capacity or potential. BELL wants to make a case statement that all individuals need to do is challenge children, support them, have rigor, hold them to high expectations, and love them. He believes children will rise to the highest of highs, and BELL wanted to build a body of evidence to prove that even though these are the lowest-income urban communities, the lowest-performance schools, the children in the program are doing very well.

The second phase of BELL's motivation to collect extensive outcomes came in the 1990s. People began to realize school alone was not enough to appropriately educate the youth of America. The new question became how to help all students achieve high marks. Those who originally had objected to BELL's use of afterschool time and summer time were now recognizing these as valuable times that were underused. Individuals began researching this topic and found BELL had already established some significant statistics. Now, when foundations were looking for the outcomes, BELL was able to provide relevant statistics for evaluation to support this initiative.

This rigorous collecting of outcomes has set BELL apart from other organizations. BELL's scientific study put it in the top one-tenth of 1 percent when measuring outcomes. This has separated BELL and helps the organization acquire resources and funding today. People now know if you want a serious academic after-school or summer program, BELL is the one that has been doing it and doing it well for fifteen years.

BELL'S SUCCESS

BELL measures success by reviewing two main areas: outcomes and scholars' success.

As mentioned earlier, BELL is very rigorous about assessment and evaluation. BELL recognized the need to develop its own system to evaluate the scholars' academic abilities. BELL found many scholars received As and Bs in school, but none were able to read or write on grade level, and in fact, only one of its fifth graders was able read above a first-grade reading level. These children were doing "well" on their report cards, their parents thought they were doing well, and even the children thought they were doing well. BELL is aggravated with the false sense of confidence that has been developed in children—and that most, without some intervention, will lack even the most basic skills they will need in life.

Therefore, in the beginning, BELL tried to prove the case to itself, the scholars, their families, the school systems, and society at large. BELL was attempting to prove that when scholars are given academic rigor, encouragement, structure, and love, they are going to meet and exceed high standards. So ever since, BELL uses a nationally normed diagnostic test (pre- and post-) to measure where program scholars start and where they end up (see Figure 10.4). There are monthly quizzes given during the after-school program as well as mid-summer quizzes given during the summer program to plot scholars' individual progress. BELL does not hide from these data but instead use them to improve programs.

Children in the six-week summer program gained an average of four and half months in reading, writing, and math skills. Two years ago, BELL realized its own outcomes looked promising and began looking into hiring an independent evaluator, the Urban Institute, to see if the outcomes could be duplicated. The study proved what BELL already knew: BELL's programs have a statistically significant impact on reading scores, and the programs also increased parental involvement in children's education, two of BELL's top goals.

Acquiring long-term data to support BELL's success is more anecdotal. For example, it is known that 100 percent of BELL's first class of twenty scholars are in or have graduated from college because BELL did a Where Are They Now survey of those scholars. After the first few years, it became difficult to remain in touch with scholars as the organization grew. BELL recognizes the missed opportunity for gathering outcomes, so it is now in the third year of tracking "alumni"

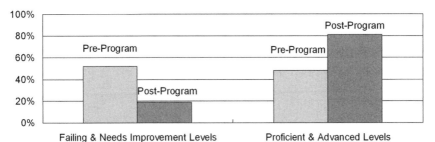

Figure 10.4   Reading performance levels.
Source: Tiffany M. Cooper (2005), "BELL Outcomes Report: After School Program 2004–2005."

scholars. BELL has started an initiative to track where the scholars are now, how they are doing, how they are progressing long-term, and how they were impacted by the program. BELL would like to maintain contact with each scholar roughly twice a year to obtain updates on the scholars' lives.

One Scholar's Story: Kourtney Lewis

Although Kourtney always believed she was academically talented, her performance did not place her anywhere near the top of her class. She spent first, second, and third grades at a public school in her neighborhood, where she felt her teachers were ill equipped to feed her curiosities. "When I was in elementary school, my teachers didn't push me," she says. "They knew that I was different from other students, and that school wasn't a challenge for me, but they couldn't do anything for me."

At the age of ten, Kourtney transferred to a new school district as part of Metropolitan Council for Educational Opportunity (METCO), a voluntary desegregation program. The move ultimately afforded Kourtney opportunities she never had at her local school. Her new school district had a smaller student-to-teacher ratio and provided more resources per student than Kourtney's neighborhood school.

When she arrived at her new school, Kourtney was placed in a remedial program. For a student who craved greater intellectual challenge and stimulation, being in remedial education was difficult. "When I was in the remedial class, I wanted to be independent and I wanted to learn more, which made it really hard for me." It took the help of her mother, a mentor, and an intensive summer program to move Kourtney from the remedial program into advanced courses, where she has since excelled. With high expectations from those around her, Kourtney now says, "I know what I have to do to get an A." And Kourtney has found earning top marks not just possible but probable. In 2006 she was recognized by METCO for earning the highest grade point average of all students in her grade in the Boston-area program.

Now in her sophomore year at a public high school in Lincoln, MA, Kourtney has her sights set on attending Stanford University or a historically black college or university when she graduates. She wants to pursue a career in law.

BELL'S STRUGGLES WITH FUNDING

BELL has undergone three phases of funding over the past fifteen years. The first phase of funding for BELL was the initial funding of the organization with an echoing green foundation grant. This foundation funds many young social entrepreneurial organizations, such as Teach for America, City Year, Jump Start, and ACE. Many of these organizations, both then and now, were started by students just graduating from college who were willing to do high-risk work. The echoing green Foundation finds young, hungry students whom they think are talented and have a solid idea that will significantly improve society. They gave Phalen and BELL an award of $12,500, which was BELL's budget for the first year of operation. At that time, BELL consisted of two employees: Phalen and Arlene Hudson. The salary budget was split between the two equally, and the remaining money was spent for educational supplies, food, and field trips. Some supplies, such as books, were donated.

The first year was not sustainable. Phalen admits that an annual income of $5,000 is not enough for an individual to live successfully. Phalen calls Hudson a saint because she had complete faith and trust in him and in the mission of BELL. They both strongly believed in BELL's concept, so they both felt the sacrifice was worth it. Phalen's parents owned a condo and were able to allow him to live there rent free. It immediately became BELL's headquarters.

A big break for BELL came in the second year and brought the organization to the second phase of funding. An article in the *Boston Globe* was published in October 1993 pertaining to BELL. It ran on the front page of the learning section. This was at a time where BELL had just sent out proposals to 100 local foundations. BELL received a couple of no's, and then some other foundations wanted to know what other funders were supporting BELL. BELL did not have any, so it was not able to provide any names. Nevertheless, the State Street Bank stepped forward and said it would invest $15,000. The Charles Hayden Foundation also came forward and donated $33,000. A third significant donation of $15,000 came from the Boston Foundation. These and several individual gifts increased the budget from $12,500 the first year to $87,500 the second year.

This funding allowed the organization to survive and provided basic sustenance pay to its employees. BELL took on an additional staff member but kept each salary at $20,000 a year. BELL never wanted people to question the organization's integrity or motives. The three employees then accounted for $60,000 of the annual budget, and the rest was put into programming. The infusion was actually a lifesaver for the staff, who were just scraping by.

The following year, BELL's budget went up to $212,000. Cambridge College, a local college, served as an incubator for BELL. BELL now had six staff members working out of Phalen's living room and one-bedroom apartment. It was over-crowded and did not provide good working conditions. Cambridge College said they loved the work BELL was doing. They offered BELL a professor's office and covered phone, fax, mailing, and office space for BELL for the next four years.

The first two funding phases for BELL consisted of a "hold tight and the money will come" mentality. The significant donations were regarded as BELL's salvation by Phalen. The next phase of funding for BELL was to continue to have great out-comes, but to share those outcomes and raise money based on those outcomes: a sign of business maturity.

Phalen admits that his belief set was partly to blame for BELL's initial funding struggles. He always had believed nonprofits should not make money. Phalen admits not recognizing at that time that being nonprofit is a tax status, and that if you do not have some kind of surplus, programs cannot be offered. BELL came to the realization in the last four years that. like any good business, it needed a business model. The business model BELL settled on allows it to take advantage of supplemental educational services under the No Child Left Behind Act. The children who qualify for these services are children in low-performing schools who are income eligible for free or reduced price lunch; those are exactly the chil-dren BELL serves. BELL has now set itself up so it can receive vouchers parents have and use the vouchers as the primary economic driver for its work.

Currently, BELL's funds are 60 percent from government and 40 percent from philanthropy. Since BELL made the conscious choice of finding a business model and delivering on it, in the last four years, its business has gone from $4 million to $31.4 million in annual revenue.

This steep growth obviously entailed several other simultaneous developments within the business. BELL had to build the infrastructure and build organizational capacity to realize this growth in service to scholars and revenues. During this period, BELL expanded from 1,000 scholars to 12,000 scholars.

Phalen believes the last phase has really been about understanding how to run a business, and understanding that every business needs a strong economic engine if it wants to succeed. He now understands it is not about how much money an organization makes, but rather it is about the predictability and the reliability of renewing those funding sources. Phalen also believes that how an organization invests resources is critical. Investment in providing superior services and building the organization for long-term sustainability is the key to success.

BELL'S BIGGEST CHALLENGE

BELL's growth and expansion were not always this simple and easy year after year. BELL's biggest challenge, thus far, was in their middle years of 1996 and 1997. During this time, BELL had two years of $200,000 plus deficits. BELL had to have board members, friends, and supportive individuals dig into their own pockets to help keep the organization afloat. This was a very difficult period for BELL.

BELL's motivation and drive as an organization was not dampened. Everyone involved simply believed that if BELL was destined to exist, it would succeed. They simply focused on how many children they were going to serve the following year. Once that was decided, they would simply not stop until the money was raised, and they accepted the deficit budgets. BELL would take into consideration which schools were interested, and this is how the organization would budget: this school wants us and this school wants us, so we're going to grow to X number of kids this year. This approach was not like BELL's current financial planning, where the organization has a budget, staff tracks budget versus actual monthly, and a reasonably well-developed system is in place to help forecast revenues. BELL makes some reasonable assumptions about the funding it can raise, but that is based on ten years of historical evidence. It is also based on a percentage of the renewals the organization will get back from the previous year, given the fact it delivered on its promise. BELL admits that this method is not fully predictive, but it is much more so than in the past. In the past, the organization may not have always met its goals because of a lack of funds.

For a period of two and half years, the organization basically survived from pay period to pay period, but the determination and faith mentality that everything would work out helped pull BELL through this period.

BELL'S APPROACH TO CREATIVE PROBLEM SOLVING AND OVERCOMING CHALLENGES

BELL thinks everyone's complete faith in their organization's success is quite creative itself. They refused to accept no for an answer. Where others might have crumbled, BELL persisted. BELL has also learned to create opportunities. For example, Professor Ogletree, board chair and Harvard Law School professor, secured a meeting with the new owners of the Red Sox baseball team when they came to town looking for an educational program to support. As a result, now every year, up to twenty-five BELL graduates each receive a $10,000 college scholarship from the Boston Red Sox. BELL also created a flag football event with the New England Patriots, called the BELL Bowl, which raises hundreds of thousands of dollars to support BELL's summer program.

BELL has also been very good about creating partnerships. The Urban Institute study was a way to do that. Despite educating 12,000 scholars annually, BELL knows that over 13 million children in the United States live in poverty. Those involved at BELL wanted to know what they could do to reach these other children. They wanted to find an avenue that would get their knowledge out to the rest of the world.

BELL staff members went on a conference circuit where they knew there would be educational influencers. One such individual was Senator Barak Obama of Illinois. He picked up on BELL's idea and helped create legislation known as the STEP UP Act. The STEP UP Act points out that America's youth are undereducated and in school less time per year than students in some other countries.

Obama was interested in a great summer learning model to help children in America compete. He picked up the BELL Summer model, and it is now written into legislation. The Act became law on August 9, 2007, as part of the America COMPETES Bill. Now each year, $100 million worth of summer funds will go to approximately 70,000 children throughout the United States.

As an organization, BELL is opportunistic about improving its program, but it also wants to help the 13 million children in this country living in poverty. BELL staffers feel responsible to take what they know and help more and more of those children realize their potential and have access to the American dream.

Another example of BELL's creative outreach is the partnership with Houghton Mifflin, a book publishing company. When BELL wanted to improve its curriculum, it sought out Houghton Mifflin and asked about a partnership. This partnership, and the curriculum, evaluation materials, and assessment tools, have taken BELL's educational services to an even higher level.

BELL is also extremely thankful for its partnership with New Profit Inc. (NPI). NPI helps organizations scale. NPI was critical in helping BELL revamp the structure of its board of directors, refine its growth strategy (with the support of Monitor Group), attract several major six- and seven-digit donors, and use policy as a way to expand social impact. This partnership was the key to BELL's capacity efforts and to BELL's rapid growth.

BELL's continued growth and expansion were accelerated by the newly reconstructed board of directors. From 1992 through 2004, BELL's board served in an advisory capacity. Directors helped facilitate entrée into new communities, informed the program model and service objectives, and reviewed quarterly and annual financial statements to ensure the organization's health. As BELL began to standardize and apply business practices to its operations, this board was restructured and became an active governing body with subcommittee working groups.

Since 2004 BELL's governing board has been responsible for holding the organization accountable and helps the senior management team think through critical issues of strategy, fundraising, finances, and social impact. Subcommittees comprised of directors and a senior management liaison carefully analyze policies, goals, and results for each functional area of the organization.

The Red Sox Program in Further Detail

Imagine the excitement of walking onto the field at Fenway Park in front of a sell-out crowd. David Ortiz pats you on the back and Manny Ramirez gives you a high-five. You have reason to celebrate: you are a Red Sox Scholar.

The Red Sox Scholars Program is an innovative partnership between BELL, the Boston Red Sox, and presenting sponsor Beth Israel Deaconess Medical Center. Centered on the basic premise that every child can excel and reach his or her full potential given support and the right resources, the Red Sox Scholars Program provides $10,000 college scholarships to twenty-five fifth-grade scholars each year. In addition, doctors, nurses, and staff members from Beth Israel Deaconess

Medical Center, the program's presenting sponsor, volunteer to serve as mentors to support the scholars through middle school, high school, and on to college.

Every year, the Boston Red Sox kick off the program with an annual ceremony at Fenway Park to honor the scholars' hard work and commitment to their education in front of the entire Red Sox Nation. The ceremony is also televised on the New England Sports Network, reaching the scholars' peers, teachers, principals and approximately 3 million other homes in New England. During the academic year, Beth Israel Deaconess Medical Center hosts professional "Shadow Days" and other educational and experiential activities for the scholars and their mentors.

To ensure the ongoing success of the program, BELL and the Red Sox Foundation host the annual Field of Dreams Gala fundraiser, a gathering of business executives, community leaders, and Red Sox owners and legends. On this inspirational night, Boston welcomes the new class of Red Sox Scholars and reaffirms its commitment to providing children with the support they need to succeed in the classroom and in life.

In the three years since the program's inception, seventy-five shining stars have become Red Sox Scholars. BELL, the Red Sox, and Beth Israel Deaconess look forward to continuing this amazing partnership and helping many more future leaders achieve their full potential in school and in life.

IF I HAD KNOWN THEN WHAT I KNOW NOW

As mentioned earlier, Phalen once believed that in order to show your commitment and success, you had to act like a saint. He does not think so anymore; rather, commitment and success are what BELL delivers to children, families, and the nation. BELL started by trying to just raise enough to get by and not to have too much in the coffers. Phalen uses the organization Teach for America to exemplify his point. This organization originated around the same time as BELL, but the founder raised $300,000 before the organization opened its services up to the public. With those resources in place, the founder could focus more energies on building an organization and executing the plan. With BELL's initial $12,500, the vast majority of BELL's early years were focused on survival.

Phalen recognized success is about a good business plan. An organization needs to create a well-written plan and then market that plan. Individuals need to go out and get the money they need to in order to execute the plan. He believes smart people raise the money as fast as they can, gather what they need to run the business (or at least close to that), and then they grow the business. Phalen believes an organization needs to understand what its business model is, raise the funds to support the business plan, be passionate about the plan, and not make it about the leaders' personal sacrifice—make it about what the organization brings to the community, what the end result is for children and families.

Phalen also said he had the false belief that money would cure all the organization's problems, and that once BELL had the money, everything else would fall into place. Phalen found this did not hold true. When BELL doubled the size of the staff, the organization actually became less productive, outcomes and quality went down, and the culture was lost. All this happened because he did not know how to manage people effectively. Phalen mentioned the social entrepreneur myth. Many people who engage in social justice work do it because they love kids, for instance. They are not great business people, and they are not entrepreneurs, but they are great educators. They are not passionate about building a business that can educate children; they are passionate about working directly with children. In the early years, Phalen wished he would have gone to business school rather than law school. He recognizes he built a business that focuses on education, and that business skills would have come in helpful in the long run. He has picked up many of the skills along the way, but feels BELL's growth could have been accelerated if it had been guided better.

Phalen feels the social entrepreneur myth helps account for the fact that there are a million and a half nonprofit organizations in the world, and 92 percent of them have budgets of less than $1 million. Other than museums, hospitals, and universities, fewer than 1 percent of nonprofits have budgets over $20 million. Only 144 of these nonprofits have grown since 1970 to revenues of $50 million dollars or more. Many people do not have the desire or skills to grow an organization. The nonprofit capital markets—how organizations are funded—also prevent others who do have the desire and skill from realizing their dreams.

There are also some misconceptions regarding how to acquire funding. Stanford University released a study that is counterintuitive to common beliefs. Most people believe organizations should diversify their funding in order to succeed. Stanford studied those 144 nonprofit organization mentioned above and found that 142 had only one major stream of funding, either from the government or individuals.[1] Phalen encourages organizations to get professional support to help them understand the economics of their business, and help them learn what their economic engine is. This has the potential to have a transformative impact on their work.

BELL'S NEXT STEPS

In terms of BELL's next steps, the organization just finished its strategic plan for 2008. BELL plans to double in size from 12,000 scholars to 25,000 scholars over the next five years. BELL also wants to expand into three to five new communities throughout the country.

BELL hopes to continue to use both partnerships and politics to expand its social impact. BELL looks to be a major player under the STEP UP Act. BELL plans on helping to ensure that legislative bills are passed to provide training, technical assistance, and quality assurance accreditation to those who will receive the $100 million from this Act. BELL wants to help maintain best practices in the field and make sure children receive great services.

BELL was excited to launch a new program in the summer of 2006: BELL BOYS. This is partnership with the Charles Hayden Foundation. BELL is developing the summer enrichment program, modeled after BELL Summer, specifically to address the interests and needs of black and Latino boys, the most vulnerable student population. Implementing innovative and effective models such as this, and researching the impact, continues to be important to BELL's future.

BELL'S AFFILIATE PROGRAM

Another attempt at reaching more children and expanding BELL's impact is through its affiliate program. Nonprofit organizations have affiliates just as for-profit organizations have franchises. BELL maintains partnerships with affiliates, which further expands and promotes BELL's after-school and summer programs.

BELL signs up affiliates who want to take the BELL program content, training, technical assistance, and assessment tools and implement the BELL model in their own facilities or programs. The affiliates pay BELL a small fee for these services. Last year BELL had a pilot program with the Boys and Girls Club in Palo Alto, California, for 500 children. It was very successful. As a result of this success, BELL hopes to gain five to ten more affiliate partners in the coming year. BELL will continue to work out any kinks in this program and hopes to continue its expansion. BELL is excited about this program because it has the potential to reach many more children than BELL programs alone. BELL will be serving approximately 25,000 children directly, but then potentially serving an additional 25,000 children through their affiliates.

The affiliate program would then create a network that would bring organizations together to share best practices and discuss new trends in the field.

AWARDS AND HONORS BELL HAS RECEIVED

BELL was awarded the 2006 Social Capitalist Award by *Fast Company* magazine and the Monitor Group. The award recognizes the top organizations changing the world that use innovation and entrepreneurship to create sustainable solutions to urgent social issues.

BELL was selected by President Bill Clinton from a national pool of 3,600 nominees to receive the 1997 President's Service Award, the most prestigious award for national community service. The award reflects the importance the president placed on community service, and is presented in recognition of outstanding service directed at solving critical social problems.

The BELL Summer Program was recognized as one of the best educational summer programs in the nation by Johns Hopkins University's Center for Summer Learning.

BELL CEO Earl Martin Phalen won the Red Cross of Massachusetts Bay's Clara Barton Humanitarian Award in recognition of his service to children and families.

BELL'S BOARD OF DIRECTORS

and is a Founding Board Member of the Canada Wide Virtual Science Fair. Mr. Oberg serves on BELL's Finance Committee.

Professor Charles Ogletree Jr., chair emeritus of BELL's board. Professor Ogletree is a professor of law at Harvard Law School and the founder of the Charles Hamilton Houston Institute for Race and Justice. He is a highly esteemed legal scholar, civil rights lawyer, and leader. Professor Ogletree is deeply committed to serving public schools and institutes of higher education.

Earl Martin Phalen, co-founder and CEO of BELL. Earl Martin Phalen serves as the organization's president. He is a graduate of Yale University and Harvard Law School. Mr. Phalen has earned several awards in recognition of his commitment to children and the achievements of BELL, including the President's Service Award and the 2006, 2007, and 2008 Social Capitalist Awards.

Chris Piela, regional vice president of Montgomery Insurance and a member of the Liberty Mutual Group. Mr. Piela brings a wealth of business and financial experience to BELL's board of directors. He is a former CFO of Specialty Risks at Liberty Mutual. Mr. Piela sits on the Governance Committee and oversees BELL's fiscal management as chair of its Finance Committee.

Dr. Lauren Smith, pediatric hospitalist and the medical director of the Medical-Legal Partnership for Children at Boston Medical Center. She is focusing her research on the impact of public policy on vulnerable children's health. Dr. Smith also serves as medical director of the Massachusetts Department of Public Health and as associate professor of pediatrics at the Boston University School of Medicine. Dr. Smith is the chair of BELL's Program Committee.

Laurene Sperling, BELL's current board chair. Ms. Sperling is an accomplished philanthropist with a background in corporate finance and investment banking. She is the former vice president at Cowen & Company. Ms. Sperling lends her expertise to universities, independent schools, and public schools as well as to BELL's Governance, Development and Program committees.

ORGANIZATIONAL SNAPSHOT

Organization: Building Educated Leaders for Life (BELL)

Founder: Earl Martin Phalen

Mission/Description: BELL (Building Educated Leaders for Life) recognizes that the pathway to opportunity for children lies in education. BELL transforms children into scholars and leaders through the delivery of nationally recognized, high-impact summer and after-school educational programs. By helping children achieve academic and social proficiency during their formative elementary school years and embrace their rich cultural heritage, BELL is inspiring the next generation of great teachers, doctors, lawyers, artists, and community leaders. By mobilizing parents, teachers, and young adults, BELL is living the idea that "it takes a village to raise a child."

Website: www.bellnational.org
Address: BELL Headquarters
60 Clayton Street
Dorchester, MA 02122 USA
Phone: +1.617.282.1567
+1.800.305.0671 (Toll Free)
Fax: +1.617.282.2698
Email: Ephalen@bellnational.org

NOTE
1. See http://www.ssireview.org/articles/entry/creating_high_impact_nonprofits/.

11

The Hybrid Vigor Institute: Relevant Knowledge, Innovation Solutions, and Better Decisions through Collaboration

Denise Caruso

The Hybrid Vigor Institute is dedicated to the proposition that collaboration is the key to solving society's most complex problems.

Introducing experts to each other's work has long been known to be a powerful catalyst for breakthroughs in scientific research. But Hybrid Vigor's operating belief is that systematic, skillful collaboration can also speed solutions to the intractable problems that exist outside the lab, in the real world. Whether addressing such pandemic diseases as avian flu, the threat of biological terrorist attacks, or our growing need for secure and sustainable food and energy supplies, research shows that experts and stakeholders working together can produce the most relevant knowledge and innovative solutions to address such problems. Together, they also can make the best possible decisions about how those solutions should be adopted and used by society.

An independent nonprofit founded in 2000, Hybrid Vigor was named to represent metaphorically the cross-pollination between the wild and the cultivated at the edges of a field, which can increase the strength and vitality of crops. In that same way, a systematic approach to collaboration can infuse new vitality and creativity into the process by which problems are solved.

This approach requires a new mechanism for producing knowledge that works in conjunction with, but does not depend upon, the university, the corporation, the government, the philanthropic sector or any other institution. That new mechanism might best be thought of as networked communities of practice, each a kind of Roman forum for research, organized around a series of individual topics or problems.

Although Hybrid Vigor's projects and program areas have evolved over the years, the organization has remained steadfastly focused on its original, twin goals: one, to build a global network of diverse thinkers who embrace collaborative, boundary-crossing inquiries; and two, to establish new methods and best practices for collaboration by and across many sectors—including academia, private industry, philanthropy, and public policy.

While adamant about the need for and advocating the advantages of interdisciplinary research, Hybrid Vigor does not pit collaboration against expertise. Specialized knowledge is, should be, and will remain vitally important. But at the same time, collaborative approaches are required to synthesize and contextualize society's vast stores of specialized knowledge in service of real-world problems and issues.

BEGINNINGS

The catalyst for what was to become the Hybrid Vigor Institute was a 1998 meeting between Denise Caruso and Richard Solomon. Caruso, a veteran technology analyst and journalist who was then serving as the technology columnist for the *New York Times*, had known Solomon for many years as a senior scientist and telecommunications policy expert at the Massachusetts Institute of Technology. Long interested in machine vision systems, he had been a key figure in the development of the high-definition television standard in the United States.

Solomon also had been instrumental in the creation of the first super-high-resolution video camera, for the Polaroid Corporation. At their 1998 meeting, he told Caruso that something about the camera had been troubling him. Its imaging capabilities were beyond anything else in the world at that moment in time, but why was it that this powerful new device still could not replicate the properties of human vision?

To answer his own question, Solomon had begun prowling the literature of disciplines that studied vision. He discovered that many fields—including neurophysiology, psychophysics, quantum mechanics, and biochemistry—study aspects of vision, but none of them were communicating with each other about their findings. In fact, those whose fields were related enough to even know each other's work existed tended to consider each other as competitors for scarce research funding, and guarded their findings rather than pooling their knowledge.

But Solomon, not beholden to any particular disciplinary perspective, found a treasure trove of new ideas in the context of his questions. As he synthesized them, he was inspired to begin working with a trio of colleagues—one from the private sector, one from academia, and one from a government agency—to design an entirely new set of machine vision technologies based on their research. Today, he is the chief technology officer at Creative Technology LLC, where he is working to commercialize the new technologies that his interdisciplinary foray yielded.

Inspired by Solomon's story, Caruso began designing an organization that could bring experts together to address their common problems. Also a successful publisher, editor, and conference producer, she had founded and produced three executive newsletters and conferences that had chronicled the nascent convergence of computers, communication, and information and had introduced its executives. Two years later, with $225,000 in seed funding from three private donors, she resigned from the *Times* and incorporated Hybrid Vigor as a nonprofit.

Within weeks, Diana Rhoten, an associate professor at Stanford University with a PhD in social sciences, policy, and educational practice, approached Caruso. She had heard about Hybrid Vigor through a colleague and wanted to join the organization. Her interdisciplinary approach had already been funded by grants from the Fulbright Commission, the Stanford University Center for Latin American Studies, and others. Rhoten's knowledge and experience in academia were the critical ingredients to move Hybrid Vigor from a project to a real research organization; as co-founder, she grounded Caruso's vision in the realities of modern interdisciplinary practice.

Hybrid Vigor has made its mark by selecting topics of practical relevance and bringing together the best people to work on them. Its first project, with Diana Rhoten serving as principal investigator, was born of the idea that although interdisciplinary research has tremendous anecdotal value, no common evaluation metrics had yet been developed to reflect the improved results with which collaboration is credited. In order to start to understand the problem, Rhoten designed a one-year pilot study of the social networks and anthropological conditions at eight interdisciplinary research centers in the United States. Funded by an interdisciplinary program at the National Science Foundation, *A Multi-Method Analysis of the Social and Technical Conditions for Interdisciplinary Collaboration* was one of the very first studies to provide empirical data on how interdisciplinary research is practiced on the ground.[1]

Although Rhoten has since left the organization, she continues her affiliation as a Hybrid Vigor Fellow and serves as director of the Knowledge Institutions program area at the Social Science Research Council in New York. In addition to an ongoing NSF-funded project studying interdisciplinary graduate students, during 2007 and 2008 she took a temporary position with the National Science Foundation as a program director in the areas of Virtual Organizations and Learning & Workforce Development for the Office of Cyberinfrastructure, and works with various academic and non-academic organizations on the design, implementation, and assessment of new organizational forms of research and training.

Denise Caruso's ongoing study of risk and technological innovation has also brought the institute to the attention of scientists, policy makers, and non-governmental organizations (NGOs) around the world. In February 2002, Hybrid Vigor published a monograph by Caruso, titled "Risk as Continuum: A Redefinition of Risk for Governing the Post-Genome World,"[2] an unconventional, interdisciplinary argument for redefining risk in the context of biotechnology that included expert findings in the fields of molecular biology, sociology, communications, science and technology studies, law, public policy, ecology, and economics.

The article was selected as a Book of the Month and was distributed to members of the Global Business Network. Based on the findings in "Risk as Continuum," in October 2002, Hybrid Vigor published a Rockefeller Foundation–commissioned white paper by Caruso that further explored the terrain, titled "Risk: The Art and the Science and Choice."[3]

In 2006, as a direct result of this work, Caruso completed the book *Intervention: Confronting the Real Risks of Genetic Engineering and Life on a Biotech Planet,* which won the silver medal for science writing in the 2007 Independent Publisher Book Awards. Published under the auspices of Hybrid Vigor Press, *Intervention* was reviewed by a wide range of publications, including the international science journal, *Nature.*

FOCUS ON THE SHARED TOPIC

A hybrid itself, the Hybrid Vigor Institute today is part think tank, part research institute, and part consultancy. Whether it is working to change public policy, conducting a research project, or helping a client assemble the right group of people for a collaboration, the organizing principle for all the institute's work is the shared topic or problem.

An ideal Hybrid Vigor topic is one that is studied by several disciplines (preferably in both the social and natural sciences), affects multiple sectors of society, and has the greatest need or potential for a shift in traditional thinking by way of collaboration or integrating disciplinary knowledge. Using the topic or problem as its focal point, the institute actively seeks out and connects experts and stakeholders from a range of fields to exchange information and/or work together.

This approach calls into service three complementary activities to encourage learning, deliberation, and collaboration. They include publications, working symposia, and the development and deployment of methods that support or require collaboration.

Publications lead the list for one simple and obvious reason: research and problem solving are as much about literature as they are about inquiry. No matter what tools or metrics individuals may use to gather data for their work, no matter whether they "agree" with collaborative approaches or not, they all write—and read others'—reports about their findings. Publications that bring together a variety of perspectives are the best and most universal way to engage experts' and the public's interest in a particular issue or problem. And because all experts are laypeople when outside their home disciplines, all Hybrid Vigor publications are written and edited to be understood by a non-technical, non-academic audience.

With the exception of its books, Hybrid Vigor's publications are free and available from Hybrid Vigor's website to anyone with an Internet connection. Books and other media are available at market costs far below the cost of books from a traditional academic press.

So far, Hybrid Vigor has published one book (the previously mentioned *Intervention*) and several well-received journals, study reports, and white papers on topics ranging from the role of clouds in climate change to the role of collaboration in philanthropy and the definition of risk in the context of technological innovation.

The institute's first publication, in 2001, was a white paper written by Caruso and Rhoten on the roadblocks to interdisciplinary research, titled "Lead, Follow or Get Out of the Way: Sidestepping the Barriers to Effective Practice of Interdisciplinarity." In it, they detailed the latest data and thinking about specific roadblocks to interdisciplinary practice, including the strong institutional bias against interdisciplinarity at most universities, the challenge of getting access to cross-disciplinary data and publications, and competition and the "geopolitics" of knowledge within the academy.

In addition to Caruso's risk reports, Hybrid Vigor released three other publications in 2002. One was the findings from a Surdna Foundation–funded study by Rhoten, which examined the workings of the internal networks of individuals, teams, and programs within a foundation, called "Organizing Change from the Inside Out: Emerging Models of Intra-Organizational Collaboration in Philanthropy." Given that such collaborations are not formal or typical enough to study directly, Rhoten's study and report focused on more preliminary issues, including emerging forms of collaboration within foundations, and if (and how) internal collaborations affected the process and performance of grantmaking.

The Institute's next publication, titled "The Living Skies: Cloud Behavior and Its Role in Climate Change," was authored by the London-based Hybrid Vigor fellow Oliver Morton, a well-known science writer, who is presently news and features editor for *Nature*. Morton tapped the work of researchers in several disciplines for a fascinating exploration of the climatic effects of clouds—the second largest source of energy for the atmosphere—on an atmosphere with significantly higher levels of greenhouse gases.

In "The Living Skies," Morton explained why today's computer-driven models of the climate system, which make use of a physics-based understanding of its various processes, may be producing large errors. He also explored other, more controversial potential problems with the models—for example, the possibility that bacteria and various aerosols may also play a critical, yet unexplored role in climate change. The month after Morton's report was released, CNN published a news story about the British scientists he had cited, noting their theory that certain bug species may have evolved the ability to manipulate the weather in order to secure their own survival.

"As If You Were There: Matching Machine Vision to Human Vision" was authored by Richard Solomon when he was serving as a senior scientist for the Program on Vision Science & Advanced Networking at the University of Pennsylvania's Center for Communications and Information Science and Policy. The paper explores the themes he discussed with Caruso in 1998—specifically that compared to older theories based on psychophysical measurements, many of the results recently published in the neurological literature about how the human vision system works are surprising and counterintuitive. The new research challenges long-held assumptions about how electronic transmission components, cameras, displays, processors, and even audio speakers should work. With this new information, engineers could begin to design more accurate electronic systems that would replicate a scene as if the observer were present.

To complement its publication strategy, the institute hosts or co-hosts invitation-only working meetings or symposia, each organized around a focal topic or problem. Attendees include experts and established researchers from a range of disciplines and, as funding permits, their graduate students and protégés, as well as relevant stakeholders. These meetings are generally organized as either a prelude to a formal project collaboration, or as part of the collaborative learning process for an ongoing project.

For example, the institute has co-hosted two meetings on risk and genetic engineering—one in advance of submitting a grant proposal, and one to present findings from its NSF-funded methodology study. Along with the epidemiologist Larry Brilliant (now the director of Google.org), Global Business Network, the Seva Foundation, and several schools of public health from several major universities, including Columbia and Stanford, Hybrid Vigor also co-hosted one of the earliest meetings on preparedness for pandemic influenza, Pandefense 1.0. The meeting was attended by top influenza experts from academia, government, and the World Health Organization, as well as by representatives of private industry, the investment community, and public health organizations such as the Red Cross.

Hybrid Vigor also develops and deploys sophisticated techniques to improve collaboration across both disciplinary and/or geographic boundaries. Most recently, the institute began a collaboration with Carnegie Mellon University to test the feasibility of a new methodology for assessing and characterizing unprecedented risks. To pursue this, the Decision, Risk, and Management Sciences program of the National Science Foundation awarded Hybrid Vigor an exploratory research grant for the project, called "Understanding Genomics Risks: An Integrated Scenario and Analytic Approach." Since the project's completion and subsequent publication of its findings, the published results have attracted the attention of practitioners in government and private industry who are considering the approach for cases ranging from bioterrorism to health care and identity theft.[4]

CATALYTIC COLLABORATION

Although it is one of the only organizations that is focused wholly on the practice of collaboration, Hybrid Vigor is far from the only voice that insists upon its value. Its benefits, and the shortcomings of deconstructing and "understanding" the world primarily through the narrow filters of specialization, have been apparent for several decades. Great discoveries and shifts in traditional thinking are commonly attributed to researchers crossing disciplinary boundaries. Interdisciplinarity has been hailed as the wellspring for innovation by many of the most respected intellectuals and scientists of history, including the biologist and theorist Edward O. Wilson, the physicist Werner Heisenberg, and the philosopher of science Thomas Kuhn.

Upon learning that he had received a 2000 Nobel Prize in chemistry, Alan MacDiarmid of the University of Pennsylvania said unequivocally that the challenges and stimulation of struggling to exchange ideas with people from other disciplines will lead to major scientific breakthroughs. "When people with completely different scientific backgrounds get together to solve a common problem, you have to learn a different way of speaking, a different language," said Dr. MacDiarmid. "It's much tougher. It takes you out of your comfort zone. But it's more rewarding."[5]

But interdisciplinary research and collaboration is not important simply because it is personally rewarding, or even because it will lead to the discovery of more interesting ideas. Because it so dramatically increases the explanatory power, the immediate relevance, and the practical application of research to real-world problems, it can no longer safely be considered as just an option. Instead, Hybrid Vigor maintains that collaboration across disciplines should be considered as the required partner to traditional, specialized inquiry.

Within the university, the best immediate evidence of the popularity and utility of crossing disciplinary boundaries comes from the growing numbers of new, hybrid disciplines that are being formed. Given the growing acceptance of such fields as bio-anything, industrial ecology, the cognitive sciences, and scores of others, there is obviously great potential for relevant discourse and discovery in the spaces between traditional disciplines.

The Human Genome Project is a relatively recent example, where physicists, computer scientists, biologists, and others worked together to invent better methods for determining the sequence of the hereditary information encoded in human DNA. In fact, the entire field of biotechnology is a cross-disciplinary, cross-sector endeavor.

An older but equally powerful example is the now-ubiquitous graphical user interface for computers that drove consumer acceptance of personal technology, as well as the laser printer and many other now-commonplace devices. The staff of Xerox Corporation's Palo Alto Research Center, the birthplace of these advances, notably included cognitive psychologists, anthropologists, computer programmers, architects, cultural theorists, artists, and others from many more fields of expertise.

Even far outside the realm of science and technological innovation, child welfare groups also insist that interdisciplinary, collaborative discussions in child protection cases—which include judges, administrators, case workers, healthcare providers, and defense counsel—yield substantively better outcomes for abused and neglected children.

Many other successful examples exist outside the traditional research setting as well, such as the ongoing National Atmospheric Deposition Program, formed in 1978 to determine trends in the chemical climate of the United States. Composed of a group of scientists from many different disciplines, public and private universities, industries, and environmental protection organizations, the data the group gathered via agreed-upon sampling and methodology protocols were an important part of the motivation and scientific foundation for the Clean Air Act amendments of 1990.

Yet despite the hosannas offered to the practice, our culture continues to overwhelmingly favor specialized expertise. Hybrid Vigor's first challenge was to understand this paradoxical phenomenon: What forces are at work here? Why do so many continue to pay such high praise to collaboration, while at the same time they consistently make decisions based on tightly bounded, limited expertise?

It found that most of today's existing institutions throw up barrier after barrier to collaborative research and problem solving, and the problem starts on the training ground for specialized expertise: the university. For example, collaboration emphasizes the goal rather than individual achievement,[6] but a university department confers professional legitimacy solely upon the basis of individual achievement, and provides both funding models and the rewards and requirements for career advancement—including tenure and publishing quotas—to sustain them.

In this context, the march toward institutional acceptance of hybrid disciplines, such as the cognitive sciences, makes sense. When they were still considered "interdisciplinary," their practitioners were dancing on the razor's edge of illegitimacy. But when they yielded sufficient individual achievement that a funding structure, rewards, journals, and publishing requirements could be snapped into place around them, they then became "accepted" disciplines in their own right.

The myriad of ways in which universities strongly discourage the crossing of disciplinary boundaries are too lengthy (and disheartening) to list, but one of the most problematic roadblocks is the logistics and the semantics of collaboration, particularly for obtaining funding or publishing research results. In some fields, collaborative research is not even tolerated.

For example, the *Journal of the American Society for Information Science* published a survey of authors from various scientific disciplines who published papers with an interdisciplinary focus.[7] What they discovered was that co-authors who were in the same discipline or subject area were officially considered "collaborators," while researchers outside that discipline were listed as "consultants," no matter how integral their contribution. The authors claimed this was only way they could circumvent the roadblocks of peer review and not damage their chances to be considered for tenure and promotion.

Another sticky cultural problem is that what constitutes a success for practicing interdisciplinarity is often radically different from success in disciplinary work. Scientific disciplines in particular usually require quantitative or measurable results, but a successful collaboration is based upon exploration and curiosity in the service of solving a problem or answering a question, which may or may not yield the kind of tangible "product" expected from traditional research.

The prevailing, disciplinary approach to problem solving is often tightly bounded, simplistic, and linear, calling into play what Margaret Somerville and David Rapport call the "symptom-treatment" coupling, which most often fails to address the more fundamental issue of basic causes. Collaboration by definition encourages more iterative, "out of the box" thinking, since the boxes (i.e., areas of expertise) have been at least mightily perforated, if not removed entirely.[8]

In the preface to their 2000 book, *Transdisciplinarity: reCreating Integrated Knowledge,* Somerville and Rapport also noted that disciplinary projects are often so tightly defined that it would be unusual *not* to produce a result, but it is difficult to confidently predict whether a proposed collaborative project will succeed. Instead of setting up a traditional result as a condition of success, they said, it might be more useful for collaborators to pinpoint the larger, meta-reasons why a collaborative project might fail—the personal, organizational, psychological, or intellectual barriers that could cause a project to implode. In that way, they can set the boundary conditions for success by avoiding obvious disaster.

THE CHALLENGE OF COMMON TOPICS AND LANGUAGE

From an organizational perspective, the identification of a topic common to all participants—as opposed to the transfer of an accepted problem from an already established discipline, to be solved by the group—is considered a prerequisite for the success for any collaborative endeavor.[9] Working on a common problem has been the de facto mode of successful collaboration in the technology industries, and more recently in biotechnology, where the intricacies of designing and building computers and software—and now, adapting them for use in biological systems—bring together people of disparate backgrounds to solve complex problems as a team.

Within the university setting, the International and Area Studies program at the University of California–Berkeley has met with great success by conducting a regular workshop, using faculty from several disciplines, to help doctoral students hone their dissertation theses. The workshop, according the program's executive director, has "accelerated the completion of dissertations; created intense and highly productive inter-disciplinary discourse across the social sciences, humanities, and professional schools; fostered wider audiences for their individual projects; and created on-going intellectual communities and collegiality on campus, and beyond."[10]

Workshop participants do significantly better in some funding competitions, and other organizations are using the workshops as a model for their own projects. Most encouragingly, numerous participants say that the workshop "charged, or re-charged, their intellectual batteries and significantly accelerated their research and writing."[11]

A more cautionary tale comes from the Intergovernmental Panel on Climate Change (IPCC), established by the United Nations in the late 1980s to advise governments of the processes and likely consequences of global climate change. The group was composed of a diverse group of scientists who, according to observers, were overly concerned with assessment orthodoxy and political propriety, and thus never managed to rise above the level of their disciplines to agree on how to approach and/or narrow the common problem.

As a result, researchers did not consult each other about extremely complex questions, such as how to achieve an integrated assessment of the cost and impact of climate change, thus the phenomenon was never discussed in a way that allowed policy makers and interested lay people to appreciate the nature of the problem. Although much disciplinary data and committees and subgroups have since been generated, no synthesis has taken place to date, and overall, the IPCC is perceived as a wasted opportunity.

The lack of common understanding between disparate fields and sectors that use different vocabularies and modes of inquiry is widely acknowledged as the most significant personal challenge to collaboration for experts who are accustomed to great fluency and literacy within their own specialized areas.

What may be even worse than simply not understanding the jargon of another's discipline is another problem that surfaces frequently: disciplines may use a common pool of language to construct their unique metaphors.

For example, the economist David Wear points out, when an economist says "competition," or an ecologist says "niche," the economist thinks "neoclassical production theory" and the ecologist thinks "identifiable components of ecosystems." But an ecologist's use of "competition" is about the forces that exclude all but the best-suited species from a "niche"; for the economist, the niche is a competitive market that supports several firms.

There are countless similar examples in the literature. Needless to say, this can be not only very confusing, but can lead to serious misapprehensions, project evaluations gone awry, and unwarranted assumptions of ignorance by (and about) the unwary boundary-crossing researcher.

As a result, members of a collaborative team, or a researcher who intends to communicate results to an interdisciplinary audience, must reach agreement not only on the interpretation of the data (which already highlights differences in backgrounds and traditions) but also on the way every term is defined and used. As one researcher wrote, "This certainly increases the heaviness of the research process, not to mention the difficulties in communicating the results. I am tempted to mutter, 'If one can only speak to those who use the same words as oneself'"[12]—which, of course, would defeat the purpose of collaborating in the first place.

Unfortunately, there is no silver-bullet solution to this problem. The best practice for collaborators is to first invest in a common understanding of disciplinary jargon and methods. Beyond that, or outside of a team environment, researchers must be hyper-vigilant about language, taking extra effort to explain themselves rather than expecting their team members to translate between the various shorthands of lingo and metaphor, shared scholarly references, and assumptions.

Related but separate from the issues of common language, gaining access and familiarity with other experts' published work is also a serious barrier for collaborative work. When asked how they seek interdisciplinary information, only 52 percent of the scientists interviewed in a 1997 study published in the *Journal of the American Society for Information Science* said they scan journals in other subject areas themselves.

The reason is astonishingly prosaic. Physically, the journal collections of different disciplines are generally housed in departmental libraries, usually within departmental buildings. Constraints of time and attention seem to dictate that these geographic boundaries are seldom crossed by those from outside disciplines or subject areas. In addition, very few of the thousands of academic journals published today are available in full text via the Internet and World Wide Web, narrowing their accessibility even more. When they are available, subscriptions tend to be prohibitively expensive—even more so than their print counterparts.

Conceptually, it is an unspoken but well-known practice that researchers generally "don't go where they don't know." Thus, the journals of other disciplines are often terra incognita, presenting vast foreign landscapes of linguistic, theoretical, and methodological difference.

What is more, these journals may continue to be unknown for other, more dire reasons. Because of the high (and rising) cost of academic journals, each year university libraries reduce their journal and monograph collections—even as the production of scholarly information is growing exponentially. Create Change, a project sponsored by the Association of Research Libraries, the Association of College and Research Libraries, and the Scholarly Publishing and Academic Resources Coalition, claims that "the free flow of scholarly information, the lifeblood of scholarly inquiry and creativity, is being interrupted."[13] As a consequence, scholars and students around the world have access to less and less intellectual output each year.

Ironically, at the same time that access to quality material is narrowing, the influx of unfiltered, unsolicited publications to the inboxes of researchers is increasing. How to cull the wheat from the chaff for anyone wanting to reach across disciplinary boundaries presents a significant challenge and opportunity for the practice of collaborative work.

COMPETITION, TURF, AND TRUST

The ability for individual researchers to overcome the psychological barriers of turf and competition—dubbed "the geopolitics of knowledge" by a leading transdisciplinary scholar, Julie Thompson Klein—is key to the success of any interdisciplinary venture, and a key to Hybrid Vigor's "institute without walls" approach. In fact, good interdisciplinary work is more likely to occur when there are several persons present who have both eclectic knowledge and a disregard for boundaries of others' intellectual turf.[14]

On an institutional level, "de-turfing" these boundaries is the idea behind the growing number of university-hosted interdisciplinary centers, including recent entrants such as Stanford University's Bio-X Program for Bioengineering, Biomedicine, and Biosciences; the McGovern Institute for Brain Research at the Massachusetts Institute of Technology; and UC–Berkeley's Health Sciences Initiative.

A long-running example of how transcending boundaries can work is the McGill Centre for Medicine, Law, and Ethics, established in 1986. At the start of the process, three faculty deans, from medicine, law, and religious studies, were fully committed to transdisciplinarity and to "unselfish cooperation beyond their faculties," according to the center's founding director. Several other important reasons were also responsible for its success, including the trust that McGill University placed in individuals and the center as an institution, and the risks they allowed the center to take by launching into large, complex, controversial, highly sensitive, and difficult projects, including assessment of the threat of the HIV/AIDS epidemic in the mid-1980s.[15]

The Natural Resources Research Center at North Carolina State University was less fortunate. Despite a promising start, when three schools joined together—and quickly obtained funding—to build a center to house an interdisciplinary program, it did not take long before internal wrangling over the allocation of equipment grants and space, as well as internal politics, began chipping away at the cooperative spirit between the schools. Today, there are some collaborative contacts and cooperative programs, but as one faculty observer noted, "the dream of a highly creative Natural Resources Research Center is dead—killed off by continuing worry and unhappy memories about . . . trying to work together when there was not enough communication and trust among the parties to overcome the inevitable problems of living together in the same outstandingly useful physical facility." The verdict: opportunity lost.[16]

The nascent university centers mentioned above, and others of their ilk, would do well to heed the warnings inherent in both these examples. Obtaining the funds and building an interdisciplinary center are apparently the easiest parts of the task; keeping the key players on equal footing, all pulling toward the same goals, requires ongoing and sustained effort in order to achieve long-term success.

Trust is closely related to issues of turf and competition, particularly since it may be true that disciplines serve to discipline trust more than anything else—by their distinctive vocabularies, the ideas they advance, and the standards of proof they accept.[17] This explains why one specialist's perspective is often greeted skeptically by another. It has little to do with the "other" per se; it has to do with the degree of trust we confer upon those whose perspectives we already know.

But learning to trust is absolutely essential if collaboration is to consistently yield the kinds of discoveries and unexpected connections that it has in the past. Those working together to solve a common problem cannot look for the similarities or matching patterns between their works and others' unless they are willing to risk their position as "experts" long enough to actually focus on another expert's perspective. We will never know how many significant discoveries have never seen the light of day because of this brand of intellectual insecurity.

Although trust may seem like an intangible, excessively psychological goal, it is cited consistently in the literature as a reason many collaborative projects break down. The various participants in a collaboration must trust that they are respected and considered as equals to those outside their fields—and that they are, in fact, in the presence of equals—in order to feel secure enough to engage in the process. (This is particularly true with researchers from the natural sciences, who tend to believe their focus on quantitative data is superior.) Cultivation of trust also creates a critically important aura of credibility around any collaboration.

FUNDING PROCESS, NOT PRODUCT

Given the breadth and depth of the kinds of challenges that an individual or team faces entering a collaboration, it is obviously *not* the easier, softer approach. Collaborative work requires tenacity and a tolerance for ambiguity that many traditional thinkers find difficult to maintain.

Unfortunately, that tenacity must extend to finding sustainable ways to finance collaborative inquiry. Despite its many significant successes in biological systems, in social and economic interactions, in artificial life and evolutionary dynamics—successes that have truly changed the course of how research in many disciplines is conducted—organizations such as Hybrid Vigor continue to struggle with convincing funders of the value of collaborative processes.

Most funding organizations, from government agencies to private foundations, clearly prefer discrete, narrowly focused projects with unambiguous, measurable results to those that put an equal emphasis on the process by which a project is accomplished. Even if they are inclined toward a process-oriented proposal, reviewers generally make their evaluations based on the expectations and metrics of traditional expertise, rather on the more inclusive philosophies and practices of collaboration. This practice more often than not prevents interdisciplinary and collaborative projects from being funded, and continues to relegate them to undeserved, second-class status.

For example, in 2001, the National Cancer Institute (NCI) invited grant applications for Centers of Excellence in Cancer Communications Research (CECCR). The Request for Applications stated that CECCR applicants were expected to propose and conduct research that would lead to major scientific advances in knowledge about cancer communications and their translation into practice. This mission included several overarching goals that were specifically interdisciplinary in nature and criteria.

Of the twenty proposals submitted—including one in which Hybrid Vigor was a participant—none were funded. According to reports from NCI and rumors from informants, none received high enough scores from the peer review because of the turf wars, disparate expectations, language issues, and so on—all well-known barriers to interdisciplinary research, but apparently not factored into the review process.

We expect that, eventually, agencies and foundations will learn how to evaluate and adequately fund these kinds of inclusive approaches. But in the meantime, like many other organizations that focus on a process rather than a product, Hybrid Vigor has had to become adept at maximizing impact on a small and perpetually uncertain budget. Its early decision, for example, to keep the institute "virtual"—that is, bringing together collaborators only on a per-project basis, rather than maintaining a full-time staff and office—was designed to keep Hybrid Vigor always pushing for the freshest and most relevant topics and co-investigators, but it has proven to be a wise financial strategy as well.

The institute continues to receive project grants from foundations and government agencies, but has also begun actively seeking out general operating funds from select philanthropies and private individuals that understand the importance of promoting and supporting collaborative problem-solving processes. A newly minted consulting practice is also helping to underwrite the organization's less lucrative projects and operations, while allowing clients to exploit the organization's expertise in a variety of areas, including facilitating collaborations and meetings, writing white papers and articles, and assembling research teams. And at the end of 2006, the institute transformed its website, Hybridvigor.org, from a resource center for publications into a blog. It is building a roster of guest bloggers known for their affiliation with various interdisciplinary topics or methods, such as risk assessment. As they bring their constituents to Hybrid Vigor, they will raise their own profiles as well as the organization's.

No one anticipated that an organization such as Hybrid Vigor, designed from the ground up to be collaborative in nature, would end up dealing so directly with the same realities—that is to say, the same difficulties—of established institutions that are trying to learn the art and the science of collaboration. But its enthusiasm for the task it has undertaken is undiminished by the slings and arrows of fortune, or lack thereof. It remains committed as ever to developing the methods and facilitating the collaborations that will result in a new knowledge ecology—one that conjoins specialized information and expertise with accountability, complex understanding, and enduring impact.

ORGANIZATIONAL SNAPSHOT

Organization: The Hybrid Vigor Institute

Founder and/or Executive Director: Denise Caruso

Mission/Description: The Hybrid Vigor Institute is an independent, not-for-profit research organization and consultancy based in San Francisco that is dedicated to interdisciplinary research and collaborative problem solving. It is focused on two goals:

1. To establish new methods, tools, and best practices for collaboration and knowledge sharing that can satisfy the demands of both the natural and the social sciences, and that can accommodate the important and underused contributions of the arts and humanities

2. To build a global network of diverse thinkers from both public and private sectors who are comfortable with these kinds of boundary-crossing inquiries, and who meet the highest standards of professional performance in their respective fields

As a result, the Hybrid Vigor Institute will make significant contributions toward solving some of today's most intractable problems threatening the health, well-being, and quality of life of people and the communities in which they live.

Website: www.hybridvigor.org

Address: Hybrid Vigor Institute

1459 18th Street, Suite 189

San Francisco, CA 94107 USA

Phone: N/A

E-mail: info@hybridvigor.org

NOTES

1. Diana Rhoten, *A Multi-Method Analysis of the Social and Technical Conditions for Inter-disciplinary Collaboration*, Final Report, National Science Foundation BCS-0129573.
2. Denise Caruso, "Risk as Continuum: A Redefinition of Risk for Governing the Post-Genome World," *Hybrid Vigor Journal* (February 2002), http://hybridvigor.net/health-determinants/publications/.
3. Denise Caruso, "Risk: The Art and the Science of Choice," *Hybrid Vigor Journal* (October 2002), http://hybridvigor.net/health-determinants/publications/.
4. Baruch Fischhoff et al., "Analyzing Disaster Risks and Plans: An Avian Flu Example," *Journal of Risk and Uncertainty* 33 (2006): 131–149; W. Bruine de Bruin, et al., "Expert Judgments of Pandemic Influenza Risks," *Global Public Health* 1.2 (June 2006): 178–193.
5. Denise Caruso and Diana Rhoten, "Lead, Follow, Get Out of the Way: Sidestepping the Barriers to Effective Practice of Interdisciplinarity," Hybrid Vigor White Paper, April 2001; 7.
6. Desmond Manderson, "Some Considerations about Transdisciplinarity," in *Transdisciplinarity: reCreating Integrated Knowledge*, ed. Margaret Somerville and David Rapport, 86–93 (Oxford: EOLSS Publishers, 2000).
7. Jian Qin, F. W. Lancaster, and Bryce Allen, "Types and Levels of Collaboration in Interdisciplinary Research in Sciences," *Journal of the American Society for Information Science* 48.10 (1997): 893–916.
8. Caruso and Rhoten, 9–10.
9. S. T. A. Pickett, William Burch Jr., and J. Morgan Grove, "Interdisciplinary Research: Maintaining the Constructive Impulse in a Culture of Criticism," *Ecosystems* 2 (1999): 302–307.
10. David L. Szanton, "Dissertation Workshops at U.C. Berkeley," March 2001 (accessed at http://www.grad.washington.edu/envision/practices/practices/dw2.html, July 2008).
11. Ibid.
12. Liora Salter and Alison Hearn, *Outside the Lines: Issues in Interdisciplinary Research* (Montreal: McGill-Queen's University Press, 1996), 53.
13. Caruso and Rhoten, 12.
14. Anthony McMichael, "Transdisciplinarity in Science," in *Transdisciplinarity: reCreating Integrated Knowledge*, ed. Margaret Somerville and David Rapport, 207.

15. Margaret Somerville, "Transdisciplinarity: Structuring Creative Tension," in *Transdisciplinarity: reCreating Integrated Knowledge*, ed. Margaret Somerville and David Rapport, 100.
16. Ellis Cowling, "Transdisciplinarity: Philosophy, Practice, and Future," in *Transdisciplinarity: reCreating Integrated Knowledge*, ed. Margaret Somerville and David Rapport, 154.
17. Roderick Macdonald, "Transdisciplinarity and Trust," in *Transdisciplinarity: reCreating Integrated Knowledge*, ed. Margaret Somerville and David Rapport, 61–76.

12

Our Voices Together

Marianne Scott

> We should offer an example of moral leadership in the world, committed to treat people humanely, abide by the rule of law, and be generous and caring to our neighbors . . . we can offer parents a vision that might give their children a better future.
>
>

9/11 Commission Report recommendation

> The task of changing a hate-filled world belongs to each one of us.
>
>

Mariane Pearl,
A Mighty Heart: The Brave Life and Death of My Husband Danny Pearl

Early on September 11, 2001, Norma Steuerle boarded Flight 77 at Dulles Airport outside of Washington, D.C. She was heading west to cross the Pacific for a family vacation. Her husband, Gene Steuerle, an economist, was attending a conference in Asia where their daughter, Kristin Steuerle, a pediatrician on active duty with the U.S. Navy, was stationed. A little over an hour after takeoff, terrorists took control of the plane carrying Norma and crashed it into the Pentagon.

Following 9/11, in the wake of initial widespread global solidarity against terrorist tactics and the outpouring of goodwill they received from strangers as well as neighbors, Gene and his daughters, Kristin and Lynne, realized they now had a special voice. It was one that they did not ask for or even want, one they would gladly give up to get Norma back, but a special voice nonetheless. This voice could effectively transmit a message that was so very different from the message the terrorists were trying to send. This voice was most evident in action. By responding in ways that demonstrated the oneness of humanity, that reciprocated the outpouring of generosity they had received, and that were in line with the way

Norma had lived her life, they could defy the terrorists' intent to divide through fear, and they could honor her. Acts of compassion could send an alternative message to the message of hate propagated by terrorists. Their voices and actions could help build a safer, more compassionate world. It was this global spirit of community and the power of these simple acts of compassion that motivated the family of Norma Steuerle to form Our Voices Together.

The Steuerle family began reaching out to other families who had lost loved ones on September 11 (see Table 12.1). They found people working to improve conditions in Afghanistan because of the direct tie between that country's tragic history and the loss of their loved ones. Joyce Manchester and David Stapleton were supporting healthcare for mothers in Afghanistan in honor of friends also killed on Flight 77. Sally and Don Goodrich were building a school in memory of their son Peter, a passenger on the second plane to hit the World Trade Center. Susan Retik, widowed and pregnant on 9/11, was reaching out to widows in Afghanistan.

Table 12.1   Our Voices Together Family Profiles

Terrorist acts create devastating loss. Nonetheless, these families, like many others, are determined to generate more good in the world out of tragedy. These are the stories of a few of the families who make up Our Voices Together.

The Steuerle Family

Norma Steuerle was a passenger on American Airlines Flight 77; her plane was hijacked and flown into the Pentagon. In response to the outpouring of goodwill her husband Gene and daughters, Lynne and Kristin, received and to honor the goodness and understanding Norma brought to the world, Gene, Kristin, and Lynne Steuerle decided to donate 100 percent of their federal Victim Compensation Fund settlement to start two charities: Our Voices Together and the Alexandria Community Trust, a community foundation that serves as a catalyst to increase charitable investment in Alexandria, VA.

Eric Gardner

Eric Gardner's brother, Jeff, was an insurance executive with an office in the World Trade Center. Jeff also was an avid participant with Habitat for Humanity both at home in New Jersey and in Latin America. Asked why he volunteered, he remarked that he knew his life was privileged and he did not want to forget that. After his death on September 11, 2001, the Gardner family—parents, the late David and Eileen Gardner, and siblings, Eric Gardner and Amy Beth Kassan—established the Jeffrey Brian Gardner Scholarship fund to allow college students to continue Jeff's work with Habitat for Humanity International's Global Village program. To date 174 college students have received Jeff Gardner scholarships to enable them to help build homes in Central America, the Caribbean, and Africa.

The Alderman Family

Elizabeth and Stephen Alderman lost their youngest son at the World Trade Center. To honor his life, the family created the Peter C. Alderman Foundation to help walking-wounded victims of terrorism and mass violence who had survived but because of traumatic depression could no longer function. They realized they could not bring Peter back but could help heal others as a living memory to him. One billion people, one sixth

Table 12.1 *(Continued)*

of the world's population, have directly experienced terrorism, mass violence, ethnic cleansing, and genocide. The Peter C. Alderman foundation has trained doctors from twelve countries on four continents to heal the wounds of victimized populations. It runs Peter C. Alderman Mental Health Clinics in Cambodia and Uganda. Their goal is to train doctors and establish a network of clinics in post-conflict countries. As the Aldermans say, "It's a personal matter: we are victims of terrorism helping victims of terrorism." www.petercaldermanfoundation.org

Sally and Don Goodrich

Sally and Don Goodrich's son Peter was on United Airlines Flight 175 on 9/11; it was the second plane flown into the World Trade Center. Don Goodrich, an attorney, serves as the chair of the board of Families of September 11th, working to prevent terrorism while preserving civil liberties in the United States. Sally, an educator, wanted to respond with the kind of love and cross-cultural exploration that Peter had shared with the world. She has been the driving force in the development of the Peter M. Goodrich Memorial Foundation, which works primarily in the Pashtun provinces of Afghanistan supporting education and addressing the fundamental needs of fragile populations. Among its activities, the foundation has built a school for girls, supports orphans in Wardak, and hosts several Afghan exchange students at high schools and colleges in the United States. www.goodrichfoundation.org

Susan Retik

Susan and her husband, David, were expecting their third child when David was killed on September 11. In November 2001, Dina was born. After David's death, Susan was very appreciative of the financial and emotional support she received from around the world. Recognizing the importance of a generous community, she realized that many Afghan widows are victims of the same war that had claimed the David's life. Susan co-founded Beyond the 11th to reach out to widows in war-torn areas, especially in Afghanistan, and offer mutual support. Beyond the 11th began with an annual fundraising bike ride from Ground Zero in New York City to the Boston Commons. www.Beyondthe11th.org

Joyce Manchester and David Stapleton

David and Joyce were close friends of Leslie Whittington, Charles Falkenberg, and their young daughters, Zoe and Dana, all of whom were passengers on American Flight 77 that was flown into the Pentagon. Read about their ongoing philanthropic efforts to support education in Afghanistan in the story of the Afghan Education Giving Circle of Northern Virginia in Appendix 1 of this chapter.

Len Burman

Len Burman and Leslie Whittington had been colleagues and fellow economists on the faculty at Georgetown University's Public Policy Institute. A few years after her death, Len read Tracy Kidder's book *Mountains Beyond Mountains,* about Paul Farmer's medical work in Haiti. Inspired by his work and in memory of the Whittington-Falkenberg family, Len and his son, Paul, cycled across America in 2005 raising over $100,000 for Dr. Farmer's organization, Partners in Health. www.Ride4Haiti.org

Marilynn M. Rosenthal (deceased)

Joshua Rosenthal, son of Dr. Marilynn M. Rosenthal, professor emerita at the University of Michigan–Dearborn, worked in the World Trade Center's south tower. After his death,

Table 12.1 *(Continued)*

she established the annual Rosenthal Lecture at the University of Michigan's Gerald R. Ford School of Public Policy and traveled to the United Arab Emirates to meet with the family of the young hijacker who had piloted the plane that crashed into the south tower. When she lost her battle with cancer in August 2007, she was turning her investigation into a book. "I'm not justifying what he did. He's a murderer. But if you just hate . . . and you don't try to understand, all you do is perpetuate the hate and the wars and the killing over and over again. I don't know any way to do it except through understanding. That doesn't mean forgiving. For me, it's not a matter of forgiveness. It's a matter of understanding." Her intellect, her warmth, her courage, her determination, her optimism, and her search for truth and understanding are greatly missed.

The Steuerle family already knew Len Burman, who was bicycling across the United States to raise funds for Haiti in memory of a friend and colleague killed on 9/11. He introduced them to Eric Gardner, whose family had set up a scholarship to enable college students to volunteer abroad building homes in poor communities, one of his brother's passions before he was killed at the World Trade Center. They recognized that coming together could amplify these voices, and in the long run, help to diminish terrorism by reaching out in friendship to those very communities around the world from which terrorists recruit.

With a few more families and friends of 9/11 victims, this core group formed Our Voices Together in Washington, D.C. As Gene Steuerle said when launching Our Voices Together on the fourth anniversary of 9/11 in 2005, "Terrorists today are using their resources to do enormous harm. We are trying to use our resources to do enormous good."

Our Voices Together advisory board member Nikki Stern, whose husband worked on the ninety-fourth floor of 1 World Trade Center, aptly noted that on September 11, the plane went crashing into her husband's life briefly and into her own life permanently.

Those planes went crashing into all of our lives permanently. Our Voices Together recognizes that we do not have to allow those who sought to destroy to be the ones to wholly define the legacy of this permanent crash. We can shape the legacy of that day by bringing good out of tragedy and building a safer, more compassionate world.

THE GLOBAL CHALLENGE AND OUR VOICES TOGETHER'S VISIONARY RESPONSE

At no point in history has America's national security depended as much on our ability to be a respected and integral part of the world community. Effective counterterrorism requires more than military force, intelligence, law enforcement, and homeland security measures. These efforts, while significant, do little to diminish the popular appeal of violent tactics or the underlying hatred that excuses such actions.

We know terrorists lose their ability to coerce if they lose their ability to recruit. The message and strategy of global extremist groups such as al Qaeda can be powerful only as long as they gain supporters. In *Dying to Win: The Strategic Logic of Suicide Terrorism*, Robert Pape of the University of Chicago observed, "An individual can die. Only a community can make a martyr."[1]

The challenge is more than just stopping those who are bent on destruction through terrorist tactics. Of course, these individuals must be stopped before they take more lives. A comprehensive counterterrorism strategy also must include engaging communities in those places where would-be martyrs find fertile support—in other words, helping to build a world where the appeal of lives lived in dignity, opportunity, and safety triumphs over the allure of extremism and its terrorist tactics.

In the sixth year of the War on Terror, the U.S. military finally institutionalized this doctrine. The December 2006 Army and Marine Corps' Counterinsurgency Field Manual says, "At its core, [counterinsurgency] is a struggle for the population's support. The protection, welfare, and support of the people are vital to success."[2] Among the paradoxes of counterinsurgency, it notes that "sometimes, the more force is used, the less effective it is."[3] This new counterinsurgency field manual was followed in October 2007 by the first ever joint Navy, Marine Corps, and Coast Guard cooperative strategy for sea power. It focuses on humanitarian missions and stresses "that preventing wars is as important as winning wars."[4] In November 2007, Secretary of Defense Robert Gates delivered the Landan Lecture at Kansas State University and became the first secretary of defense to call for "a dramatic increase in spending on the civilian instruments of national security." He said, "One of the most important lessons of the wars in Iraq and Afghanistan is that military success is not sufficient to win: economic development, institution-building and the rule of law, promoting internal reconciliation, good governance, providing basic services to the people, training and equipping indigenous military and police forces, strategic communications, and more—these, along with security, are essential ingredients for long-term success."[5]

Secretary Gates also noted that the military had taken on these burdens but that this was no replacement for "the real thing—civilian involvement and expertise." Our Voices Together is part of a growing number of people who know that "citizen involvement and expertise" is our nation's best asset. Ordinary citizens are one of the most powerful and most underappreciated elements of our national influence abroad. Our Voices Together understands that to achieve a safer future, we must build mutual trust and respect around the globe. Our Voices Together recognizes the vast potential in engaging our entire nation in diplomacy by connecting communities. A nonprofit, nonpartisan network of people and organizations, Our Voices Together promotes the vital role of people-to-people efforts to help build better, safer lives and futures around the world through three principal program areas.

1. The "Agenda of Opportunity"—promoting global philanthropy and volunteerism to empower Americans to respond to terrorism with meaningful,

positive global action, such as hosting foreign students, engaging in interfaith and international service projects, or providing job skills, school supplies, and medical care to communities abroad in need.

2. A network of good out of tragedy—Our Voices Together supports and helps others support a growing network of organizations and individuals providing hands-on services as a constructive civilian response to terrorism. Many of these organizations have grown out of 9/11.

3. Building a safer, more compassionate world—Our Voices Together is working to reframe the public discussion concerning terrorism away from fear and toward actions that engage rather than disenfranchise communities world-wide. The Safer, More Compassionate World public awareness campaign promotes citizen diplomacy as a critical part of our nation's efforts to counter terrorism.

Our Voices Together is not so naïve as to believe that such efforts are the single antidote to terrorism. They are a component of a comprehensive strategy. As 9/11 Commission chairman Thomas Kean and vice chairman Lee Hamilton wrote in the *Washington Post,* "America's long-term security relies on being viewed not as a threat but as a source of opportunity and hope."[6]

1. An Agenda of Opportunity: Promoting Global Philanthropy & Volunteerism

Recommendation: A comprehensive U.S. strategy to counter terrorism should include economic policies that encourage development, more open societies, and opportunities for people to improve the lives of their families and to enhance prospects for their children's future.

9/11 Commission Report[7]

Poverty and lack of education are not root causes of terrorism. Most terrorist leaders are not poor or uneducated, and poor, uneducated people are not more likely to become terrorists. Yet the final report of the National Commission on Terrorist Attacks Upon the United States (the *9/11 Commission Report*) called for the United States to offer an "Agenda of Opportunity" of education, employment, and the prospect of a brighter tomorrow. Poverty, exclusion, and ignorance create fragile conditions and foster resentment, which extremists then exploit and use to rationalize terrorist tactics. As the *9/11 Commission Report* noted, "When people lose hope, when societies break down, when countries fragment, the breeding grounds for terrorism are created."[8]

Gene Steuerle wrote in a letter to the editor published in the July 17, 2007, edition of the *Wall Street Journal*:

There are two reasons to fight poverty as a response to terrorism. First, it offers an alternative vision of how to work for a better society and how to unite those who are divided. Second, terrorists depend upon the emotional support of their communities, and these communities are much less likely to exhibit hatred toward those who are actively engaging with them to construct better lives.

I work with a group of families who have lost loved ones to terrorism and are trying to make a difference by devoting their own resources to activities like building schools or clinics in poor areas of the world, often those communities most affected by terrorists. Our work complements, not competes with, the sacrifices of those who serve as police or firefighters or military.[9]

Terrorists realize that in our modern world, each one of us has tremendous power. They use theirs to hurt others. Our Voices Together asks people not to downplay their own power to make better the lives of many others. What more powerful statement can there be about our nation that that of our people, interested in the world around them, personally reaching out to provide education or medical care or jobs? Our Voices Together offers tools to help people to engage in global philanthropy and actively promotes international volunteer opportunities.

Gifts That Count is Our Voices Together's alternative, online gift shop that encourages people to change the way they "gift." The idea is simple: instead of buying birthday, holiday, or other gifts that friends may not need, give something in their name to those in need. When individuals donate through Gifts That Count, they are giving directly to the projects of Our Voices Together network organizations and can customize an e-card to be sent to the person in whose name the gift was selected. Gifts That Count has raised over $200,000 for featured projects in two and a half years.

Global Giving Circles offer an opportunity for small groups of friends to get more substantially engaged in global philanthropy. A giving circle is commonly defined as "a group of individuals who pool grant making resources to pursue common goals in a particular interest area and who commit to learn with each other and with leaders and activists in the field."[10] In partnership with the Clarence Foundation, Our Voices Together promotes giving circles as a response to terrorism. For example, the Afghan Education Giving Circle of Northern Virginia, started by Our Voices Together board members David Stapleton and Joyce Manchester, is committed to supporting two primary schools outside of Kabul over three years. (See the story of the Afghan Education Giving Circle of Northern Virginia in Appendix 1 of this chapter.)

Think Big, Act Big FunRaisers are online tools set up by Our Voices Together to enable community and youth groups to hold local fundraising events for the charities and causes featured in Gifts That Count. During the program's first year and a half, two basketball Hoop-a-thons in California to support anti–child slavery efforts in the carpet industry in India, a long-distance bike ride in Canada for schools in Pakistan, and an art event in Wisconsin for women's projects in Afghanistan, took place.

Our Voices Together also points people toward volunteer opportunities in the United States and abroad, such as the Jeffrey Brian Gardner scholarship for college students who want to volunteer with Habitat for Humanity International. From

2002 to 2007, 174 college students—mostly of them low income who would not have otherwise been able to afford the experience—received Jeffrey Brian Gardner scholarships to build homes in Latin America, Africa, and the Caribbean. In 2003 this scholarship helped finance a special youth exchange: twelve students from Haiti and twelve from the Dominican Republic built for a week in the Dominican Republic and then traveled together to Haiti to build for a second week.

2. A "Counterterrorist" Network of Good out of Tragedy

Al-Qaeda, Arabic for "the base," is an international terrorist network today only nominally led by Osama bin Laden. As leading terrorism expert and Our Voices Together advisory board member, Bruce Hoffman told Congress in early 2006, "It has become a vast enterprise—an international franchise with like-minded local representatives, loosely connected to a central ideological or motivational base, but advancing the remaining center's goals at once simultaneously and independently of each other."[11] It is a coalition of extremist groups and individuals who have chosen to use terrorist tactics to achieve common aims. Al-Qaeda holds the twisted view that force, intimidation, and hatred are the way to improve the lives of Muslims around the world. And they have shown, they are willing to make extraordinary personal sacrifices of their own resources and lives to do so.

Out of the horror of their violent methods another network is growing. This network of "counterterrorists" is a network of private citizens using largely their own resources to generate good will and hope (see Table 12.2). These are people who understand that the battle against terrorism is a very long one, and who recognize that people everywhere around the world are looking for ways to improve lives. They see that alternatives to the extremists' message of hatred and their agenda of violence occur when one village meets another in acts of compassion. The Our Voices Together network empowers people with ideas and opportunities to take positive, concrete actions. Our Voices Together is nothing more and nothing less than people reaching out in kindness to other people around the world. As families meet families, networks of friendship, understanding, and mutual respect are formed.

Our Voices Together started from a core group of families who are making a positive difference in honor of lost loved ones. The formal network has grown to more than twenty-four organizations providing hands-on services as a constructive civilian response to terrorism. These groups provide education in rural regions of Afghanistan and Pakistan, facilitate interfaith dialogue, organize global volunteering opportunities, run international exchange programs, provide physical and mental health care to people who are suffering, conduct global public opinion polling, and in many other ways increase cross-cultural understanding.

By fostering collaboration across these groups and spreading word about their work, Our Voices Together is working to increase their impact and to multiply the

Table 12.2   Our Voices Together Network Organizations

- Alfred Friendly Press Fellowships
- American Councils for International Education: ACTR/ACCELS
- Beyond the 11th
- Central Asia Institute
- Clarence Foundation
- Daniel Pearl Foundation
- Families of September 11
- GlobalGiving Foundation
- Global Volunteers
- Grassroots International
- Green Village Schools
- Help the Afghan Children
- Institute for International Education
- Interfaith Youth Core
- Manjari Sankurathri Memorial Foundation
- Peter C. Alderman Foundation
- Peter M. Goodrich Memorial Foundation
- Project on Middle East Democracy (POMED)
- Save the Children
- Seeds of Peace
- Terror Free Tomorrow: Center for Public Opinion
- Unity Productions Foundation—20,000 Dialogues
- Women for Women International
- Zade Foundation for International Peace and Understanding

number of people engaged in responding to terrorism in this way. Our Voices Together provides the following free services to organizations in the network:

- *Visibility for the work of network organizations as a response to terrorism.* The work of network nonprofits is featured on the Our Voices Together website and in Our Voices Together's nationwide campaign promoting citizen diplomacy.
- *Networking.* Opportunities to collaborate on innovative solutions to common challenges, including an annual conference in Washington, D.C., and periodic peer-to-peer support and networking virtual meetings are available through Our Voices Together.
- *Online fundraising portal.* Our Voices Together encourages international philanthropy as a practical and innovative response to terrorism and promotes network participants' fundraising efforts via online tools.
- *Online action portal.* Our Voices Together's online community of people interested in responding to terrorism through positive actions has grown to nearly 6,000. Our Voices Together enables organizations to take full advantage of this

community by disseminating opportunities for the public to get involved with their work. The Action Center is divided into four major categories:

Build Understanding—opportunities to reach out in friendship through interfaith service projects, select books for book clubs, and participate in music and other events of network organizations

Give/Donate—online tools to facilitate financial support for projects organized by organizations in the network through alternative gifts and other forms of philanthropy

Volunteer—opportunities to host an exchange student or international visitor, volunteer abroad, or organize a Safer, More Compassionate World event

Raise Your Voice—advocacy and other efforts whereby individuals can engage their elected officials, the media and the general public

• *Tailored organizational support services.* Our Voices Together also supports the smaller organizations in the network through tailored organizational, marketing, and media support. This has included help designing their websites, brochures, and other outreach materials, as well as organizational support. A good example of this was the 2006 "Roads to You: Celebration of One World" international young musicians' assembly sponsored by the Zade Foundation. Our Voices Together organized the Washington, D.C., leg of this tour of thirty young adult musicians from Tunisia, Iran, Turkey, Canada, the UK, China, Malaysia, Mexico, the United States, and elsewhere. The Assembly's month-long tour to Washington, D.C., Houston, and Los Angeles used music to combat cultural ignorance and intolerance, and to promote respect for diversity. To increase direct cross-cultural interaction, Our Voices Together worked with a team of Washington, D.C., area groups to organize home stays with local families and visits to local schools, community centers and places of worship for the musicians. The home stays and concerts sparked lasting interfaith and cross-cultural friendships, and the effort reached close to 4,000 people in the Washington area.

3. Building a Safer, More Compassionate World Awareness Campaign

Our Voices Together's signature program, the Safer, More Compassionate World campaign, is aimed at reframing public dialogue about counterterrorism from an overwhelmingly fear-based focus on strategies of force and coercion, to include strategies of positive action and global partnerships, and to offer substantive opportunities for citizen action (see Table 12.3).

This effort began with the fifth anniversary of September 11 in 2006. Our Voices Together members realized early that year that on college campuses across the United States, tensions and differences were running very high over the war in Iraq and concerns about the impact of the War on Terror on civil liberties and human rights. University administrators were asking themselves how they could

Table 12.3   Terrorism

Terrorism is

- A tactic used by extremists to coerce opponents and to gain supporters.
- The use of violence by an organization other than a national government to cause intimidation or fear among a civilian target audience.
- A global threat to human rights, fundamental freedoms and democracy, as well as the territorial integrity and security of nations.
- Condemned by every single member of the United Nations. The United Nations Global Counter-Terrorism Strategy was adopted on September 8, 2006.
- Supported by some groups who see violent acts as justifiable.

Terrorism isn't

- Associated with any particular religion, nationality, or ethnic group.
- Caused by poverty. Most terrorists are not poor, and poor people are not more likely to use terrorist tactics. Yet exclusion and poverty give rise to grievances that are often exploited by terrorists. The UN's Counter-Terrorism Resolution recognizes that development, peace, security, and human rights are interlinked and mutually reinforcing.
- Quelled through one nation's military or homeland security measures alone. International cooperation is required to disrupt terrorist financing, expose networks, and bring terrorists to justice. The resonance of extremists' message must also be addressed. Economic and educational opportunities, interfaith and cross-cultural respect, and international exchanges are effective ways to do so.

mark this anniversary in a way that did not inflame these tensions. Our Voices Together reached out to colleges to encourage them to think beyond memorial services and disaster preparedness training in order to rekindle the solidarity and goodwill that existed in the days following the attacks. Our Voices Together proposed that universities organize panel discussions on/around September 11 with scholars and family members of 9/11 victims talking about responding to terrorism through a multipronged strategy with an emphasis on positive actions individuals could take to help diminish the hatred underlying the attacks.

The fifth anniversary forum series asked and answered the question, What can I do to help stop terrorism? The series fostered a paradigm for individuals to respond to terrorism through positive works and to encourage a comprehensive strategy of global engagement and understanding. Topics included engaging communities abroad, sustainable development, building international understanding, and U.S. relations with the Muslim world. Through fairs or expos in conjunction with the panel discussions, the events also sought to increase student participation in study/volunteer abroad opportunities in developing countries, to encourage cross-cultural studies and study of international development issues, and to engage more students in interfaith dialogue and alternative gift giving.

In September 2006, on eighteen university campuses nationwide, students and faculty explored these issues through town hall meetings, information fairs, and good-deeds events. Build a Safer, More Compassionate World events reached approximately 2,500 people directly and thousands more indirectly via C-SPAN and other media coverage, offering concrete actions that students—indeed, everyone—could take to act as forces for positive change. Participating universities were large and small, public and private, and included Brandeis University, the University of Michigan, American University (Washington, D.C.), Cornell University, East Central University (OK), and others. In addition, on and around September 11, 2006, organizations that are part of Our Voices Together were featured in almost thirty print, television, radio, and Internet news outlets around the world.

Fifth anniversary activities were not limited to college campuses. Our Voices Together encouraged people everywhere to mark the fifth anniversary of 9/11 by helping to build a safer, more compassionate world; community events included a concert and talk at the American Center in Munich, Germany. Our Voices Together offered the first step of signing the Statement of Global Responsibilities petition (see Table 12.4.) Over 6,000 people signed the petition that fall.

In this successful series, Our Voices Together recognized the kernels of a larger Safer, More Compassionate World campaign. Public opinion polling was consistently showing that people around the world viewed Americans as hardworking but also arrogant, greedy, selfish, and violent. Polling indicated that majorities in developing countries, in particular, felt left out of the world's growing economic prosperity, trampled by America's overwhelming presence globally, and not listened to by the United States. When terrorist tactics are employed to "make" the United States pay attention or to pull back internationally, these negative perceptions of our nation turn lethal.

Table 12.4 Our Voices Together: Responsibilities in the Global Community Statement

We believe in an interdependent world there is a pressing need to recognize and act on moral obligations to the global community. These responsibilities include

- Striving to create opportunities for longer life, dignity, prosperity, equality, and freedom for all people
- Promoting cross-cultural and interfaith understanding
- Protecting individuals from pervasive threats

We believe that addressing the existing disparity in living standards worldwide is central to reducing terrorism—not because terrorists are poor or because poor people are more likely to become terrorists, but because poverty creates fragile conditions and resentment which extremists exploit. Over time, greater equity, greater interfaith and cross-cultural interaction, and acts of goodwill neutralize the ability of terrorists to polarize communities and manipulate popular support for their actions. And they offer a contrast to terrorist tactics as forces for change.

We believe that we can and must learn from our past. Each of us can make a difference. While terrorists use their resources to cause enormous harm, each of us can marshal our resources and pool them to generate enormous good.

We, the undersigned, join Our Voices Together in building a safer, more just and compassionate world.

By using our nation's core strengths—generosity, volunteerism, and entrepreneurship as well as our diversity of religions, ethnicities, cultures, and countries of origin—to build relationships one person at a time, these perceptions could be changed. This is the basic tenet of the concept of citizen diplomacy: in a vibrant democracy, "the individual citizen has the right, even the responsibility, to help shape United States foreign relations, one handshake at a time."[12] Many of today's major international exchange organizations (such as the Institute for International Education, an organization in the Our Voices Together network) were founded in the aftermath of World War I by private citizens as part of the effort to seek ways to prevent future wars. In this same spirit, Our Voices Together designed its Safer, More Compassionate World campaign, consisting of nationwide forums, online strategies, and advocacy.

The 2007 forum series started with a panel discussion featuring four international journalists from Egypt, Bangladesh, Brazil, and Kenya discussing anti-Americanism worldwide, xenophobia in the United States, and strategies for bridging the gaps and fostering understanding between the United States and the world. "Hearts and Minds: Foreign Perceptions of the U.S. & American Understanding of Foreign Cultures" took place at the National Press Club in Washington, D.C., before a standing-room-only crowd of approximately 150 people and was broadcast live on C-SPAN, where thousands more watched it.

Over the fall of 2007, twenty-three more Safer, More Compassionate World events took place on university campuses and in community centers from upstate New York to southern California, reaching approximately 1,500 people directly and thousands more via media coverage of the events. Sixteen of these were hosted and coordinated by each state's local and state League of Women Voters, through a formal collaboration with the League of Women Voters Education Fund. Our Voices Together wrote a Forum Toolkit and offered it free to any community or student group interested in exploring these themes through a public discussion. The toolkit offers step-by-step instructions to organize a forum, including discussion questions for panelists, tips for working with the media, checklists for organizers, evaluation forms, and strategies for moving the audience beyond discussion into action. By spring of 2008, fifty Safer, More Compassionate World events had taken place across the country.

Using the forums as a starting point, Our Voices Together employed online methods to further engage the public. The Our Voices Together Blog continues provocative, in-depth conversations about long-term security, citizen involvement, and counterterrorism. Our Voices Together experimented with many of the online social networking websites, asking people to send in their stories of how they are helping to build a safer, more compassionate world, encouraging people to spread the word to their friends, and challenging them to take action.

Our Voices Together also adopted its first targeted advocacy efforts, lobbying for the Global Service Fellowship Act as a member of the Brookings international service coalition that catalyzed this legislation. Introduced in the House and Senate in 2007 as part of efforts to confront terrorism, the bill seeks to establish a new Federal fellowship program to provide funding for lower-income international volunteers.

OUR VOICES TOGETHER: ORGANIZATIONAL EVOLUTION OF AN IDEA

The Steuerle family started with an idea. When Our Voices Together launched in 2005, it was among the first organizations to recognize and to try to harness the vast potential in engaging our entire nation in helping to create a safer, more compassionate world as a response to terrorism. In less than three years, Our Voices Together has

- Pioneered the role of individuals to counter terrorism through compassionate actions globally, such as visionary philanthropy, interfaith understanding, and international volunteerism and service
- Led by example by providing critical financial, media, and in some cases, operational support to save lives, educate children, protect the environment, and in other ways make a vital, positive difference in the world
- Provided millions around the world with a different image of 9/11 families and an alternative vision of how to counter terrorism
- Succeeded in giving people concrete ways to respond to terrorism that get them beyond the fear
- Provided critical elements of an innovative and truly comprehensive paradigm for counterterrorism to policy makers and citizens alike

The Steuerle family recognized that there were already inspiring people and organizations making a huge difference on the ground around the world addressing international poverty, building international understanding, and engaging in interfaith dialogue. There were also families that had been directly affected by terrorism and wanted to help address the underlying hatred and poverty so often used as an excuse to justify terrorist tactics. The Steuerles saw the value in not creating yet another direct service organization, but in networking those existing organizations and voices. Together, they could provide an answer to all those people who had been asking, "What can I do?" that was not based in fearful, defensive actions, but on creating goodwill, much as Norma Steuerle had done during her life.

The Steuerle family provided start-up funding for Our Voices Together from the September 11 Victim Compensation Fund settlement they received. The Our Voices Together organization began as a project of the Community Foundation of the National Capitol Region and became independent in 2005. Over the organization's short lifespan, individuals have sustained the organization; most of the major donors have lost a family member or friend to an act of terrorism. In 2007 the Wallace Global Fund supported Our Voices Together's operations through a small general support grant.

With an operating budget below $300,000 annually, including direct financial support for network organizations through fundraising, Our Voices Together has relied on a tremendous amount of volunteer time from an extremely dedicated board of directors as well as others, and on in-kind and discounted services. A small, all-volunteer core consisting of Gene, Lynne, and Kristin Steuerle; Eric Gardner; Joyce Manchester and David Stapleton; Len Burman, along with Norma Steuerle's best friend, Rev. Claudia Merritt; and Leslie Whittington's sister-in-law, filmmaker Susan Koch, worked with nonprofit and international service consultant Zahara Heckscher and Marianne Scott, an accomplished former Foreign Service officer and former executive director of the Daniel Pearl Foundation, as well as with interns to set up the organization and develop the website and early programming. Throughout, this team relied on wisdom and suggestions from an illustrious advisory committee. (See list and bios of committee members at the end of this chapter.) As of this writing, the organization has two staff, Marianne Scott as executive director and Cecilia Snyder, an experienced nonprofit communications specialist, talented graphic artist, and webmaster, as director of communications and e-initiatives. Three members of the 9/11 Commission are members of the honorary committee: Chairman Thomas H. Kean, Vice Chairman Lee Hamilton, and member Bob Kerrey.

As a pioneer, the organization had to learn some things through trial and error. For example, Our Voices Together's model of offering fundraising tools for events turned out to be extremely labor intensive on a small scale. Although events such as the Hoop-a-Thon organized by a California high school student enabled him to use his love of an American sport to help children he has never seen, in a country he has never visited, and planted the seeds for his long-term interest in eliminating child labor around the world, a few of these events annually were just not financially sustainable for Our Voices Together.

Another example of trial and error was the structure of the citizen diplomacy awareness campaign. Our Voices Together initially unveiled a Learn, Act, Share structure to the online campaign, encouraging people to begin a journey that starts with becoming globally informed, moves to taking actions at home or abroad, followed by sharing what they have done with their communities, elected leaders, and others. Feedback indicated this structure was catchy and understandable. Our Voices Together collected online curriculum, news, and book resources for all ages on topics ranging from fostering tolerance and cross-cultural understanding to undermining terrorist networks. However, since Our Voices Together is focused on the second step—Act—people moved away from OurVoicesTogether.org to other websites and organizations for the first step and then did not come back to take steps two and three; as a result, Our Voices Together was unable to track whether people had continued along the three-step journey. As a network that promotes direct service and giving abroad, Our Voices Together needed to measure actions in order to evaluate its own effectiveness. A new, online Action Center solved this problem, and Our Voices Together found that the critical challenge is moving Americans from embracing the concept of citizen diplomacy as an important part of countering terrorism to becoming citizen diplomats themselves.

The major challenges faced by Our Voices Together have been in scale and resources. Collaboration with other organizations and an incredible group of committed volunteers and wonderful interns have very successfully stretched its impact and helped spread the core message, but exponentially, more Americans will need to take personal responsibility for citizen diplomacy to make a major difference in global public opinion.

Our Voices Together has continued to look for more "voices." Many people who did not suffer a personal loss on September 11, 2001, still found it to be a profound turning point in their own lives. Our Voices Together has heard from students studying Arabic to be able to communicate directly with people in a part of the world they just had not given much thought about before; professionals who left the corporate sector to follow a passion for international service; international journalists who renewed their commitment to their profession as they realized the vital role balanced reporting plays in informing the world; people who reached out to estranged family members in a spirit of reconciliation; and many people who recommitted themselves to their own faith and, in so doing, gained new respect for other faiths. It is the potential power of bringing these individual experiences together in a way that amplifies their impacts and thus blunts the long-term effectiveness of terrorist tactics that Our Voices Together seeks to harness. Terrorist tactics will cease to be used when they are no longer effective. The more we can show that each of us refuses to be cowed by these tactics and that instead of driving us apart, they drive us together, the closer we will get to the day when terrorist tactics are no longer used.

In late 2007, Our Voices Together began thinking more creatively about how to address these challenges and about expanding its reach and impact exponentially. As a result, Our Voices Together decided to take another bold and rather unusual move: During the summer of 2008, Our Voices Together will merge with fellow nonprofit Americans for Informed Democracy (AID), a student-focused, Baltimore-based group that seeks to build a new generation of globally conscious leaders; AID works on more than 1,000 university campuses across the United States and in more than ten countries worldwide.

Both Americans for Informed Democracy and Our Voices Together were born out of the tragedy of 9/11 to encourage citizens to build bridges internationally and to recognize their individual power to make a positive difference in our interdependent world. Beginning in the fall of 2008, a new "Rethinking Counterterrorism" initiative at AID will continue Our Voices Together's Safer, More Compassionate World forum series on university campuses, and AID will launch new programming aimed at reframing the public discussion concerning terrorism. The merger will also provide greater opportunities for students, in particular, to get involved with the organizations that have been the heart of the Our Voices Together network.

Parallel to this merger, Our Voices Together's global philanthropy program will unveil a new home at www.GlobalGiving.org as the Safer, More Compassionate World Fund. The Global Giving Foundation uses online technology to link grassroots projects improving lives and driving change in communities around the world with the people who can support them. Global Giving has been part of the Our Voices Together network and Gifts that Count since 2005. Enabling them to grow the Safer, More Compassionate World global philanthropy initiatives will provide an economy of scale to expand online giving as a response to terrorism.

Thus, although the voices of Our Voices Together will move into two new homes, the expectation is that this will make them even more effective at building a safer, more compassionate world. Our Voices Together believes that, although government policies and support are absolutely vital, ultimately it is ordinary people who are most effective at building trust across cultures and in stimulating the hope that is required to build a better, safer future, one in which people do not embrace tactics that destroy but adopt tactics that construct. In the eloquent voice of Argentinean bilingual poet, novelist, peace activist, and educational psychologist Maria Cristina Azcona that she lent to Our Voices Together, "peace needs hope to grow" ("Peace and Hope" by Maria Cristina Azcona. Our Voices Together, 2005. http://www.authorsden.com/visit/viewpoetry.asp?AuthorID=2933&ID=131894. Reprinted with permission).

Peace and Hope
By Maria Cristina Azcona, Argentina

Peace needs hope to grow.
Hope is an open window.
Through it, pain breathes.

A sorrowful heart
Needs a mouthful of air,
Nothing more than that.

The North and the South,
The West, the East and the rest
To be only one.

An emerald sea,
A golden sun reflected.
Humanity hand by hand.

Special thanks to Teresa Barttrum for her outstanding effort in compiling the initial draft of this story of Our Voices Together.

APPENDIX 1: THE STORY OF THE AFGHAN EDUCATION GIVING CIRCLE OF NORTHERN VIRGINIA.
Joyce Manchester and David Stapleton

On September 11, 2001, we lost good friends and a former colleague on the plane that terrorists crashed into the Pentagon. Leslie Whittington, Charlie Falkenberg, and their two small children, Zoe (8) and Dana (3), were on their way to Australia where Leslie was to spend a semester on sabbatical.

Around the time of the first anniversary of 9/11, David felt strongly that he wanted to do something in memory of Leslie and her family. The war in Afghanistan was in the news, but people like us—upper-middle-class and upper-middle-aged Americans—had not been asked to contribute to the effort in any substantial way. We decided to honor Leslie, Charlie, and their family through a response that would be in keeping with Leslie's life work and help address the conditions in Afghanistan that had allowed terrorists to take hold there.

Leslie Whittington taught at Georgetown University. Her academic research often focused on how public policy affects the lives of women and their families. She was one of many economists who argue that providing economic opportunities to women in developing countries and investing in them through education and health care are critical to establishing their rights, improving living standards, and promoting political stability. Since we are both also economists, supporting a real-life implementation of such an approach appealed to us. We initially supported the Safe Motherhood Initiative in Afghanistan, a program that trains women to be birth assistants. This program offers career opportunities for women and has already contributed to substantial reductions in Afghanistan's extraordinarily high maternal and infant mortality rates.

Soon another fellow economist, Gene Steuerle, contacted us about Our Voices Together. We became founding board members and helped develop the online alternative gift shop known as Gifts That Count. We saw the gift shop as a way to encourage middle-class households to do what we had done: support development in countries that were, or could become, hotspots for terrorism. At the same time, the gifts would raise awareness of the needs of the developing world. But the gift shop did not catalyze the larger donations we knew those households were capable of making, the kind that would have a profound people-to-people impact. So we kept investigating other ways to get those households involved.

We were convinced by Greg Mortensen, author of *Three Cups of Tea* and founder of the Central Asia Institute, and by a volunteer with a small nonprofit, that providing better educational opportunities for Afghans was more than an act of good will. We felt strongly that opportunities based on education would have greater appeal to young people and their communities than opportunities offered by the extremists. We were taken by the idea of building a school in Afghanistan.

We also learned about giving circles, found the concept appealing, and decided to organize one for the purpose of building schools in Afghanistan. Marc Manashil of the Clarence Foundation, a nonprofit dedicated to supporting global giving circles and a member of the Our Voices Together network, gave us practical advice about organizing our giving circle. We invited four households, mostly in our northern Virginia region, to join our giving circle with the understanding that each would make a substantial contribution to one or more mutually agreed-upon projects. The group decided on a six-month time frame of monthly potluck dinners, rotating homes until we had made our first grants.

At our first meeting in January 2007, over a delicious dinner of Afghan food from recipes we found on the Internet, we talked about what we wanted to do, our desire to establish a long-term connection with the project(s) we supported, and how we could best evaluate our impact and effectiveness. We agreed that as we learned more about Afghanistan, our own approach might have to adjust, but that we wanted concrete evidence that we were making a positive difference in people's lives. We agreed to focus on supporting one or more community education projects in Afghanistan and to consider funding complementary community infrastructure projects if needed. We wrote a Points of Agreement document to solidify our starting position.

At our second potluck dinner in February, we agreed to make decisions by consensus. We developed a process to put together a formal Request for Proposals (RFP), identify organizations to receive the RFP, and work formally with the Clarence Foundation. Members of the giving circle took on individual assignments. Members spent the next month drafting the RFP, reading, searching the Web, and calling nonprofit organizations working on educational projects in Afghanistan.

At our third dinner meeting in March, we discussed the draft RFP. We agreed to emphasize the ongoing nature of the relationship we would like to build with the chosen organization, as well as a requirement of strong community support for the project. Our original idea of building a school was challenged as we found many existing schools in need of structural repairs and improvements, curriculum development, teacher training, or other academic support. We also thought hard about the security situation in the location of our project. Children in areas that continue to be hit by violence desperately needed education, but did we want to jeopardize their lives, the lives of their teachers and families, and the success of the investment by providing American funding for a school? We considered starting in an area that was reasonably secure and where the probability of establishing a long-term relationship with a community was relatively high. With those issues in mind, we narrowed the list of organizations to five and sent our draft RFP to Marc Manashil of the Clarence Foundation for comment and review.

At our fourth meeting in late April, good weather allowed us to enjoy an outdoor barbecue together. Our RFP was now in excellent shape. We agreed to send it to the five organizations we had identified and ask for responses by June 1 so that we could make our decision by the end of the month. We discussed ways to ask foundations and corporations for support of giving circles with an international focus. We realized that our circle needed a name and brainstormed possibilities.

By our fifth meeting in June, we had received four attractive proposals. One organization declined to submit. Because two of the proposals were substantially closer to what we were looking for than the others, it was not difficult to reach consensus on the two winning projects. We decided also to make small grants to the other two organizations, to show our support for the work they are doing for the children of Afghanistan and our appreciation of their effort to submit proposals. Although we had not made our June deadline, we were very pleased to have come so far in a little over six months.

As it turned out, our two winning projects also allowed us to conduct a small grant-making experiment. One project was organized by a large, well-established, widely respected international NGO, and the other was the initiative of a talented and energetic American woman who had been working in Afghanistan as a volunteer for several years. That contrast presented an opportunity for us to better understand the relative strengths of those two types of nonprofits in connecting our giving circle to a school and its community, and putting our grant funds to good use.

By the end of August 2007, the Clarence Foundation had received signed agreements from the two nonprofits and had sent the initial grant money to each of them. The grants call for the two organizations to report on progress periodically, with the first reports due within six months.

At the time of writing the grant letters, we finally settled on our name. We are the Afghan Education Giving Circle of Northern Virginia. We look forward to helping the children and communities of our two schools for a long time to come.

Summaries of the Two Selected Projects

The exact names and places of the schools are not mentioned to protect their security.

School #1 under the Direction of a Small Nonprofit

The small nonprofit works in the economic hub of northern Afghanistan, a "melting pot" of languages, cultures, and religious practices. The area is relatively secure, and the nonprofit has developed strong relationships with the communities and the Ministry of Education. In 2007 we contributed $20,000 to pay for water systems and hygiene training at three rural schools north of Mazar-i-Sharif that together serve about 3,000 boys and girls. We also promised additional support for a co-ed school of 800 students, built in 2005 with the help of a U.S. corporation. The school is located in a village that is home to two ethnic communities. Abandoned during decades of war, it now has a high percentage of returned refugees. The village elders had shown a strong commitment to establishing a school for their children, allowing classes to be held in a mosque, then later in an abandoned house, until the new school was completed.

School #2 under the Direction of a Large International Nonprofit

The large nonprofit proposed that we help an existing girls' primary school in a community outside of Kabul that needs significant support. Despite the area's close proximity to Kabul, only two thirds of boys and one third of girls in the area are enrolled in school. The girls' school offers grades one through seven but has been unable to provide an acceptable level of education because of inadequate funds. Our group is committed to providing $74,000 over a three-year period to enable the staff of the large nonprofit to work with school staff, the community, and the Ministry of Education to repair and maintain the school, train and support school staff, promote community-based activities to support enrollment and attendance, and design and start to implement an approach aimed at increasing the number of female teachers. We also hope to fund the addition of grades eight and nine.

APPENDIX 2: CELEBRATE THEIR LIVES: OUR INSPIRATION

Our Voices Together is inspired by the lives and spirits of loved ones lost to acts of terrorism.

Peter C. Alderman

Elizabeth and Stephen Alderman

Our son Peter was twenty-five years old, standing on the threshold of a bright and promising life. Suicidal terrorists stole his future. That it would have been glorious was guaranteed by his history.

Peter literally had hundreds of friends. People gravitated toward him. He was bright. He was witty. And he knew how to have a good time. But most importantly, Peter deeply cared for his friends. Each of them believed that they had a special connection to him. Eight days after Peter was killed, we held a party for his friends at our home. More than 200 friends came from all over the United States, many of whom he had known since kindergarten. We celebrated Peter's life, toasting him with champagne and beer (his preferred drinks), eating his favorite foods, and telling Pete stories. We laughed and we cried, and no one slept and no one seemed able to leave. The celebration began at one in the afternoon and lasted well into the next day.

We knew that Peter enjoyed and was challenged by his job at Bloomberg LP, but we never really knew how he was regarded at work. We should have known. Not only was he responsible, but people at all levels looked to Peter for support. He was generous with his time: solving their problems, helping them to learn new techniques, getting them through training programs and even helping them find new apartments. His superiors expected great things from him. Taking his job seriously, Peter arrived early for the Risk Waters conference at Windows on the World on September 11, 2001.

Peter died too young to leave his mark on the world. We believe that the work of the Peter C. Alderman Foundation will leave a profound and indelible mark that Peter existed on this earth. Peter would be proud. (Excerpts from Elizabeth and Stephen Alderman, Celebrate Their Lives: Our Inspiration—Peter C. Alderman. Our Voices Together website, 2006. Reprinted with permission.)

Jeff Gardner

Jeffrey Brian Gardner was born on June 1, 1965, and was raised in Livingston, New Jersey. Although he received his bachelor's degree in Food Science from

Rutgers University in 1987, Jeff spent his professional career in the insurance industry with an office in the twin towers in New York City.

Jeff was an avid participant with Habitat for Humanity. On any given weekend he could be found at a Habitat build site in Newark, New Jersey, but he had also gone to Honduras and Brazil to build homes with Habitat's Global Village Program. Asked why he did so, he remarked that he knew his life was privileged and he didn't want to forget that.

At the time of his death on September 11, 2001, Jeff had already planned his next Global Village build. He was preparing to head back to Latin America, this time as a team leader to raise awareness of the burden of poverty and to build a decent, affordable house for a family.

Peter Goodrich

The following reading from the Qur'an, preceded by remarks from Peter Elvin, close family friend and Rector of St. John's Church, Williamstown, MA, are from the Vermont memorial service held for Peter Goodrich:

> In the early hours of recoiling from the news that Peter Goodrich was on board Flight 175, someone was heard to say, "For Christ's sake, he read the Qur'an!" I saw his copy of the Qur'an on Monday. It is full of markers, where passages crossed his threshold of wondering. Would that our Bibles had as many markers. His Bible does, by the way. It is in tribute to Peter's wide-embracing search for answers, as well as for his profound respect for questions, that our first reading today is from the Qur'an, which we have cause to say Peter did read for Christ's sake, to be a peacemaker in our time.
>
> This is a reading from a portion entitled "The Dinner Table":
> In the name of Allah, the Beneficent, the Merciful.
> "O you who believe! Be upright for Allah, bearers of witness with justice, and let not hatred of a people incite you not to act equitably; act equitably, that is nearer to piety, and be careful of your duty to Allah; surely Allah is aware of what you do. Allah has promised to those who believe and do good deeds that they shall have forgiveness and a mighty reward."

Daniel Pearl

Danny, as everyone called him, was born on October 10, 1963. He grew up in Los Angeles and attended Stanford University, where he co-founded a student newspaper and graduated at the top of his class.

A gifted writer and musician from a very young age, Danny joined the *Wall Street Journal* in 1990 and traveled around the world with his violin and his laptop, searching for truth and making friends along the way. He started in the *Journal*'s Atlanta bureau and then moved to the Washington bureau, followed by the London bureau, where he served as a Middle East correspondent. He met his wife, Mariane, a Buddhist, French-Dutch-Cuban journalist, in Paris in 1998 and moved there; a year later, they were married. In 2002 Danny and Mariane moved to Bombay, India, where Danny became the South Asia Bureau Chief for the *Wall Street Journal.*

Danny was in Karachi, Pakistan, in January 2002, retracing the steps of "shoe bomber" Richard Reid when he was abducted by terrorists for being a journalist, an American, and a Jew. For weeks, millions around the world—from heads of state, to religious leaders and ordinary people—rallied for Danny's release. His murder was confirmed on February 21, 2002. Two days before his abduction, Danny learned that Mariane, who was expecting their first child, was carrying a baby boy. He chose a universal name for their universal son. In May, just three months after his murder, Mariane Pearl gave birth to Adam Pearl.

David Retik

Dave Retik, a general partner and founding member of Alta Communications, was one of the few people who was able successfully to strike the perfect balance between work and family life. Although Dave enjoyed numerous career successes in his eight years as part of the Alta/BEDCo family, everyone within the Alta family most remembers Dave for his warm smile, loyal friendship, hard work, and relentless practical jokes, and for his dedication to the benefits of casual dress within the office.

The true joy of Dave's life was his family, which included his wife, Susan, and children, Ben (4) and Molly (2). Dave was excitedly awaiting the birth of his third child, for Susan was seven months pregnant at the time of his tragic death on September 11, 2001. Dave was a devoted father who was most happy when playing with children. He had the unique gift of being able to put a smile on any child's face.

Joshua Rosenthal

Josh had a natural talent for negotiating the big and the little exigencies of life, and he had a streak of the whimsical as well. More than anything, he had a gift for friendship, and he treasured the many friends he had in his lifetime. Josh was working at Fiduciary Trust International when his life tragically ended at the World Trade Center in New York City on September 11, 2001.

Josh grew up, safe and suburban, in Michigan. His was a sunny childhood. He was much influenced by a family tradition of interest in public affairs. Majoring in political science and economics, he spent two summers as a congressional intern in Washington, D.C., and a year as an aide to a member of the British parliament. Josh received his AB from the University of Michigan in 1979.

Josh's first job was as special assistant to the new president of the New York Mercantile Exchange. He then moved on to Amarada Hess, JP Morgan, the New York Metropolitan Museum of Art (as associate treasurer), Grantham, Mayo in Boston, and back to New York City. Continuing his work in the field of international finance, Josh was a senior vice president at Fiduciary Trust International.

Norma Steuerle

Norma Steuerle was a talented family therapist, a loving mother and wife, and a dedicated volunteer with her church and community.

Born in Pittsburgh, Pennsylvania, the oldest of three daughters of Norman and Helen Lang, Norma loved to discover the world around her from the very beginning. In 1970 Norma Lang married Gene Steuerle, and early in 1971, they moved to Madison, WI, where Norma literally talked her way into the psychology department midyear. With her indomitable spirit, Norma managed to finish within four years, earning her PhD in social psychology. Norma and Gene also started a family at this time. Their first child, Kristin, entered the world in 1973, and their second daughter, Lynne, arrived in 1977. Norma established a thriving counseling private practice when the family moved to Alexandria, VA.

Norma loved her work, combining deep concern for her patients with common-sense wisdom and a great sense of balance, conveying a deep spiritual notion about what is important in life. Her dedication, skill, and competence were evidenced by the number of those who sought her out. Most of all, she loved her family, and nothing excited her more than to visit or be visited by them.

Leslie Whittington, Charles Falkenberg, Dana, and Zoe

Leslie Whittington's passions included family, teaching, and a quest for knowledge. Leslie had a heart full of love for her husband, Charles, whom she had met in high school in Colorado. "Charles was a bike-riding, mountain-climbing, love-to-be-at-home-with-his-girls kind of dad," says Reverend Barbara Wells. He promoted his vision of socially responsible business though his work at ECOlogic. Their daughters, Zoe and Dana, were a source of delight and the center of their lives. Dana, age three, loved dressing up as a princess. Zoe, age eight, enjoyed soccer, singing, dancing, and Girl Scouts. "I would hope that all families could learn to live together with as much joy as this family did, and that all children could be as cherished as these children were," says their grandmother, Ruth Koch.

Leslie was so full of life and energy and so skilled as a teacher that she won awards even for teaching statistics—part of her work as associate professor and associate dean at the Georgetown Public Policy Institute (GPPI). According to GPPI Director of Policy, Judith Feder, "She believed profoundly in educating students that wanted to change the world. She saw it as her job to be sure they had the skills to do so."

One of those students was Alan Berube. "Most people remember their favorite teacher in life as an elementary or high school teacher. I had my favorite teacher at age twenty-five in Leslie," says Alan. "There are some people who just make the world function better. Leslie was one of them."

The family was traveling to Australia, where Leslie planned to spend her sabbatical furthering her research on women, families, and work. As always, her own family was an integral part of her journey. Kenner Stross, best friend and godfather says simply, "They were a family, and they left as a family."

APPENDIX 3: WHO IS WHO AT OUR VOICES TOGETHER
Board of Directors

Eric Gardner is the data analysis advisor at the Georgetown Public Policy Institute, where he was a colleague of Leslie Whittington, who was killed on American Airlines Flight 77. His brother, Jeffrey Brian Gardner, was killed at the World Trade Center on 9/11. His family established the Jeffrey Brian Gardner Memorial Scholarship Fund at Habitat for Humanity International in Jeffrey's memory. They are also supporting the building of a house with the Newark, NJ, chapter of Habitat for Humanity. He received a BA in history from Rutgers College and an MPP from Georgetown University.

Joyce Manchester is a supervisory economist at a federal agency in Washington, D.C. She has a PhD in economics from Harvard University and graduated from Wesleyan University. She previously served as an economist at the Social Security Administration, Congressional Budget Office, the World Bank, and as assistant professor at Dartmouth College. She and her spouse, Our Voices Together board member David Stapleton, have two teenage daughters. Joyce Manchester is a co-founder of the Afghan Education Giving Circle of Northern Virginia.

Rev. Claudia W. Merritt is an Episcopal priest serving at St. Paul's Episcopal Church in Miller's Tavern, VA. She received a BA in economics from Carnegie Mellon University, an MBA from Vanderbilt University, and an MDiv from Princeton Theological Seminary. She has been involved with organizations addressing issues of homelessness, racial equality, and poverty. She currently resides in Richmond, VA.

Lynne Steuerle Schofield is special assistant to the dean of the College of Education at Temple University. Lynne holds two master's degrees from Carnegie Mellon University: an MS in statistics and an MPhil in public policy. Lynne is working on her doctorate in statistics and public policy.

David Stapleton is an economist and the director of the Center for Studying Disability Policy at Mathematica Policy Research in Washington, D.C. He holds a PhD in economics from the University of Wisconsin. He and his spouse, Our Voices Together board member Joyce Manchester, have two teenage daughters. Together they started the Afghan Education Giving Circle of Northern Virginia which funds school projects in Afghanistan.

Gene Steuerle is a founder of Our Voices Together, and the Alexandria Community Trust, a community foundation. He is a senior fellow at the Urban Institute, the author or co-author of eleven books, a former deputy assistant secretary of the treasury, and former president of the National Tax Association.

Kristin Steuerle Swanson is a pediatrician in northern California. Until late 2007, she was on active duty with the U.S. Navy. A native of Alexandria, VA, she graduated from Princeton University with a BA in molecular biology and from the University of Virginia Medical School in 2000. Since medical school graduation, she has been on active duty in pediatrics and also spent one year overseas with the Marines, organizing medical support for a small humanitarian mission to Pohnpei, Micronesia.

Staff

Marianne Scott, executive director, came to Our Voices Together from the Daniel Pearl Foundation. She was the first executive director of that nonprofit organization, which she helped the Pearl family start in honor of her college friend Daniel Pearl, the *Wall Street Journal* reporter kidnapped and murdered in Pakistan in 2002. Before working with the Daniel Pearl Foundation, Marianne worked with the American Committees on Foreign Relations and served sixteen years as a career Foreign Service officer specializing in international academic and professional exchanges and cultural affairs. From the late 1980s to the late 1990s, she lived and worked in Latin America and Africa. She was the executive director of the Instituto Guatemalteco Americano, an educational and cultural binational center in Guatemala City, Guatemala, and served in the cultural affairs sections of the American embassies in Mexico City, Mexico, and in Nairobi, Kenya. She is the author of *A Citizen's Guide to Global Economic Policymaking,* published by the League of Women Voters Education Fund in December 2002. She is a Stanford University graduate.

Cecilia Snyder, director of Communications and e-initiatives, has worked for fifteen years in the international development field using electronic media as an advocacy tool, and focusing on education and outreach through new technologies. Prior to joining Our Voices Together, Cecilia Snyder was director of new technologies at the Communications Consortium Media Center and executive editor of several online news services for journalists, including PLANetWIRE.org, PUSHJournal.org, and SavingWomensLives.org.

Cecilia used websites, electronic listservs, RSS feeds, and targeted e-mail bulletins while working at Bread for the World Institute, the Panos Institute, the Centre for Development and Population Activities (CEDPA), and the Population Council.

Cecilia has also designed several print publications and scientific posters for hard copy and electronic distribution. These products reflect an informatics perspective, which values effective dissemination of data. She received a master of liberal arts degree from Georgetown University in 2002 (focusing on image ethics of nonprofit advocacy organizations) and a bachelor's of science in sociology from Virginia Tech in 1992.

Honorary Board

The Honorable Lee H. Hamilton

Member, Homeland Security Advisory Council, 2002–present
President and director, Woodrow Wilson International Center for Scholars, 1999–present

Co-chair, Iraq Study Group, 2006
Vice Chairman, 9/11 Commission, 2002–2004
U.S. Congress, Ninth District, Indiana, 1965–1999

The Honorable Thomas H. Kean

President, Drew University, 1990–2005
Chairman, 9/11 Commission, 2002–2004
Governor of New Jersey, 1982–1990

The Honorable Bob Kerrey

President, The New School, 2001–present
Member, 9/11 Commission, 2002–2004
U.S. Senator, Nebraska, 1989–2001
Governor of Nebraska, 1983–1987

Advisory Board

Ambassador Akbar S. Ahmed, the Ibn Khaldun chair of Islamic Studies and professor of international relations at American University. Washington, D.C., is the former high commissioner of Pakistan to Great Britain. He has advised Prince Charles and other world leaders on Islam. Dr. Ahmed is a distinguished anthropologist, writer, and filmmaker. He has been actively involved in interfaith dialogue for many years. He has published many books, including *Journey into Islam: The Crisis of Globalization,* and co-edited *After Terror: Promoting Dialogue among Civilizations.* The Daniel Pearl Dialogue for Muslim-Jewish Understanding features Dr. Ahmed and Daniel Pearl's father, Dr. Judea Pearl.

Stephen J. Alderman co-founded the Peter C. Alderman Foundation (PCAF) with his wife, Elizabeth, his daughter, Jane, and his son, Jeffrey. He was a member of the steering and executive committees of 9/11 Families United to Bankrupt Terrorism. Dr. Alderman graduated from the State University of New York Upstate Medical Center–Syracuse with an MD. He chaired the Radiation Oncology departments at Roosevelt–St. Luke's Hospital and Catholic Medical Center in New York City, and at the White Plains Hospital Center in White Plains, NY.

Elizabeth Alderman, co-founder of PCAF, has served as co-chair of the Memorial Committee for Families of September 11th. Since September 11, 2001, Ms. Alderman has made numerous appearances on television, including *NOW* with Bill Moyers, the *Today Show* with Katie Couric, and *American Morning* with Paula Zahn. On November 4, 2004, Ms. Alderman was honored by Court TV with their annual Everyday Heroes Award. Ms. Alderman graduated from Syracuse University with a BS degree in special education. She taught mentally challenged and emotionally disturbed children for ten years.

Bob Boisture is a member of Caplin & Drysdale's Washington, D.C., office. Mr. Boisture is the leader of the firm's exempt organizations practice group and currently serves as president of the firm. Mr. Boisture joined the firm in 1979; from 1986 to 1992, he served as associate general counsel and then director of public policy for the YMCA of the USA, rejoining Caplin & Drysdale in 1992. Mr. Boisture also serves as director of YMCA Activate America, a national leadership initiative to strengthen YMCA's capacity to help Americans find healthier ways to live. Mr. Boisture is a graduate of Oxford University and Yale Law School.

Leonard E. Burman is a senior fellow at the Urban Institute and co-director of the Urban-Brookings Tax Policy Center. He is also a visiting professor at Georgetown University's Public Policy Institute, where his friend and colleague, Leslie Whittington, who died on American Airlines Flight 77, was associate dean. Dr. Burman is an expert in public finance and modeling the effects of government policies. He has held high-level positions in both the executive and legislative branches, serving as deputy assistant secretary for tax analysis at the Treasury Department from 1998–2000 and as senior analyst at the Congressional Budget Office.

Mimi Evans's extensive experience in philanthropy includes strategic planning, major gifts, foundation and corporate relations, special events, public relations, and marketing. She is currently the director of development at *NOW*, a public affairs show seen weekly on PBS. She has directed fundraising efforts and raised millions of dollars for many prestigious institutions, including the International Fund for Animal Welfare, the Hunger Project, the U.S. Fund for UNICEF, the New York Philharmonic, Yale University, Williams College, and Trinity College. Prior to her fundraising career, she founded Bailey & Company Communications in Albany, NY, which specialized in corporate and association public relations. A graduate of the State University of New York–Albany, Ms. Evans is also a freelance consultant and a talented graphic designer, editor, and writer. She is the mother of two sons who have served in Iraq and Afghanistan (one as a U.S. Marine and one as a humanitarian aid worker).

Elliot Gerson is responsible for the Aspen Institute's seminars and public programs and activities, including programming for the International Freedom Center to be created at the World Trade Center site. He is a graduate of Harvard College and Oxford University, where he was a Rhodes Scholar, and Yale Law School.

Louis W. Goodman is dean and professor of international relations at American University's School of International Service, positions he has held since 1986. Previously, Dr. Goodman served on the faculty of Yale University's Department of Sociology and as director of the Latin American and Caribbean programs of the Social Science Research Council and the Woodrow Wilson International Center for Scholars. The author of numerous books and articles, Dr. Goodman currently focuses on research on democracy building and civilian control of the armed forces in Latin America.

Sarah W. Goodrich is a Title I/Reading First coordinator and reading specialist in the North Adams, MA, public schools. She is a member of the Bennington School District Board, the board of the Reading Institute in Williamstown, MA, and deacon of First Congregational Church, Old Bennington. Ms. Goodrich lost her son, Peter M. Goodrich, on 9/11. She co-founded the Peter M. Goodrich Memorial Foundation. She is the mother of Foster Hetherington and Kim Trimarchi and grandmother to Ben, Sarah, James, and Eamon. She is married to Don Goodrich, chair of the board of Families of September 11th.

Bruce Hoffman has been studying terrorism and insurgency for thirty years. He is currently a tenured professor in the Security Studies Program at Georgetown University's Edmund A. Walsh School of Foreign Service, Washington, D.C. Professor Hoffman previously held the corporate chair in counterterrorism and counterinsurgency at the RAND Corporation and was also director of RAND's Washington, D.C., office. From 2001–2004, he served as RAND's vice president for external affairs, and in 2004, he also was acting director of RAND's Center for Middle East Public Policy. Professor Hoffman was adviser on counterterrorism to the Office of National Security Affairs, Coalition Provisional Authority, Baghdad, Iraq, during the spring of 2004, and from 2004–2005 was an adviser on counterinsurgency to the Strategy, Plans, and Analysis Office at Multi-National Forces-Iraq Headquarters, Baghdad. He was also an adviser to the Iraq Study Group (Baker-Hamilton Commission), serving on the Military and Security Experts Working Group.

Thomas S. Johnson is chair of the board for the Institute for International Education, an organization in the Our Voices Together network. His son, Scott, worked at the World Trade Center, where he was killed on September 11, 2001. Mr. Johnson has served as president and director of Chemical Bank and Chemical Banking Corporation, Manufacturers Hanover Corporation, and chairman and CEO of GreenPoint Financial Corporation and GreenPoint Bank. Mr. Johnson is the chairman of the board of trustees of Trinity College and a trustee of the Asia Society, the Cancer Research Institute of America, Religion in American Life, the United Way of New York City, and WNET Channel 13. He is a member of the Council on Foreign Relations and former chairman of the board of directors of Union Theological Seminary. Mr. Johnson is also a director of the Lower Manhattan Development Corporation board.

Christopher Koch has an extensive experience producing, writing, and directing nonfiction programming and documentaries for television and radio. Mr. Koch has directed and produced award-winning programs on history, science, technology, current events, and the environment. His documentary film *Blacklist: Hollywood on Trial* received the first presidential Emmy Award for superior programming. He directed and wrote *Normandy: The Great Crusade,* which received the prestigious George Foster Peabody Award. He is the former executive producer of NPR's evening news program, *All Things Considered,* and public television's series on journalism, *Inside Story.* He began his television career at KQED, the public television station in San Francisco, and at the

ABC documentary unit, Close Up. Mr. Koch received a master's degree with honors from Columbia University on a Woodrow Wilson National Fellowship and a BA from Reed College. He is a member of the Producers' Guild of America. He is a relative of Leslie Whittington and her family, passengers on American Flight 77.

Susan Koch, Emmy and Peabody Award–winning documentary filmmaker, has produced and directed award-winning documentaries and nonfiction programming for worldwide distribution and television broadcast. Her work has appeared on ABC, NBC, HBO, PBS, MTV, the Discovery Channel, National Geographic, American Movie Classics, and the Learning Channel. Ms. Koch directed *City at Peace,* which premiered at the Kennedy Center in Washington, D.C., and at Lincoln Center in New York City, and was broadcast on HBO. Before forming her own company, Susan Koch was a producer at NBC News. Susan Koch began her television career at WETA-TV, the public television station in Washington, D.C. In September 2002, Koch produced an ABC/Nightline special, *Remembering a Family,* on her four family members who were killed on the flight that crashed into the Pentagon. The program focused on what family and friends are doing to honor their lives. Ms. Koch serves on the board of the Women's Commission for Refugee Women and Children.

Charles MacCormack is currently president and CEO of Save the Children Federation, a nonprofit, nonsectarian, humanitarian organization. He currently serves as co-chair of the Basic Education Coalition and the Campaign for Effective Global Leadership, and is a member of the Council on Foreign Relations, the Executive Committee of InterAction, the Advisory Committee on Voluntary Foreign Aid, and the Food Security Advisory Committee. He received his doctorate and master's degrees from Columbia University and graduated from Middlebury College. He was a Fulbright Fellow at the Universidad Central de Venezuela in Caracas. He has also participated in a special three-year program at the Harvard Business School on Leadership of Global Nonprofit Organizations.

Susan Retik is the co-founder and director of Beyond the 11th, a charitable organization devoted to supporting widows in war-torn areas, especially in Afghanistan. She received her BA from Colgate University. While living in New York City, she worked in marketing at Scholastic. On September 11, Ms. Retik already had two children, Ben (3) and Molly (2). She was seven months pregnant, and two months later she gave birth to a second daughter, Dina.

Nikki Stern was most recently executive director for Families of September 11th, a national outreach and advocacy group founded by families of victims of the September 11, 2001, attacks. A communications consultant, Ms. Stern, whose husband was killed on 9/11, has been active in facilitating discourse among and between various constituencies on issues ranging from Ground Zero in New York to the recommendations of the National Commission on Terrorist Attacks Upon the United States (the 9/11 Commission). Ms. Stern is currently consulting on communications and organizational development while working on a book.

Zade Dirani is a young Jordanian composer and pianist, passionate about playing his compositions that blend Eastern Arabic scales with Western contemporary influences. Dedicated to using his music to bring people together, his efforts have resulted in his CDs charting on Billboard, prestigious awards, friendships forged worldwide, and accolades, including a feature in *People* magazine. To continue cross-cultural understanding through the arts, Zade launched the Zade Foundation for International Peace and Understanding, aimed at helping young musicians share with the world a deeper understanding of their cultures by offering them a unique opportunity to expand their roles from musicians to become proactive peace builders and future community leaders.

ORGANIZATIONAL SNAPSHOT

Organization: Our Voices Together

Founders: C. Eugene Steuerle, Lynne Steuerle Schofield, and Kristin Steuerle

Mission/Description: Our Voices Together holds a vision of a world where the appeal of lives lived in dignity, opportunity, and safety triumphs over the allure of extremism and its terrorist tactics. Our Voices Together sees a future where terrorist tactics are not condoned by any community worldwide and understands that to achieve this, trust must be built on mutual respect around the globe. It recognizes the vast potential in engaging the people of the United States in diplomacy by connecting communities. To this end, Our Voices Together promotes the vital role of people-to-people efforts to help build better, safer lives and futures around the world.

Website: www.ourvoicestogether.org

Address: Our Voices Together

1730 Rhode Island Ave. NW, Suite 712

Washington, DC 20036 USA

Phone: +1.202.223.0080

NOTES

1. Robert A. Pape, *Dying to Win: The Strategic Logic of Suicide Terrorism* (New York: Random House, 2005), p. 80.
2. David H. Petraeus, *The U.S. Army/Marine Corps Counterinsurgency Field Manual, FM3-24/MCWP3-33.5*, James F. Amos (Foreword) (Department of the Army, December 15, 2006), pp. 1–28.
3. Ibid., pp. 1–27.
4. Marine Corps, U.S. Navy, U.S. Coast Guard, *A Cooperative Strategy for 21st Century Seapower* (October, 2007, http://www.au.af.mil/au/awc/awcgate/maritime/maritime_strat_oct07.pdf), p.4.

5. Robert M. Gates, Landan Lecture, Kansas State University, Manhattan, KS (November 26, 2007).
6. Thomas H. Kean and Lee H. Hamilton, "Are We Safer?" *Washington Post* (September 9, 2007), B01.
7. National Commission on Terrorist Attacks, *The 9/11 Commission Report: Final Report of the National Commission on Terrorist Attacks Upon the United States* (New York: W.W. Norton & Company, 2004), p. 379.
8. Ibid., p. 378.
9. *Wall Street Journal,* Letter to the Editor by Gene Steuerle, July 17, 2007.
10. S. J. Clohesy, *Donor Circles: Launching and Leveraging Shared Giving* (San Francisco, CA: Women's Funding Network, 2004).
11. Bruce Hoffman, "Combating Al Qaeda and the Militant Islamic Threat: Testimony before the House Armed Services Committee, Subcommittee on Terrorism, Unconventional Threats and Capabilities on February 16, 2006" (RAND Corporation, 2006).
12. Coalition for Citizen Diplomacy, http://www.coalitionforcitizendiplomacy.org/.

13

IESC Geekcorps: Development for the New Millennium

Donald Bernovich II
and Kathy M. Tin

Picture a Peace Corps volunteer working in some far, remote area helping improve crop production or teaching children in a small schoolhouse. Now picture the volunteer with a pocket protector and laptop working to connect a remote village to the digital community. This is a volunteer from IESC Geekcorps. Founded in 1999 by Ethan Zuckerman and Elisa Korentayer, IESC Geekcorps follows the Peace Corps' model of sending volunteers and consultants to countries lacking digital infrastructure to help build up their information/communication technology (ICT) capacity. Essentially, the goal is to move a country from being a technology backwater to becoming a leading ICT-enabled country.

INSPIRATION

The inspiration for Geekcorps originally came from Ethan Zuckerman, who studied music in Ghana on a Fulbright Fellowship (Dewan, 2000). In 1993, while visiting the University of Ghana library, he noticed that it did not have any books newer than 1957, the year Ghana had gained its independence from Great Britain. He thought that if only there were an Internet connection, the library could virtually double its collection. Thus, Geekcorps was started to help countries lacking in ICT resources. When Geekcorps goes into a country, the Geek staff works with private and public companies and provides technological training and resources so that these organizations can function digitally.

PREPARING THE GEEKS

Just sending a group of Geeks into a developing country is not enough. They need to be prepared for the new culture they will be living in and learn other skills as well. IESC Geekcorps recognizes that the Geeks they recruit already have the technical know-how to get the job done, but they may need some training in how to teach their skills to others (Harkins, 2001); thus, there is a need to prepare the volunteers about the culture they will be living in before they leave. Most of IESC Geekcorps volunteers and consultants do only brief assignments in-country, so there is no luxury for providing cultural immersion training once they arrive. Therefore, cross-cultural training begins before they leave on their assignments. Once they arrive, a short in-country orientation is provided that teaches the basics of living and working in the new culture.

A second component of the training for every Geek is focused on teaching exercises (Harkins, 2001). Since the volunteers and consultants are only spending a short time developing the project, they need to train locals on how to maintain and work with the technology afterward. Finally, training on expectations—those of the IESC Geekcorps managers, the volunteers and consultants, and the businesses—is provided. This is done to ensure that volunteers and consultants remain realistic and do not become disheartened because of overblown expectations and goals.

FIRST FEW YEARS

Geekcorps' first project was in Ghana since that was where the idea for the organization originated. Called Ghana 2000, this project envisioned sending in six tech volunteers to set up an operating base, and then rotating groups of volunteers in and out over short periods of time. When the call went out for the first six volunteer slots, Geekcorps received almost 150 applications. Over the next three years, seven teams of approximately six volunteers each were sent to Ghana to help local partnering agencies gain Internet connections, improve computer infrastructure, and become current with the digitized world. These partnering agencies included an art gallery, a graphic design firm, and Ghana's Internet service provider (ISP).

Geekcorps began with about $300,000 from the founder's own pocket as well as donations from others within the dot.com community at the time (Grow, 2001). These funds did not last long with all the work going on in Ghana. Donations were requested from private donors and foundations, but something more was needed for Geekcorps to survive and grow. In August 2001, the International Executive Service Corps (IESC) acquired Geekcorps, which turned it into IESC's Information and Technology Division. IESC is a nongovernmental organization (NGO) that specializes in economic development programs worldwide. IESC started in 1964, sending American business experts on missions to furnish, upon request, technical and managerial advice to businesses in developing countries. Over the years, IESC has implemented more than 200 integrated development programs in more than 130 countries, generating over 25,000 technical assistance activities using both volunteers and consultants.

Like Geekcorps, many of IESC's core programs use volunteers, thus enabling IESC to take advantage of the synergy in the acquisition of an ICT division into its portfolio. Likewise, by joining IESC, Geekcorps expanded its reach through

IESC's international programming experience via IESC's United States Agency for International Development (USAID)–funded projects, which totaled $22 million a year (Grow, 2001). In return, IESC benefited from Geekcorps' technology skills to help ensure that IESC would develop projects geared for the information age. Therefore, the integration into IESC has been a tremendous benefit in allowing Geekcorps to expand its mission and reach far more places than previously. This was the beginning of the new chapter in the life of Geekcorps, now called IESC Geekcorps.

SINCE IESC'S ACQUISITION OF GEEKCORPS

In the beginning of 2002, IESC Geekcorps began one-month placements for software engineers and programmers in Armenia. These volunteers engaged in information technology (IT) development and marketing projects with small- to medium-size firms that had been identified as potential up-and-comers in the global market. About the same time, opportunities arose in Sofia, Bulgaria, for volunteers to go in, carry out assessments, and make recommendations to improve IT for four local firms.

In mid-2002, a total of eight Geeks were sent to Mongolia over the course of twelve months to provide networking and programming/software expertise for local businesses. Rapidly, over the next few years, Geeks were also sent to Thailand to work on an ambitious database development project, to Zimbabwe to implement a new high-tech communication tool (Control-F1), and to begin work in Lebanon to help bring the local tourism industry into the information age.

In November 2003, IESC Geekcorps began a unique adventure in Mali. There, Geekcorps set up a new office and was tasked with finding technological options to connect more than 145 radio stations in Mali. This connected network would enable the radio stations to exchange development information and content, and strengthen the reach that radio had in this West African nation.

In 2003 IESC Geekcorps went to Senegal. Senegal's financial services infrastructure was primarily limited to the main urban centers, with little or no penetration in rural areas. As a result, the majority of small- to medium-size enterprises (SMEs) in rural areas faced major challenges when trying to access even the most basic financial services. This situation led to nonuniform economic development concentrated in Senegal's major urban centers and an associated rural-to-urban population migration. In addition, a large section of the Senegalese population remained "unbanked," with little knowledge of or insight into even the most basic financial instruments, such as interest-based saving, investing, and other services available on an individual or community basis. IESC Geekcorps deployed approximately fifteen volunteers over the next year to Senegal to work in the following areas: initiating e-finance, strengthening operations and management of SMEs through ICT, improving SME access to market via ICT tools, and strengthening telecenters and cyber cafés.

GEEKCORPS TODAY

Although Ethan Zuckerman left IESC Geekcorps in 2004 to work for the Berkman Center for Internet and Society at Harvard Law School and the Open Societies Institute (OSI), IESC Geekcorps continues to grow and prosper.

In 2005 IESC Geekcorps volunteers started working with USAID's East and Central Africa Trade Hub to create a common interface between systems in order to share and store information between the Kenyan and Ugandan border control agencies in Mombasa, Nairobi, the Malaba Border Post, and Kampala. A team of four Geeks was sent out to do field research on existing systems, and to design a platform to meet international standards as per World Customs Organization rules in the Revised Kyoto Convention.

IESC Geekcorps proved to be as busy throughout 2005 and 2006 as in previous years. The organization had great success in Mali by empowering community radio stations with Internet connectivity, and along the way made technological leaps in the process with the development of BottleNet, a do-it-yourself antennae designed to be constructed from basic materials easily found in Mali (i.e., plastic water bottles, window screen mesh, used valve stems from motorbikes, television and low-cost coaxial cables) that could receive wireless transmissions up to 2–3 GHz. The organization also designed a software integration system to ease transportation bottlenecks in East Africa; coordinated a "Who's Who" of Sudanese Diaspora for the government of southern Sudan; developed training courses to make technology fun, exciting, and most importantly, profitable for microentrepreneurs worldwide; and designed the Desert PC to withstand a high-heat, high-dust, low-electricity environment.

Continuing the momentum into 2007, IESC Geekcorps was able to send Microsoft development experts to Lebanon to participate in IESC-led Access to International Markets through Information Technology (AIM-IT) program, which worked to improve the capacity of SMEs specializing in technology products or services, and also harnessed technology to increase tourism into the region. Also in Lebanon, an ICT Academy program was developed to mobilize ICT skills in the country so that Lebanon could recover from recent devastation and provide affordable access to the Internet in rural areas by connecting ICT training centers to the Internet, and by providing ICT training to residents in rural areas in Lebanon.

Other successes include further building of radio stations in Mali for USAID in several regions throughout the country. Through IESC Geekcorps assistance, these community radio stations have become self-sustaining by using established connections primarily to send e-mail, access the news, and deliver information. To make the stations more sustainable, IESC Geekcorps also developed the Cybertigi, a mini cyber café that allows affordable and accessible ICT services. The Cybertigi design allows Malians in even the remotest regions to have access to laser printers, scanners, digital cameras, and photo printers, as well as to have the ability to play video games, burn CDs, and transfer music from cassette tapes to CDs or MP3 players.

Currently, IESC Geekcorps is expanding opportunities for both ICT volunteers and consultants to participate in its programs through short-term assistance. ICT usually finds its way into many of IESC's core practice areas, such as trade, SME development, tourism, and financial services. IESC Geekcorps has expanded its programming to include developing financial service software, working with education centers to help them incorporate ICT into their students' curriculum, and finding ways to introduce ICT into programs to bring about peace and prosperity around the world. Thus, what started as one man's dream to bring ICT resources to developing countries has evolved into a reality where IESC Geekcorps Geeks are paving new paths and bridging the digital divide in those countries.

STAFF

IESC Geekcorps has program staff in the Washington, D.C., headquarters of the International Executive Service Corps and full-time field staff managing the larger country programs.

Washington, D.C.:

- Merove Heifetz, Geekcorps associate
- Gladys Villacorta, AIM-IT program manager
- Lina Parikh, Smarter Seminars consultant

Bamako, Mali:

- Olivier Alais, Geekcorps Mali program manager

Beirut, Lebanon:

- Mohammed Bensouda, AIM-IT country director
- Mahmoud Elzein, AIM-IT deputy country director

ORGANIZATIONAL SNAPSHOT

Organization: IESC Geekcorps

Founders: Ethan Zuckerman and Elisa Korentayer

Mission/Description: IESC Geekcorps is an international 501(c)(3) nonprofit organization that promotes stability and prosperity in the developing world through information and communication technology (ICT). IESC Geekcorps' international technology experts teach communities how to be digitally independent: they are able to create and expand private enterprise with innovative, appropriate, and affordable ICTs.

International technical volunteers are the Geekcorps difference, offering a significant focus on the transfer of skills—a task that is often not possible with consulting agreements where specialists focus only on deliverables, not on capacity building or sustainability.

Website: www.IESC.org
Address: IESC Geek Corps
1900 M St. NW Suite 500
Washington, D.C. 20036
Phone: 202-326-0280

REFERENCES

Dewan, S. (2000, October 19). A techie volunteer corps. *New York Times*. Retrieved January 8, 2008, from http://www.nytimes.com/learning/general/featured_articles/001019thursday.html

Grow, B. (2001, August 15). Trying to spread the tech wealth. *Business Week*. Retrieved January 8, 2008, from http://www.businessweek.com/technology/content/aug2001/tc20010815_833.htm

Harkins, A. M. (2001, May 1). Training digital divide warriors. *Linux Journal*. Retrieved January 8, 2008, from http://www.linuxjournal.com/article/4595

Afterword

Keith Ferrazzi

If you take the ingredients of social entrepreneurship, venture philanthropy, and social networking, liberally mix with individuals who hold a passion for making a true difference in various aspects of people's lives throughout the world, and then take a sample of some of the best, the result you have is *The New Humanitarians*. Chris Stout has served as a uniting thread to connect these organizations in this three-volume set. While these organizations are all different in their approaches and goals, they share a common aspect of their work: innovation. Indeed, they are the *new* humanitarians. They are born from the power of the individual taking action in a novel way, and then using the power of their relationships to effect impactful change. After all, giving back is a huge part of a life well led.

In the spirit of *Three Cups of Tea*, Chris's adventuresome life has taken him to a variety of exotic and often not-so-safe locales, and the work he has done in these venues has resulted not only in his Center for Global Initiatives, but also *The New Humanitarians*. He has done well with many of the aspects I wrote about in *Never Eat Alone* but applied them in the milieu of humanitarian work. He and I share a kinship, as Chris was a reviewer for the ABE Awards that I founded, a fellow Baldrige Award reviewer, and a fellow "TEDizen" during the Richard Saul Wurman era; was elected as a Global Leader of Tomorrow by the World Economic Forum; and served as faculty with me in Davos. So it is no surprise that Chris has the brainpower as well as the horsepower to have accomplished this wonderful compilation of wunderkinder.

Chris is able to contribute to Davos talks and UN presentations, but he is much more at home working in the field and with his students. He is known for bringing people together in cross-disciplinary projects worldwide—in healthcare, medical education, human rights, poverty, conflict, policy, sustainable development, diplomacy, and terrorism. As the American Psychological Association said about him and his work: "He is a rare individual who takes risks, stimulates new ideas, and enlarges possibilities in areas of great need but few resources. He is able to masterfully navigate between the domains of policy development while also rolling up his sleeves to provide in-the-trenches care. His drive and vigor are disguised by his quick humor and ever-present kindness. He is provocative in his ideas and evocative in spirit. His creative solutions and inclusiveness cross conceptual boundaries as well as physical borders." *The New Humanitarians* serves a testament to this praise.

Simply put, these organizations are amazing. The people behind the organizations are amazing. Their stories are amazing. And as a result, this book is amazing.

Series Afterword

THE NEW HUMANITARIANS

I am honored to include Professor Chris Stout's three-volume set—*The New Humanitarians*—in my book series. These volumes are like rare diamonds shining with visionary perspectives for the fields of human rights, health, and education advocacy; charitable and philanthropic organizations; and legal rights and remedies.

The *New Humanitarians* volumes are of great value to informed citizens, volunteers, and professionals because of their originality, down-to-earth approach, reader-friendly format, and comprehensive scope. Many of the specially written book chapters include the latest factual information on ways in which the new leaders, advocates, and foundations have been instrumental in meeting the critical medical and human service needs of millions of people in underdeveloped and war-torn countries.

Professor Chris Stout has developed a pathfinding set here. A gifted and prolific psychologist who planned and edited these comprehensive volumes, Stout has developed an original concept couched in these three remarkable books. I predict that the *New Humanitarians* will rapidly become a classic, and will be extremely useful reading for all informed citizens and professionals in the important years ahead.

Albert R. Roberts, DSW, PhD
Series Editor, Social and Psychological Issues: Challenges and Solutions
Professor of Social Work and Criminal Justice
School of Arts and Sciences
Rutgers, the State University of New Jersey

About the Editor and Contributors

Chris E. Stout is a licensed clinical psychologist and founding director of the Center for Global Initiatives. He also is a clinical full professor in the College of Medicine, Department of Psychiatry; a fellow in the School of Public Health Leadership Institute; and a core faculty member at the International Center on Responses to Catastrophes at the University of Illinois–Chicago. He also holds an academic appointment in the Northwestern University Feinberg Medical School and was visiting professor in the Department of Health Systems Management at Rush University. He served as a nongovernmental organization special representative to the United Nations for the American Psychological Association, was appointed to the World Economic Forum's Global Leaders of Tomorrow, and was an invited faculty at their annual meeting in Davos, Switzerland. He was invited by the Club de Madrid and Safe-Democracy to serve on the Madrid-11 Countering Terrorism Task Force.

Dr. Stout is a fellow of the American Psychological Association, past-president of the Illinois Psychological Association, and is a distinguished practitioner in the National Academies of Practice. He has published thirty books, and his works have been translated into eight languages. He was noted as being "one of the most frequently cited psychologists in the scientific literature" in a study by Hartwick College. He is the 2004 winner of the American Psychological Association's International Humanitarian Award and the 2006 recipient of the Illinois Psychological Association's Humanitarian Award.

Teresa Barttrum attended Ball State University for her undergraduate studies. She earned a bachelor's degree in psychology and photojournalism. She worked at the *Herald Bulletin* in Anderson, Indiana, and at the *Star Press* as a staff photographer for five years before moving back to the field of psychology. She then worked at the Youth Opportunity Center, a juvenile residential treatment facility, as a frontline supervisor in the Treatment of Adolescents in Secure Care (TASC) Unit of this organization. While employed at this organization, she helped develop and facilitate a therapeutic horseback riding program, served as a therapeutic crisis intervention instructor, and completed multiple in-service trainings. She currently attends the Adler School of Professional Psychology while pursuing her doctoral degree in clinical psychology. She completed her community service practicum at the Center for Global Initiatives while working on the book project *The New Humanitarians: Innovations, Inspirations, and Blueprints for Visionaries.*

Stephanie Benjamin grew up on Long Island, New York, always dreaming of being a doctor and an artist. She earned her bachelor's degree in art history and studio art from Tulane University in New Orleans and continued her education in Northwestern University's post-baccalaureate pre-medical school program. Currently, she is at the Adler School of Professional Psychology working on a master's degree in counseling psychology and art therapy. Through her internship at the Center for Global Initiatives, she worked to help ameliorate inequalities in global healthcare by writing for *The New Humanitarians* as well as doing grant research and writing for other worldwide projects. After completing her clinical internship at Rush University Medical Center, she will be attending medical school in order to become a physician and continue working to improve healthcare around the world.

Originally from North Pekin, Illinois, **Donald Bernovich II** has traveled and worked in a number of different locations. For the past five years, he lived in Rapid City, South Dakota, where he worked as a work-life consultant at Ellsworth Air Force Base. Prior to this, he lived in Malaysia, were he worked as a volunteer English instructor and counselor for a year. He received his BA from Benedictine University in 1997 and his MS from Capella University in psychology in 2005. Donald is currently a doctoral student in clinical psychology at the Adler School of Professional Psychology, located in Chicago, Illinois.

Alice K. Johnson Butterfield is professor at the Jane Addams College of Social Work, University of Illinois–Chicago. Her scholarship includes international social work education, the nonprofit sector in Romania, participatory community change, and asset-based community development in Ethiopia. She is co-editor of *University-Community Partnerships: Colleges and Universities in Civic Engagement* (2005) and *Interdisciplinary Community Development: International Perspectives* (2007), published by Haworth Press. Dr. Butterfield is a leader of ACOSA, and a member of the Council on Social Work Education's Commission on Global Social Work Education. Her research includes international higher education partnerships in Ethiopia, funded by the Great Cities Institute and HED, and the Gedam Sefer University-Community Partnership. She is co-PI of a project with Bahir Dar

University to establish an MEd for school directors in Ethiopia. In 2007 she received the Distinguished Alumni Award from Washington University–St. Louis.

Denise Caruso is executive director and co-founder of the Hybrid Vigor Institute in San Francisco, an independent, not-for-profit research organization and consultancy dedicated to interdisciplinary and collaborative problem solving. In December 2006, she published her first book, on risk, public policy, and biotechnology, titled *Intervention: Confronting the Real Risks of Genetic Engineering and Life on a Biotech Planet*, which won a silver medal in the science category of the 2007 Independent Publisher Book Awards. She continues to work on projects both in academia and the private sector to improve critical-thinking and decision-making processes, with a special focus on science- and technology-related innovations. Caruso is a former *New York Times* columnist, an affiliated researcher at the Center for Risk Perception and Communication at Carnegie Mellon University, and a director emerita of the Electronic Frontier Foundation; she also serves on the boards of the Independent Media Institute and the Molecular Sciences Institute. Caruso also serves on the advisory boards of Public Knowledge, which advocates for a vibrant "information commons"; London-based SustainAbility.com, the world's leading business consultancy on corporate responsibility and sustainable development; and the Graduate Program in Design at California College of the Arts. She is a graduate of California Polytechnic State University–San Luis Obispo.

Keith Ferrazzi is one of the rare individuals to discover the essential formula for making his way to the top through a powerful, balanced combination of marketing acumen and networking savvy. Both *Forbes* and *Inc.* magazines have designated him one of the world's most "connected" individuals. Now, as founder and CEO of Ferrazzi Greenlight, he provides market leaders with advanced strategic consulting and training services to increase company sales and enhance personal careers. Ferrazzi earned a BA degree from Yale University and an MBA from Harvard Business School.

Originally from Trinidad and Tobago, **Annie Khan** migrated to Toronto, Canada, in 1994. She completed her undergraduate degree at the University of Toronto in neuroscience and psychology. While working in community-based organizations, she felt compelled to do more for disenfranchised populations. She pursued a master's in counseling psychology at the Adler School of Professional Psychology and is currently working on her doctorate in clinical psychology. She worked at the Center for Global Initiatives as a placement student on *The New Humanitarians: Innovations, Inspirations, and Blueprints for Visionaries* book project.

Since May 1998, **Paul Kronenberg** has been working together with Sabriye Tenberken to establish the rehabilitation and training center for the blind in Tibet. He also worked part-time as a designer and construction coordinator for the Swiss

Red Cross in Shigatse. Paul has a technical background, having completed studies in mechanical engineering, computer science, commercial technology, and communication systems. For several summers during his studies, Paul worked for different organizations in development projects in Africa, Eastern Europe, and Tibet. Paul is responsible for all technical aspects and maintenance at Braille Without Borders. He also trains people in bookkeeping, office work, and the use of computers. In addition to being responsible for communications and fundraising, Paul began the production of Tibetan Braille books and supervises all construction activities within the project.

Evan Ledyard graduated from Loyola University–Chicago. He majored in psychology with a minor in communication. He joined Invisible Conflicts in 2006 and was co-vice president from 2007–8. In the future, he hopes to continue being part of Invisible Conflicts and travel to Uganda to help further develop the Dwon Madiki Partnership.

Valeria Levit was born in Donetsk, Ukraine, and grew up in the Crimean Peninsula. Growing up in the family of doctors, Valeria was groomed for a route of excellence in education and was accepted into an academy for musically talented children at the age of seven. At the age of thirteen, she transferred to the Medical Lyceum to study medical and biological sciences with the goal of medical school in the future. However, after finishing one year at the Lyceum, Valeria immigrated with her family to Chicago, Illinois. She graduated from Stevenson High School with honors and was accepted to Loyola University of Chicago. Valeria was on the Dean's list each semester at Loyola and graduated with a major in psychology and minor in pre-medicine. During her undergraduate studies, Valeria volunteered at a hospital and several not-for-profit organizations. It did not take her long to realize that she has a passion for studying the human mind. After graduating from Loyola, Valeria was accepted to the Adler School of Professional Psychology.

During her first year in the graduate school, Valeria fulfilled her community service practicum at the Center for Global Initiatives, which is dedicated to fighting against health disparities around the world. At the age of twenty-two, Valeria is a second-year student at Adler and is greatly interested in the mind/body aspect of psychology. Valeria is a member of the Golden Key Honors Society and the American Psychological Association. Currently she resides in Morton Grove, Illinois, with her family.

Nathan Linsk is the principal investigator of the Midwest AIDS Training and Education Center at the Great Lakes Addictions Technology Transfer Center. He is professor of social work at the Jane Addams College of Social Work, University of Illinois–Chicago. Dr. Linsk has extensive clinical experience serving individuals with HIV/AIDS in a number of settings, and has been involved in the training of HIV/AIDS healthcare providers nationally and internationally for ten years.

In 1994 he co-chaired the International Society for AIDS Education conference. His international consultation includes Romania (PI on World AIDS Foundation Grant, 1991–4), Namibia, Malawi, and Ethiopia. He was awarded a Fulbright Research Award in Ethiopia in 2006. His latest work in Africa is a partnership project in Tanzania on social work education and training on HIV/AIDS and the orphan situation.

Nathan Mustain is a graduate of Loyola University–Chicago who studied biology, graduating in May 2008. He is the co-founder of Invisible Conflicts and served as president from 2005–7. Nathan is now working as a spokesperson, political advocate, and adviser to Invisible Conflicts. He plans on becoming a physician and to work with the world's poor, who are also the world's sick. In working with them, he seeks to understand what keeps them poor and sick. Then he hopes to change these "distal" causes of disease and poverty by helping people to find wellness, and by partnering with educators and lawmakers to change the educational, political, and economic systems that keep people sick and poor. Nathan also dreams of traveling the world and connecting communities of wealth and power with those living under oppression and poverty.

Amy Nemeth, a student at Loyola University–Chicago, is expected to graduate in May 2009 with degrees in history and secondary education with a focus in political science and peace studies. After joining Invisible Conflicts in the fall of 2005, she traveled to Uganda in the summers of 2007 and 2008 to volunteer at the Dwon Madiki Partnership. She was co-president of Invisible Conflicts from 2007–8. She hopes to travel back to Uganda and other war-torn areas as well as to inspire future students to get involved with Invisible Conflicts.

Steve Olweean is founding director of Common Bond Institute, a founder and president of the International Humanistic Psychology Association (IHPA), past president of the Association for Humanistic Psychology, founder of the Annual International Conference on "Engaging The Other," and co-founder of the Annual International Conference on Conflict Resolution and the Global Youth Conference on the Ecology of War and Peace.

He has written and presented internationally on concepts of "The Other," the social/psychological dynamics of group paranoia, victim identity, inherited communal trauma, negative belief systems, cross-cultural dialogue, forgiveness and reconciliation, conflict transformation, and building capacity at the grass roots and social institutional level for an authentic world culture of peace. His current book project is *Engaging The Other,* a compilation of chapters by diverse authors each exploring concepts of The Other from their unique cultural perspectives. He received his degree in clinical psychology from Western Michigan University, and is a psychotherapist with a treatment focus on recovery of victims and perpetrators of abuse, trauma recovery, and healing negative belief systems. He developed the integrated Catastrophic Trauma Recovery (CTR) treatment model for treating large populations victimized by war and violence in developing countries that are regions of conflict.

Mehmet Oz received a 1982 undergraduate degree from Harvard and a 1986 joint MD and MBA from the University of Pennsylvania School of Medicine and the Wharton Business School. He is vice-chair of surgery and professor of cardiac surgery, Columbia University; founder and director, Complementary Medicine Program, New York Presbyterian Medical Center; currently, director, Cardiovascular Institute, New York Presbyterian Hospital. Research interests include heart replacement surgery, minimally invasive cardiac surgery, and healthcare policy. He is a member of the American Board of Thoracic Surgery; American Board of Surgery; American Association of Thoracic Surgeons; Society of Thoracic Surgeons; American College of Surgeons; International Society for Heart and Lung Transplantation; American College of Cardiology; and the American Society for Artificial Internal Organs. He is the author of over 350 publications.

Myron Panchuk completed his BS degree in psychology and philosophy at Loyola University–Chicago in 1976. In 1982 he was ordained to the priesthood for the Chicago Diocese of Ukrainian Catholics and has actively served this community for over twenty years. His professional work includes designing and facilitating retreats and conferences for clergy and laity, professional development, conflict resolution, and social advocacy. He is a co-founder and member of Starving For Color, a humanitarian organization which provides baby formula for orphans in Ukraine. He is currently a counseling graduate student at the Adler School of Professional Psychology and is engaged in a community service practicum with Dr. Chris Stout at the Center for Global Initiatives. He intends to continue his studies and pursue a doctorate in depth psychology.

Earl Martin Phalen is the co-founder and CEO of BELL (Building Educated Leaders for Life), a nonprofit organization created to dramatically increase the educational achievements, self-esteem, and life opportunities of black and Latino children living in low-income, urban communities. BELL operates high-quality summer and after school educational programs for 12,000 children in Baltimore, Boston, Detroit, New York City, and Springfield, MA. BELL provides direct services to children and works to change the systems that impact children. As a result of these efforts and a partnership with Senator Barack Obama of Illinois, the STEP UP Act was voted into law in August 2007. STEP UP will bring $100 million worth of high-quality summer learning programs to children throughout the country. Mr. Phalen is unswerving in his commitment to helping children excel. As a young adult, Mr. Phalen participated in the Lutheran Volunteer Corps as the assistant coordinator of a homeless shelter for women in Washington, D.C., and served as a summer law associate at the Jamaican Council for Human Rights.

In 1997 President Clinton awarded Mr. Phalen and BELL the President's Service Award for outstanding community service. Mr. Phalen currently sits on the advisory board for the Center for Summer Learning at the Johns Hopkins University and serves on the education advisory committees of Massachusetts governor Deval Patrick. Mr. Phalen holds a BA in political science from Yale University and a JD from Harvard Law School.

Patrick Savaiano is currently enrolled in the doctoral (PsyD) program at the Adler School of Professional Psychology (ASPP) in Chicago, IL. He graduated from the University of Notre Dame in 2004 with a BA in history and Spanish, and has since worked in marketing, real estate, and music. In the summer of 2003, he had the rewarding experience of traveling to Costa Rica by himself to work with Habitat for Humanity. Although he still plays guitar in two bands, in 2006 he decided to shift his "day job" away from business and into the profession of psychology. In fall 2007, as part of ASPP's Community Service Practicum, he worked under Dr. Chris E. Stout at the Center for Global Initiatives (CGI). He became an integral member of a team of students and professionals that ultimately put together a book project titled *The New Humanitarians: Innovations, Inspirations, and Blueprints for Visionaries.* Mr. Savaiano hopes to use the experience he has gained at ASPP and CGI to fuel his desire to help the less fortunate and underserved populations throughout the world.

Marianne Scott helped start Our Voices Together and has led the organization since fall 2005. Before this she was the first executive director of the Daniel Pearl Foundation, which she helped the Pearl family start in honor of her college friend Daniel Pearl, the *Wall Street Journal* reporter kidnapped and murdered in Pakistan in 2002. Marianne spent sixteen years as a career Foreign Service officer with the United States Information Agency (USIA) and the Department of State, specializing in international academic and professional exchanges and cultural affairs. Eleven of these years, she lived and worked at U.S. embassies and American cultural and educational centers overseas in Latin America and Africa. She is the author of *A Citizen's Guide to Global Economic Policymaking,* published by the League of Women Voters Education Fund in December 2002. She is a graduate of Stanford University.

Katie Scranton is a student at Loyola University–Chicago majoring in bilingual-bicultural elementary education with a minor in Spanish language and literature. She has been involved with Invisible Conflicts since 2006 and is constantly impressed by the dedication and passion of those involved in the group. She was co-president of Invisible Conflicts from 2007–8. She plans to travel to Uganda to finally meet the children and volunteers of the Dwon Madiki Partnership. Katie expects her involvement in the work and vision of Invisible Conflicts to continue far into her future.

M. Christopher Shimkin is a *summa cum laude* master's graduate in business administration from Northeastern University. Recently, Mr. Shimkin was selected as one of the World Economic Forum's 100 Global Leaders for Tomorrow, and he currently serves on several nonprofit and engineering advisory boards. A graduate in civil and ocean engineering from the University of Rhode Island in 1989, he pursued a consulting career in environmental engineering, developing expertise in water quality evaluations, civil works infrastructure planning and design, and environmental regulatory compliance as a senior engineer.

Morgan Smith is a student at Loyola University–Chicago. She is a student in the Marcella Niehoff School of Nursing and hopes one day to use her nursing skills in Africa. She has been to South Africa to observe that healthcare system through a program called International Scholar Laureate, which deepened her interest in returning to the continent to assist in the healthcare shortage. In 2005 she co-founded Invisible Conflicts with Nathan Mustain, as well as the Dwon Madiki Partnership with Katie Scranton in 2006.

Abye Tasse is associate vice president for international affairs, and dean of the School of Social Work at Addis Ababa University. He is president of the International Association of Schools of Social Work. He has also worked to develop social work education in Romania and Cameroon. His scholarship includes research design in social sciences and in immigrant and refugee matters, comparative research on migration, policy work on social work education, and the monitoring, evaluation, and restructuring of higher education institutions. He is the author of *Ethiopians in France and the United States: New Forms of Migration.*

Sabriye Tenberken studied Central Asian Studies at Bonn University. In addition to Mongolian and modern Chinese, she studied modern and classical Tibetan in combination with sociology and philosophy. Since no blind student had ever before ventured to enroll in these kinds of studies, she could not fall back on the experiences of anyone else, so she had to develop her own methods to come to terms with her course of studies. It was thus that a Tibetan script for the blind was developed. She coordinates and counsels the Braille Without Borders project. She is responsible for the training of teachers and trainers for the blind, and she initially taught the children herself. Further, she selects and supervises all staff members. She is also responsible for fundraising and communication with official and sponsor organizations. Tenberken has written three books in which she tells about the history of the project and the way she dealt with becoming blind: *Mein Weg fuehrt nach Tibet* (*My Path Leads to Tibet*; Arcade Publishing, New York); *Tashis' New World*; and *Das siebte Jahr* [The Seventh Year]. The first book has been published in eleven languages, including English.

David Thatcher is a student at Loyola University–Chicago pursuing a dual degree in economics and international studies. He has been involved with Invisible

Conflicts since 2006, serving as Dwon Madiki Partnership's lead coordinator and financial adviser. In this capacity, he organized and led the first trip of students to Gulu, Uganda, where they spent the summer setting up the Dwon Madiki Partnership (DMP) office and documenting the program. Upon graduating from Loyola University–Chicago, Dave plans to obtain a master's degree in international development and continue to work with and develop the DMP.

Kathy M. Tin is a development professional with more than six years of experience in both new business development and program management, as well as seven years in software development. Ms. Tin's particular expertise is in developing programs using information and communications technology (ICT) as an enabling tool to promote economic and social development. She currently serves as a director with the International Executive Service Corps (IESC) Geekcorps division. Prior to joining IESC, Ms. Tin worked at CARE in several capacities and also as a Peace Corps volunteer in Romania.

John Wood is founder and CEO of Room to Read, an international nonprofit that partners with local communities in the developing world to build educational infrastructure. John left a distinguished career at Microsoft to lead the Room to Read team in constructing over 5,600 schools and libraries with more than 3 million books and sponsoring over 4,000 scholarships for girls. Author of *Leaving Microsoft to Change the World*, John marries the "scalability of Starbucks with the compassion of Mother Theresa" to create one of the fastest-growing, most effective, and most award-winning nonprofits of the last decade.

Carolyn Ziembo is a student at Loyola University–Chicago. She is expected to graduate in 2010 with degrees in English and history. She has been involved with Invisible Conflicts since 2006 and was secretary from 2007–8. In addition to helping with other Dwon Madiki and Invisible Conflicts projects, she led the development of the art exhibit at LUMA. In the future, she hopes to travel to Uganda and meet the children of the Dwon Madiki Partnership.

Diana Zurawski is a student at Loyola University–Chicago majoring in elementary education. She has been involved with Invisible Conflicts since 2005 and is visiting Uganda in the summer of 2008 to assist in curriculum development of the Dwon Madiki Partnership. Diana hopes to teach in the Chicago Public Schools and looks forward to establishing new connections between students in Chicago and Gulu.

Index

Note: A page number followed by an *f* or *t* indicates that the reference is to a figure or table respectively.

International Executive Service Corps
    (IESC), 236
  acquisition of Geekcorps, 237
International Federation of Social
    Workers (IFSW), 61
International Foundation for Education
    and Self Help (IFESH), 74
International Humanistic Psychology
    Association (IHPA), 50, 51
International Institute for Social
    Entrepreneurs (IISE), Kerala, India
  eco-friendly campus of, 11–12
  establishment of, 11
  scope of, 12
International Professional Exchange, 48
International Selection Panel, 98
International Youth Conference on
    Ecology of War and Peace, 52
Intergovernmental Panel on Climate
    Change (IPCC), 195
Internet service provider (ISP), 236
*Intervention: Confronting the Real Risks of
    Genetic Engineering and Life on a
    Biotech Planet* (Caruso), 190
Invisible Children
  formation of, 131
  mission of, 132
Invisible Children (film)
  first screening of, 133–134
  at Grant Park, public screening of, 140
  inspiration behind, 132
  on national tour, 133
Invisible Conflicts, xxv–xxvi
  actions taken in Uganda, 139–141
  beginning of, 135–137
  creating changes in lives, 154–155
  in Democratic Republic of Congo,
    153–154
  DMP, launching of, 129 (*see also* Dwon
    Madiki Partnership (DMP))
  and DMP plan, 152–153
  DRC committee, formation of, 154
  fostering relationships, 138–139
  founding members of, 141
  Gear Up Alliance and, 148–150
  guiding principle of, 139
  members of, 148, 149
  mission of, 137–138, 139
  naming of, 137

organizational snapshot, 159
peace vigil in Chicago, promoting, 140
public exhibition at LUMA, 152
Run for Congo 5K walk, participation
    in, 154
UIUC chapter of, 154
ISP. *See* Internet service provider (ISP)

Jamaica Center for Arts and Culture, 90
Jamaica Flux and CUP, 90–91
Jane Addams College of Social Work, 60,
    62
  Gedam Sefer Community-University
    Partnership, 75–77, 76*f*
  UIC-AAU-ISW in Tanzania, 77–78
Jason, 131–132
Joey, 133
John, Jeremy, 133
Johns Hopkins School for Advanced
    International Studies (SAIS), 126
Johnson, Thomas S., 231
Joshi, Sandhya, 62
Journal of Conflict Transformation, Web-
    based journal, 55
*Journal of the American Society for
    Information Science,* 194, 196

Kanis, David, 133, 136
Kean, Thomas H. 208, 217, 229
Kechene Potters Association, 69
Kelley, Kathleen, 183
Kellner, Peter
  analyzing entrepreneurs, 97
  founding Endeavor, 96
Kerrey, Bob, 217, 228
Kidder, Tracy, 205
Killassy, Natalie
  Endeavor's global impact and, 106
  Stitch Wise and, 106–107
Kim, John J-H, 183
Klein, Julie Thompson, 197
Knez, Deb, 183
Koch, Christopher, 231–232
Koch, Susan, 232
Komakech, Jimmy, 147
Kony, Joseph, 132
Kordesh, Richard, University of
    Illinois–Chicago, 67
Korentayer, Elisa, 235